advance praise for

From The Cooking School at La Campagne

"La Campagne has long been known to have the best French Provençal cuisine in New Jersey. I'm excited that they are willing to share their recipes with the rest of us!"

— Jim Coleman
Executive Chef of The Rittenhouse Hotel, Philadelphia, PA
Host of PBS's "Flavors of America" and author of its companion cookbook

"I can't wait to get a copy of *From The Cooking School at La Campagne* into the kitchen and start cooking. The recipes look great!"

— D. Herbert Lipson
Publisher of *Philadelphia Magazine*

"Love delicious food? *From The Cooking School at La Campagne* tells you how to prepare it. Your preparations will taste like a chef just dropped in to make your dinner."

— Barbara Ann Rosenberg
Philadelphia Correspondent for The James Beard House

"A class act from the classrooms at La Campagne! John Byrne has created a cookbook with scrumptious recipes and practical cooking tips, and like the best cookbooks, it teaches as well as guides."

— Ed Hitzel
Host of "Table for One" and publisher of *Ed Hitzel's Restaurant Newsletter* and *Ed Hitzel's Restaurant Magazine*

"These are fresh, inviting, sophisticated recipes that will be a pleasure for the confident cook to prepare at home."

— Lyn Stallworth
Co-author of *The Brooklyn Cookbook* and *The Country Fair Cookbook*
Culinary instructor at The New School in New York City

"This cookbook is a must for both experienced and novice cooks. The advice and tips included with the recipes are informative and helpful."

— Pam Lyons
Taste Editor of the *Courier-Post*

"Food lovers alert! This book contains all the secrets you need to turn your kitchen into a Provençal paradise. Magnifique!"

— **Kevin Meeker**, Owner of Philadelphia Fish & Co., Philadelphia, PA

"La Campagne heads the short list of really fine BYOB restaurants we recommend to our customers. Now we can suggest (once in a while) that they enjoy our authentic small farm wines in the comfort of home, along with this wonderful cookbook."

— **Gregory Moore**, Owner of Moore Brothers Wine Co.

"The easy-to-follow recipes truly show John Byrne's love of Provençal cuisine. This cookbook will make even a novice appear to be a seasoned chef."

— **Andrew Latz**, Owner of Knife & Fork Inn, Atlantic City, NJ

"The cuisine of Provence is among the world's finest, and no East Coast restaurant interprets it as well as La Campagne. How generous of them to share the recipes and culture with home cooks everywhere."

— **Leigh Donadieu**, Publisher and Editor of *Cuizine* magazine

"Reading these recipes motivates me to travel to southern France (the sooner, the better). But in the meantime, this great cookbook will tide me over."

— **Chris Fifis**, Owner of Ponzio's, Cherry Hill, NJ

"Finally a long standing tradition of Cherry Hill shares its secrets. I can't wait to get a hold of them!"

— **Joe Brown**, Chef/Owner of Melange Cafe, Cherry Hill, NJ

"When I flipped to the recipe on salt-crusted whole fish, I realized that this is a cookbook I'm taking to the shore when I entertain in the summer."

— **Frank Panico**, Owner of Panico's, New Brunswick, NJ
Past President of New Jersey Restaurant Association

"*From The Cooking School at La Campagne* contains valuable ingredient information as well as easy-to-follow technical instructions. The recipes are also clear and concise, utilizing ingredients which are readily available at most supermarkets."

— **Linda Lipsky**, President of Linda Lipsky Restaurant Consultants, Inc.

From The Cooking School at La Campagne

From The Cooking School at La Campagne

La Campagne

Provençal Recipes
from the Famed Country Farmhouse

J O H N   B Y R N E

Small Potatoes Press

This is dedicated to the one I love ... Dorothy
(The Shirelles circa 1959)

Printed in the United States of America.
10 9 8 7 6 5 4 3 2 1

Library of Congress Catalog Card Number: 99-66020
ISBN: 0-9661200-3-5

Copy Writer: Connie Correia Fisher
Cover Designer: Jennifer Frisch
Proof Reader: Joanne Correia

Small Potatoes Press
1106 Stokes Avenue
Collingswood, NJ 08108
(856) 869-5207
Connie@smallpotatoespress.com

ATTENTION ORGANIZATIONS, SCHOOLS, AND EDUCATIONAL FACILITIES:
Quantity discounts are available on bulk purchases of this book for educational purposes or fund-raising. Special books or book excerpts can also be created to fit specific needs. For information, please contact Small Potatoes Press, 1106 Stokes Avenue, Collingswood, NJ 08108. Call (856) 869-5207 or fax (856) 869-5247.

Our gratitude goes to . . .

our chefs

Through the years we've been lucky to have wonderful chefs who have shared both their talents in the kitchen and their secrets in the cooking school. Thank you for your invaluable contributions and the legacy of excellence you helped create. Particular thanks to Eric Hall for your contribution to the restaurant, the school, and this book.

our employees past and present

Thank you for helping us achieve and maintain our reputation.
You share in our success.

the media

We've been interviewed and reviewed by the best. Thanks to all who have given us their stamp of approval.

friends and family

I am grateful that after 10 years of owning a restaurant, you are still my friends and family! Thank you for all your support and encouragement.

connie correia fisher

Thanks for all your help. Without you, this book wouldn't be possible.

But most of all, thanks to our customers who continually challenge and support us as we strive to exceed your expectations.

Foreword by Elaine Tait

"From The Cooking School at La Campagne" is a delightful rarity, a restaurant cookbook that makes it possible — often easy — for home cooks to capture the essence of a beloved dining destination.

It's no accident that the recipes are user friendly.

When he first conceived the idea for a cooking school at his French country restaurant, John Byrne saw an opportunity to reinforce La Campagne's image as a source of high quality dining experiences.

But Byrne knew that he didn't want the sort of classes where students sat in awe as a dictatorial chef cooked ultra-complicated recipes on a high-powered professional range. From the very first, the school was equipped with appliances designed for home rather than professional kitchens.

Recipes were developed featuring the flavors and creative combinations that have earned La Campagne ten years of unfailingly complimentary reviews yet with a home cook's abilities and resources in mind. Every recipe in this book was tested and approved in the school. By collecting them for you, La Campagne lets you share with family and friends the joys that meals here have brought to thousands of South Jersey diners.

Elaine Tait

poultry ... 87

Chicken Tapenade   *Cotelette Au Poulet*   Poulet Au Nid   *Duck à la Orange*
Roast Duck with Figs, Dates, and Raisins   *Duck Confit*   Duck with Sour Cherries
Cassoulet   Squab with Provençal Ragoût   *Cornish Hens with Mustard
and Rosemary*   Pheasant with Red Fruits   *Goose Stuffed with Chestnuts*
Morel Mushroom Stuffed Quail with Reduced Balsamic Demi-glace
Quail Stuffed with Foie Gras and Figs in Rhubarb-Kumquat Sauce

meat and game ... 103

Filet of Beef Niçoise   *Boeuf Bourguignonne*   Beef Wellington
Ossobuco Milanese   Provençal Stuffed Pork Tenderloin   *Rack of Lamb
with Caramelized Shallot Crust*   Grilled Leg of Lamb with Sour Cherries
Leg of Lamb with Spring Herbs   Lamb Shanks Braised in White Wine
Sautéed Sweetbreads in Shiitake Cream Sauce   Seared Sweetbreads with
Sherry Balsamic Reduction   *Braised Rabbit with Garlic and Basil*
Herb Roasted Loin of Venison with Currant Sage Sauce   *Venison with
Apple, Leek, and Rutabaga Compote*

fish ... 119

Poached Salmon with Cucumber Dill Cream   *Salmon Roulade with
Roasted Pepper, Goat Cheese, and Swiss Chard*   Porcini-Crusted Salmon
Lavender and Mustard Seed-Crusted Salmon   Wild Striped Bass Niçoise
Citrus Striped Bass   Chilean Sea Bass with Herb Crust   *Sea Bass Provençale*
Pan Seared Tuna with Ginger Carrot Beurre Blanc   Pepper-Crusted
Tuna with Ginger Glaze   Potato-Crusted Hamachi with Orange Beurre
Blanc   *Prosciutto-Crusted Monkfish with Madeira Balsamic Syrup*   Pan
Seared Arctic Char with Red Butter Sauce   *Hazelnut-Crusted Pompano*
South by Southwest Red Snapper   *Tomato Confit Poached Halibut*
Skate Wing with Citrus Brown Butter and Shallot Confit   *Mahi Mahi in
Potato Crust with Morels*   Dover Sole Provençal   *Trout in Puff Pastry*
Whole Grilled Fish with Sauce Vierge   *Salt-Crusted Whole Roasted Fish*

shellfish ... 143

Crab Cakes   *Crab Galette*   Soft-shell Crabs with Roasted Garlic Risotto
Shrimp, Zucchini, and Tomato Misto   Roasted Lobster with Vanilla Ginger Butter
Lobster Pernod   Mussels in Fennel Saffron Cream   *Mussels with Tomato,
Cilantro, and Lime*   Seared Scallops in Curry Beurre Blanc
Diver Scallops with French Lentils and Balsamic

cuisine rapide . . . 155

Simple Green Salad *Weekday Fish Soup* Wild Mushroom and Chicken Sauté
Herb Roasted Chicken with Caper Oil Breast of Duck Au Poivre
Tenderloin with Roquefort Sauce Rabbit Loin with Mushroom Broth and Truffles
Lemon-Steamed Arctic Char Red Snapper with Opal Basil Buerre Blanc
Red Snapper en Papillotes Sole Meunière *Mussels with Lemon Grass*
Mussels in White Sauce *Chocolate Truffles* Chocolate Nut Truffles
Poached Pears with Red Wine

risottos
and a few pastas . . . 171

White Wine Risotto *Truffled Risotto* Porcini Mushroom and Red Wine Risotto
Roasted Garlic and Tomato Risotto Lobster Risotto *Shrimp and
Shiitake Mushroom Risotto* Herb Rice *Rice Pilaf* Tomato, Basil, and
Couscous Salad *Potato Gnocchi* Gnocchi au Gratin with Goat Cheese
and Tomatoes *Chicken and Spinach Tortellini with Sage Butter Sauce*
Fettucine with Roquefort, Lemon Zest, and Rosemary

vegetables . . . 185

Marinated Artichokes *Gratin of Artichokes and Goat Cheese*
White Asparagus in Puff Pastry *Asparagus in Vanilla Honey Sauce*
Broccoli Rabe with Toasted Garlic *Carrots Bercy* Carrot Flan *Fennel Flan*
Grilled Figs with Goat Cheese and Mint *Mushroom Ragoût*
Glazed Pearl Onions with Currants and Almonds *Provençal Onion Tart*
Pommes Soufflés *Potatoes à la Normande* Potato Morel Gratin
Garlic Mashed Potatoes Mashed Potatoes, Rutabega, and Parsnips with
Caramelized Shallots *Swiss Chard Gratin* Lavender-Scented Tomato Gratin
Root Vegetable Gratin Ratatouille *Roasted Provençal Vegetables*

tarts, tortes, and more . . . 207

Alsatian Apple Tart *Apple Walnut Strudel* Caramel Sauce
Sour Cherry Almond Tart Chocolate Strawberry Tart *Raspberry Tart*
Rhubarb-Raspberry Galette *Lemon Tart* Strawberry Tart with Almond
Cream *Vanilla Gènoise* Chocolate Gènoise *Praline Mousse Cake*
Chocolate Raspberry Cake *Chocolate Almond Torte* Cranberry Upside
Down Cake Profiteroles *Hazelnut Biscotti*

Welcome to La Campagne...

With the purchase of La Campagne in 1990, my eye was on the future and my heart set on preserving the past. Like any new owner, I wanted to put my stamp on the business but was determined to maintain the historical spirit and character of the property — a farmhouse that dates back to the 1840s. With that vision, the interior was refurbished; the landscaping restored; herbs, fruit trees, and grapevines planted; a garden terrace and a "petaque" court added. But the original pumpkin pine floor planks still remain, the fireplaces continue to warm our cozy dining rooms, and guests enjoy good food and gracious hospitality much as they did over 150 years ago.

Although our farmhouse is a celebration of the abundant resources available in southern New Jersey, it is another southern countryside that inspires our cuisine. Through the years, we have traveled often to Provence and, in fact, many of the decorations and wall hangings at La Campagne are remembrances of these trips. In addition to souvenirs, we bring back new ideas and a desire to share the flavors and foods of France with our guests. These trips are a form of continuing education and were the inspiration for the creation of The Cooking School in 1993.

Our cooking school is located on the second level of the farmhouse in a renovated demonstration kitchen. In this comfortable instructional kitchen, we have held over 200 classes for nearly 3,000 guests. Taught by our executive chef, sous chef, and special guest chefs, these classes are serious studies in method and preparation but retain an air of casualness and sociality that is representative of our restaurant.

Although the classes, like our menu, are influenced by Provence, they showcase a variety of international and regional cooking styles. Classes run from *haute cuisine* to *cuisine rapide* (quick cooking); from berries to Burgundy; from the Mediterranean to both coasts and the Far East.

All cooking school students receive copies of the recipes presented in each class, and frequent attendees have quite a collection! When we realized that *our* collection had grown to include over 1,000 recipes, we decided to compile them into a cookbook. In this book, as in our school and restaurant, we strive to bring a fresh perspective to Provençal cooking. As a result, all have a strong French flavor with the underlying knowledge and respect for the Delaware Valley marketplace.

My staff and I have enjoyed welcoming both guests and students into our restaurant and embrace the sense of community that has developed over the years. I am pleased to be able to extend that community to you and hope you will use our recipes to create memorable moments and good times for yourself and the guests you welcome into your kitchen.

Santé!

John Byrne

from the cooking school at la campagne ~ from the cooking school at la campagne ~ from the cooking school at la campagne ~ from the cooking school at la campagne ~ from the cooking school at la campagne ~ from the cooking school at la campagne ~ from the cooking school at la campagne ~ from the cooking school at la campagne ~ from the cooking school at la campagne ~ from the cooking school at la campagne ~ from the cooking school at la campagne ~ from the cooking school at la campagne ~ from the cooking school at la campagne ~ from the

starters

Black Olive Tapenade

Olive merchants in Provence sell more than a dozen types of tapenade. This is one of our favorites.

½ pound large Greek-style black olives such as kalamata, pitted
4 anchovy fillets, rinsed
3 tablespoons capers, rinsed
1 clove garlic, chopped
Pinch of cayenne
4 tablespoons olive oil

Place all ingredients, except oil, in a food processor and puree. With motor running, add oil in a slow, steady stream until mixture is homogenous. Store covered in refrigerator. Serve at room temperature.

Long summer days give us tapenade, a classic spread from Provence. Use it as a condiment for fish, meat, and sandwiches; as a topping for pizza and bruschetta; or as a spread for French bread.

Tuna and Salmon Tartare

Think of Marseilles and the fresh fish vendors.

¼ cup lemon juice
1 tablespoon olive oil
1 tablespoon sesame oil
Salt and pepper
4 ounces salmon fillet, boned and skinned
4 ounces tuna fillet, skinned, all dark meat removed
1 cucumber, peeled and cut into ¼-inch slices
Chopped chives

Combine lemon juice, olive oil, sesame oil, and salt and pepper to taste. Finely chop salmon and tuna. Combine salmon and tuna in a bowl and stir in lemon-oil mixture. Spoon tartare onto cucumber slices and garnish with chives.

Serves 10 to 12

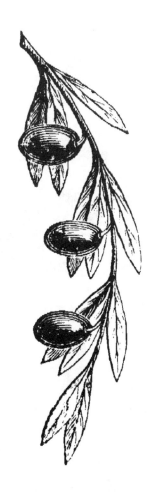

Duck Rillettes

The longer you stay in France, the more rillettes you'll eat.
It's addictive!

1 duck (6 pounds), quartered
1½ cups dry white wine
1 onion, sliced
1 bay leaf
1 clove garlic
3 sprigs fresh thyme
Coarse salt and freshly ground pepper

Preheat oven to 400°. Place duck pieces in a heavy roasting pan and cook, turning pieces so they brown evenly, until duck fat begins to melt, about 30 minutes. Transfer duck to a heavy stockpot. Add remaining ingredients and cook slowly over low heat for 3¼ hours.

Strain juices from the pot and set aside. Shred the meat into small pieces and finely chop the skin. Discard the bones. Add meat and skin to the strained liquid and beat well with a wooden spoon until the mixture resembles a hash. Season to taste with salt and pepper. Transfer to ramekins or a crock. Cover tightly with plastic wrap and refrigerate until set. Remove the rillettes from refrigerator at least 2 hours before serving. Serve spread on crackers or slices of fresh baguettes.

Yield 2½ pounds

rillettes
[rih-YEHTS]

Meat or fish that is cooked in seasoned fat and then pounded or pulverized into a paste. From the Loire Valley, rillettes resembles pâte.

Beggar's Purse with Smoked Salmon Mousse

These elegant little bundles are the perfect party food: they seem extravagant, but they're really easy to prepare.

1 bunch chives
Basic Crêpes (Recipe appears on page 273.)
1 cup Salmon Mousse (see recipe)

Blanch chives in boiling water. Submerge in an ice bath to refresh.

Cut crêpes with a 5-inch round ring mold. Place ½ teaspoon salmon mousse in the center of each crêpe round. Draw crêpes up around mousse (to resemble a purse) and tie with a chive.

Yields approximately 20 purses

Salmon Mousse

½ pound smoked or cured salmon
½ pound cream cheese
¼ cup chopped chives or scallions
¼ cup chopped fresh dill
Juice of ½ lemon
Pepper to taste
2 dashes Tabasco sauce

Combine all ingredients in a food processor and puree until smooth. Remove and transfer to a serving dish or mold to chill. Serve at room temperature.

Yields 2 cups

What to do with mousse . . .

pipe it onto buttered toast points and garnish with chopped shallots and capers

serve with watercress as a first course

spread on bread or bagel and eat like a sandwich

toss with hot pasta

New Potatoes with Garlicky Goat Cheese

Crispy potatoes form a sturdy base for this festive finger food which combines many of our favorite Provençal ingredients, including olives, goat cheese, garlic, and thyme.

Two commonly used olives are the niçoise and the kalamata. Hailing from France, the niçoise is generally cured in brine and packed in oil. The larger Greek kalamata olive offers a potent flavor and is considered by many to be "crème de la crème" of all olives.

10 slices new potato (each ¼ inch thick)

¼ cup olive oil

6 ounces goat cheese, softened

2 cloves garlic, crushed

2 tablespoons chopped fresh thyme leaves

¼ cup chopped black olives

10 slices black olive

10 sprigs thyme

Heat oil in a pan over high heat. Add potato slices and pan sear until crispy on each side. Remove potatoes from pan and reserve. Combine goat cheese, garlic, thyme, and chopped black olives. Spread or pipe mixture onto potato slices. Garnish each with a slice of olive and a sprig of thyme.

Serves 10

Profiteroles with Crab

Miniature cream puffs can be stuffed with either a sweet or savory filling. Tabasco and cayenne ensure that our crab filling is savory indeed.

8 tablespoons mayonnaise

Dash of Tabasco sauce

Dash of Worcestershire sauce

Pinch of cayenne

2 teaspoons lemon juice

1 tablespoon chopped chives

1 tablespoon diced tomato

½ pound lump crabmeat

Profiteroles (Recipe appears on page 222.)

Combine all ingredients, except crabmeat and profiteroles, in a bowl and mix well. Gently fold in crabmeat.

Slice profiteroles in half horizontally. Place 1 tablespoonful crabmeat mixture on each bottom half. Cover with remaining halves.

Yields approximately 20 profiteroles

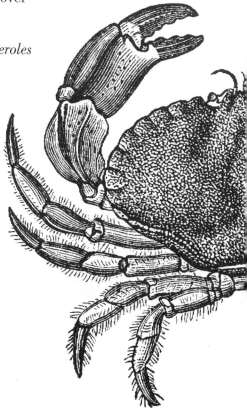

Gougere

A traditional snack in Burgundy, these warm, cheesy mouthfuls are delightfully crisp on the outside and wonderfully chewy inside. Serve them piping hot and make an extra batch because they disappear fast.

1 cup water
½ cup unsalted butter, cut into ½-inch pieces
½ teaspoon kosher salt
1 cup flour
4 eggs
1 cup grated Gruyère cheese

Combine water, butter, and salt in a heavy saucepan and bring to a boil. Remove pan from heat and stir in flour. Whisk to combine; then return to medium heat. Cook, whisking constantly, until mixture is thickened and pulls away from the sides of the pan, no more than 5 minutes. Remove from heat and beat in eggs, one at a time. Stir in cheese.

Preheat oven to 425°. Line 2 baking sheets with parchment paper. Using a pastry bag fitted with a ⅝-inch tip, pipe pastry onto baking sheets in ½-inch mounds. Mounds should be spaced at least 1 inch apart. Bake for 15 minutes. Reduce oven temperature to 300° and bake for another 20 minutes or until golden brown. Serve as is or stuff with Salmon Mousse (Recipe appears on page 18.), Duck Rillettes (Recipe appears on page 17.), or soft cheeses.

Yields 45 puffs

Plan on 6 hors d'oeuvres per person if you are also serving dinner; 12 to 15 pieces per person if you are only serving hors d'oeuvres.

Wild Mushroom Strudel with Gruyère Cheese

We created this recipe specially for a reception for New Jersey Governor Christine Todd Whitman. It's now one of the most requested items on our catering menu.

3 tablespoons unsalted butter

2 shallots, minced

10 ounces wild mushrooms such as shiitake, crimini, or cèpes, sliced

½ cup white wine

Salt and pepper

4 ounces Gruyère cheese, grated

9 sheets phyllo dough

Melted butter

Heat butter in a sauté pan over medium heat. Sauté shallots until soft. Add mushrooms and sauté for 2 minutes. Add wine and simmer until wine is absorbed. Season to taste with salt and pepper. Stir in cheese. Reduce heat to low.

Preheat oven to 350°. Lay 1 sheet of phyllo dough out on a clean, dry work surface. Brush with melted butter. Repeat process 2 more times to create 3 layers. Cut phyllo into 2-inch wide strips. Place 1 tablespoon mushroom-cheese mixture at one end of each strip and fold up like a flag to form individual triangles. Repeat with remaining phyllo sheets and filling. Arrange triangles on a baking sheet and bake for 10 to 12 minutes. Serve warm.

Yields approximately 24 triangles

phyllo
[FEE-loh]

Greek for "leaf," phyllo refers to thin sheets of pastry dough used in sweet and savory foods such as baklava. Phyllo is sold both fresh and frozen. Frozen dough should be thawed according to package instructions.

Escargot à la Bourguignonne

We found this dish at a little bistro in northern Lyon. The proprietor gave us the recipe after we ordered six portions.

1 sheet frozen puff pastry, thawed
Burgundy Herb Butter (see recipe)
24 helix snails, drained and rinsed
2 egg yolks, beaten

Preheat oven to 400°. Line a baking sheet with parchment paper. Roll puff pastry out on a lightly floured work surface. Using a 2-inch round cookie cutter, cut pastry into 24 circles.

Place a dollop of butter in the center of each circle and top each with 1 snail. Fold the edges of pastry dough over each snail and pinch to seal. Brush edges with a little bit of egg yolk to help secure the seams. Place wrapped snails, seams down, on baking sheet. Brush with egg yolk and bake for 10 to 12 minutes until golden brown. Serve hot.

Serves 12

à la Bourguignonne
[ah-lah boor-gee-NYON]

The French term for "as prepared in Burgundy," one of France's most famous gastronomic regions.

Burgundy Herb Butter

¼ cup Burgundy wine
Pinch of sugar
¼ pound butter
1½ teaspoons chopped garlic
2 tablespoons EACH chopped parsley, thyme, and chives
1 teaspoon lemon juice
Salt and pepper

Combine wine and sugar in a saucepan over medium heat. Cook until wine is reduced and almost syrupy. Cool and reserve. Put butter, garlic, and herbs into a food processor and pulse until smooth. Add reduced wine and lemon juice and blend. Season with salt and pepper. Cover and refrigerate until ready to use.

Bruschetta with Tomato and Fresh Mozzarella

This is one of our favorite uses for ruby ripe Jersey tomatoes. We make our homemade mozzarella especially for this dish.

4 medium tomatoes, diced
⅓ cup diced onion
¼ cup red wine vinegar
3 tablespoons oregano
Salt and pepper
1 baguette (about 10 inches long), cut into 1-inch thick slices
⅓ cup olive oil
6 cloves garlic, mashed
10 slices fresh mozzarella, each ½-inch thick

Combine tomatoes, onion, vinegar, oregano, and salt and pepper in a bowl. Set aside and allow mixture to marinate for at least 20 minutes.

Meanwhile, brush bread with olive oil and spread with garlic. Toast under broiler, on a grill, or in a hot oven (400°) until golden, about 2 minutes. Top each slice with 1 to 2 tablespoons tomato mixture and garnish with a slice of fresh mozzarella. Serve immediately.

Serves 10

Garlic grilled bread can be crowned with an endless array of toppings. Here are some of our favorites:

salmon mousse and dill

sun-dried tomatoes and goat cheeses

roasted garlic, prosciutto, and sharp provolone

roasted red peppers and Greek olives

brie and apple slices

pesto and pine nuts

Calamari Bruschetta

We first enjoyed light, refreshing seafood bruschetta while sitting by the water in Cannes. Calamari is our favorite.

2 pounds squid tubes and tentacles, cleaned

1 cup extra virgin olive oil

Salt and pepper

Juice of 2 lemons

1 cup chopped basil

3 plum tomatoes, diced

2 teaspoons minced garlic

12 slices Italian or French bread

Toss together squid, 3 tablespoons olive oil, and salt and pepper to taste in a mixing bowl. Place squid on a preheated hot grill. Cook tubes for 2 minutes per side and tentacles for a total of 2 minutes. Remove pieces from grill and cool until easily handled.

Cut tubes into rings and roughly chop tentacles. Place squid in a bowl. Add remaining ingredients, reserving 2 tablespoons olive oil. Allow mixture to marinate for at least 30 minutes.

Brush both sides of bread slices with remaining olive oil and grill both sides. Spoon a little mixture on each piece of bread and serve.

Serves 12

Although the squid can be sautéed, grilling really brings out the sweetness of the delicate meat.

Escargot en Croûte in Champagne Cream with Fennel Butter

Fennel butter adds a touch of herbal sweetness to this recipe. The puff pastry makes an elegant presentation.

1 sheet frozen puff pastry, thawed

1 egg, beaten

1 tablespoon butter

1 shallot, minced

1 teaspoon chopped garlic

1 cup champagne

1½ cups heavy cream

2 dozen large snails

2 tablespoons Fennel Butter (Recipe appears on page 287.)

Salt and pepper

Preheat oven to 400°. Line a sheet pan with parchment paper. Roll puff pastry out on a lightly floured work surface and cut into 6 equal-size squares. In each square, cut a square inside the square ½ inch from the edge, leaving two opposite corners connected. Brush the inside square with beaten egg and fold the cut corners over so the edges meet with the inside square. Brush top with egg and place on sheet pan. Bake until golden brown, about 10 minutes.

Melt butter in a pan over medium heat. Add shallot and garlic and sauté until translucent. Deglaze with champagne and heat until liquid is reduced by half. Add cream and cook until mixture is thick enough to coat the back of a spoon. Add snails and simmer for 1 to 2 minutes. Swirl in fennel butter. Season to taste with salt and pepper. Spoon mixture into warm puff pastry croûtes.

Serves 6

Not too long ago, home cooks had to rely on canned and packaged snails. While these are still available in gourmet stores and supermarkets, fresh snails are increasingly available year-round in specialty markets. The best known varieties are vineyard or Burgundy and *petit-gris*.

Pâté en Croûte

Pâté en Croûte can be the festive centerpiece of any buffet.
Serve it with baguettes or crostinis.

½ teaspoon juniper berries

1 bay leaf

1 teaspoon allspice

2 tablespoons salt

1 tablespoon mixed peppercorns

2 tablespoons sugar

1 pork shoulder (1 pound), cut into cubes

2 ounces port

2 ounces brandy

2 eggs

1 sheet frozen puff pastry, thawed

Place spices, salt, peppercorns, and sugar in a food processor. Process until well combined. In a bowl, combine spice mixture with meat. Cover and refrigerate for at least 6 hours.

Drain and rinse meat. Grind or cut meat into tiny cubes. Add liquids and 1 egg and mix thoroughly. Set aside.

Preheat oven to 400°. Roll puff pastry out on a lightly floured work surface and cut pastry in half lengthwise. Spread meat on center of one half. Cover with remaining pastry slice. Lightly beat remaining egg and brush on top of pastry slice. Make 4 or 5 shallow cuts into pastry with a small knife. (This allows steam to escape.) Cook for 25 minutes or until brown. Serve hot or cold.

Serves 12

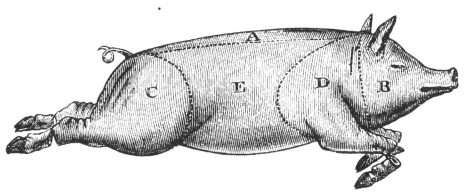

Smoked Salmon Terrine with Goat Cheese, Peppers, and Horseradish Cream

Smoked salmon, fiery horseradish cream, and tangy goat cheese make this dish an impressive and inventive first course.

¼ cup cream cheese

6 tablespoons unsalted butter

1 pound goat cheese

1 shallot, chopped

3 sprigs fresh thyme, stemmed and chopped

1 sprig rosemary, stemmed and chopped

1 red pepper, diced

1 green pepper, diced

1 pound smoked salmon, sliced

Horseradish Cream (Recipe appears on page 290.)

Sprig of rosemary or thyme for garnish

Whip cream cheese and butter together. Add goat cheese, shallot, thyme, rosemary, and peppers. Mix well.

Line a 16 x 9-inch terrine mold with plastic wrap. Place a thin layer of salmon in terrine mold, overlapping slices as necessary to fully line the mold. Top with a ½-inch layer of goat cheese. Repeat, filling mold with alternating layers of salmon and cheese, ending with a layer of salmon. Press gently and refrigerate for 1 hour.

Unmold terrine (see sidebar). Use a sharp serrated knife to gently cut terrine into ½-inch-thick slices. Spread a bit of horseradish cream on a serving plate and display terrine slices on top of cream. Garnish with sprig of thyme or rosemary.

Serves 8 to 12

To unmold a terrine

Run a thin, sharp knife along the edges of the pan. Set a platter upside down over the terrine, invert, and tap the terrine onto the platter.

Lobster and Salmon Terrine with Sauce Verte

Lobster, salmon, and truffles —
it doesn't get any better than this!

3½ quarts cold water
6 live Maine lobsters (1 pound each)
3 large egg whites
2 teaspoons salt
4½ cups heavy cream
9 ounces boneless salmon fillet
¾ ounce truffle, chopped
Sauce Verte (Recipe appears on page 285.)

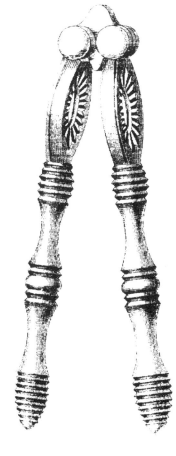

Fill a stockpot with water and bring to a boil. Plunge lobsters head first into pot and cook for 5 minutes. Remove lobsters from water and refrigerate to cool. Once chilled, remove lobster tails, claws, and knuckles from lobsters. Crack tails, claws, and knuckles and remove meat. In a food processor, puree lobster meat, 2 egg whites, and salt. Add 3 cups cream in a slow, steady stream. Transfer to a bowl and refrigerate until well chilled.

Place 6½ ounces salmon and remaining egg white in a food processor and puree. Add remaining cream in a slow, steady stream. Transfer to a bowl and refrigerate until well chilled.

Preheat oven to 250°F. Lightly butter a 12 x 3¼ x 3-inch terrine mold. Stir half of lobster mousse into salmon mousse. Stir in truffle. Spread mixture over the bottom of terrine mold. Thinly slice remaining salmon fillet and lay pieces over mousse mixture. Fill terrine with remaining lobster mousse. Cover with buttered foil. Place mold in a water bath. Bake for 1½ hours. Refrigerate overnight.

Unmold terrine. Slice and top with sauce verte.

Serves 8 to 10

Mixed Game Terrine

Although wild —it's mild.

2 pounds combination of wild boar, pork, venison, duck,
   and/or squab, trimmed of fat

4 ounces fat back, cubed

4 ounces duck liver

2 cloves garlic, minced

3 shallots, minced

1 cup breadcrumbs

2 large eggs, lightly beaten

1 tablespoon chopped fresh thyme

½ teaspoon chopped fresh rosemary

½ cup brandy

Salt and pepper

10 strips smoked bacon, blanched

3 bay leaves

1 sprig thyme

½ cup dry white wine

Finely chop or grind meat, fat back, and liver in a food processor or meat grinder. Transfer to a large mixing bowl. Mix in garlic, shallots, breadcrumbs, eggs, thyme, rosemary, and brandy. Season with salt and pepper.

Preheat oven to 325°. Line a 3-quart terrine with bacon strips. Allow the loose ends to hang over edges. Place meat mixture (also known as forcemeat) in terrine on top of bacon. Fold excess bacon over top of forcemeat. Top with bay leaves and thyme sprig. Pour wine over mixture. Cover terrine with foil and place in a water bath. Bake for approximately 1 hour or until an inserted meat thermometer reads 160°. Remove from oven; allow to cool. Refrigerate until solid.

Unmold terrine (See page 28.). Gently cut terrine into ½-inch-thick slices using a sharp serrated knife.

Serves 12

The wild boar we use at La Campagne are actually quite tame, farm raised cousins to the wild relatives. Although wild boar is available and hunted in many regions of the country, domestically raised boar are less gamey and more tender than their wild counterparts.

Sautéed Frog Legs with Oven-Dried Tomatoes, Capers, and Olives

Make sure you buy enough frog legs because they get snapped up like chicken wings.

1 tablespoon olive oil

12 sets frog legs, cleaned and split

4 oven-dried plum tomatoes, quartered and diced

¼ cup pitted and chopped black olives

1 teaspoon chopped garlic

1 tablespoon rinsed and chopped capers

¼ cup white wine

1 cup Chicken Stock (Recipe appears on page 278.)

2 tablespoons chopped fresh basil

2 tablespoons butter

Salt and pepper

Heat olive oil in a 10-inch sauté pan until almost smoking. Add frog legs and sauté for 1 minute. Add tomatoes, olives, garlic, and capers and sauté for 1 minute. Remove legs from pan, reserve, and keep warm. Add wine and heat until liquid is reduced by half. Add chicken stock and heat until sauce is reduced by half. Add basil, butter, and salt and pepper. Serve frog legs topped with tomato mixture.

Serves 6

To oven dry tomatoes

Quarter tomatoes lengthwise and place skin side down on a baking sheet. Sprinkle with salt and pepper, drizzle with olive oil, and place in a 200° oven for 4 to 5 hours or until the tomatoes take on a shriveled appearance. Herbes de Provence can be added for a nice touch!

Champagne Poached Oysters with Saffron Aïoli

We serve this on New Year's Eve. It's the perfect party food for any celebration.

12 fresh oysters, shucked
1 cup champagne
Saffron Aïoli (see recipe)
1 ounce sevruga caviar

Remove oysters from shells. Reserve juice and bottom shells. Combine oysters, oyster juice, champagne, and salt and pepper in a small saucepan over medium heat. Cook until oysters are poached, about 2 to 3 minutes. Immediately place oysters in the reserved shells. Top with a dollop of aïoli and a spoonful of caviar.

Serves 6

aïoli
[ay-OH-lee]
This garlicky mayonnaise is the unofficial garlic dish of Provence. Serve it with fish, meats, or vegetables.

Saffron Aïoli

½ teaspoon saffron
¼ cup white wine
3 cloves garlic, mashed
1 egg
½ cup olive oil
Juice of 1 lemon
Salt and pepper

Combine saffron and white wine in a saucepan over low heat. Heat gently until liquid is reduced by half. Remove from heat and cool to room temperature. Mix garlic and egg in a bowl. Slowly whisk in oil — first in drops and then in a steady stream — until fully incorporated. Add cooled wine, lemon juice, and salt and pepper to taste. Stir until aïoli is thick and shiny.

Oysters with Caviar in Lemon-Saffron Fumet

Steeping the saffron extracts its aromatic fragrance and golden color.

12 fresh oysters, shucked

Pinch of saffron

1 tablespoon warm water

Zest and juice of 1 lemon

1 small carrot, peeled and diced

2 stalks celery, diced

1 shallot, minced

½ cup dry white wine

2 tablespoons fresh chopped chives

Salt and pepper

½ ounce caviar

Remove oysters from shells. Reserve oysters and juice. Arrange bottom shells on a serving platter.

Soak saffron in warm water for 10 minutes, drain, and reserve saffron. Heat zest and enough water to cover in a small saucepan over medium-high heat. Simmer for 5 minutes, drain, and reserve zest.

Blanch carrot and celery in boiling water for 3 minutes. Plunge into ice water, drain, and reserve.

Combine saffron, carrot, celery, shallot, and wine in a sauté pan over medium-high heat. Simmer for 1 minute. Add oysters and reserved juice and simmer for 1 minute. Add lemon zest, lemon juice, and chives. Season to taste with salt and pepper.

Place oysters in the reserved shells. Spoon broth over shells and top with a spoonful of caviar.

Serves 6

Look for lemons that are smooth, bright yellow, plump, and heavy. To get more juice from a lemon, microwave for 15 seconds on high and then roll the lemon on a counter top or hard surface.

Smoked Salmon Napoleons.

An elegant crowd pleasing starter. Don't be intimidated by the recipe length; it's actually quite easy to make.

½ cup flour, sifted

3 large egg whites

3 tablespoons Clarified Butter (Recipe appears on page 287.)

½ cup clam juice

¾ pound smoked salmon, cut into 12 slices (each about 3 inches wide)

1 cup Crème Fraîche (Recipe appears on page 289.) or sour cream

3 tablespoons minced chives

1 tablespoon minced shallot

1 teaspoon lemon juice

Salt and pepper

Shallot Vinaigrette (see recipe)

Chopped chives

Place sifted flour into a mixing bowl. Make a well in the middle and pour in egg whites. Whisk until smooth. Stir in butter and clam juice. Chill for 2 hours.

Using ramekin or cookie cutter as a guide, cut a 3-inch circle from each salmon slice. Set aside. Chop remaining salmon scraps into small pieces. In a mixing bowl, whisk together crème fraîche, chives, shallot, lemon juice, and salt and pepper to taste. Fold in chopped salmon. Chill.

Preheat oven to 400°. Butter a baking sheet. Using a tablespoon, drop 12 pastry mounds about 6 inches apart onto baking sheet. Spread batter with the back of a fork into 3-inch circles. Bake for 7 minutes in center of oven, just until edges brown. Transfer pastry tiles to a cooling rack.

If possible, avoid packaged lox products. Choose high-quality smoked salmon from the deli counter or specialty shop. It should be mild and sweet and not overly salty.

Place 1 pastry tile in the center of each of 4 serving plates. Top with 1 slice salmon and 1 tablespoon salmon cream. Cover with a second tile, another slice salmon, and another tablespoon cream. Top with a third tile, a third slice salmon, and a mound of cream. Spoon vinaigrette around napoleons. Garnish with chopped chives.

Serves 4

Shallot Vinaigrette

4 shallots, thinly sliced
¼ cup olive oil
1 teaspoon Dijon mustard
¼ cup clam juice
Juice of ½ lemon
1 teaspoon minced fresh parsley
Salt and pepper

Over medium heat, sauté shallots in oil until very soft, but not brown. Whisk in mustard. Slowly whisk in clam juice and lemon juice. Stir in parsley. Season to taste with salt and pepper.

Vegetable Polenta on Tomato Basil Coulis

Polenta may be a trendy item on restaurant menus, but it is actually just a mush made from cornmeal. It can be served hot as a hearty breakfast cereal or cooled, cut into squares, and fried. At La Campagne we add cheeses, herbs, and vegetables and serve it as a side dish or first course.

5¼ cups water

3 carrots, diced

3 red peppers, diced

2 green peppers, diced

2 medium zucchini, diced

2 teaspoons salt

2 cups corn meal

7 tablespoons butter

6 tablespoons grated Parmesan cheese

2 tablespoons butter

Tomato Basil Coulis (Recipe appears on page 290.)

Bring ¾ cup water to a boil. Add carrots, peppers, and zucchini and boil for 8 to 10 minutes. Remove vegetables from water and set aside.

Bring remaining water and salt to a boil in a large pot. Add corn meal, reduce heat to low, and simmer for 30 minutes, stirring constantly. Add 5 tablespoons butter, cheese, and cooked vegetables. Mix gently and spread polenta onto a large cookie pan to about 1 to 2 inches high. Cool until firm, about 60 minutes.

Cut polenta into squares. Melt remaining 2 tablespoons butter in a sauté pan over medium-high heat. Pan fry squares until brown, about 5 minutes per side.

Cover bottom of a serving plate with coulis and stack polenta squares.

Serves 4 to 6

"Aumoniere" of Lamb

This is a tasty winter alternative to a rack or leg of lamb.

5 tablespoons butter

1 pound white mushrooms, chopped

2 shallots, diced

¼ cup cream

Salt and pepper

6 medallions lamb, cut from the saddle

6 ounces white wine

1 clove garlic

1 tablespoon tomato paste

1 teaspoon fresh herbs

6 Basic Crêpes (each 8 inches round) (Recipe appears on page 273.)

2 scallions, sliced into long strips

Melt 2 tablespoons butter in a saucepan. Add mushrooms and shallots and sauté until dry. Add cream and cook until mixture becomes a moist paste. Season to taste with salt and pepper. Remove from heat and reserve.

Melt 2 tablespoons butter in a sauté pan and pan sear lamb medallions until brown on one side and just a bit cooked on the other. Remove from pan and keep warm. Deglaze pan with white wine, garlic, tomato paste, and fresh herbs. Cook, stirring occasionally, until well blended. Reserve.

Preheat oven to 400°. Lightly butter an ovenproof platter. Place 1 lamb medallion in the center of each crêpe. Top with 1 tablespoon mushroom mixture. Roll crêpe into a cigar-shaped tube and tie with a scallion strip. Place stuffed crêpes on platter. Cook for 8 minutes.

Strain sauce and stir in remaining 1 tablespoon butter. Serve crêpes topped with sauce.

Serves 6

You'll find some of the best lamb in the world in Provence, specifically in the small town of Sisteron. Although not available in the United States, you *can* find really wonderful lamb at specialty stores. Ask the butcher (very nicely) for the best available and you'll swear you're dining in the shadow of the Provençal Alps.

Foie Gras with Diver Sea Scallops and Porcini Crêpes

*Each scallop is hand-picked by divers and dry packed to ensure a wonderful flavor and firm meat. Once considered a novelty, we now serve **only** diver scallops.*

4 large diver sea scallops

½ ounce fresh black truffle, sliced into 4 pieces

4 ounces foie gras, sliced into 4 pieces

½ cup pitted sour cherries, juice reserved

½ cup Madeira wine

Salt and pepper

4 Porcini Crêpes (Recipe appears on page 39.)

White truffle oil

Carefully dry scallops with paper towel. Cut a small pocket into each scallop and stuff each with a truffle slice. Heat a nonstick pan over medium-high heat. Add foie gras and sear each side for 45 seconds. Remove from pan and reserve. Add scallops and sear each side for 90 seconds. (Don't overcook. Scallops should be translucent in the middle.) Remove from pan and reserve. Add cherries and juice, wine, and salt and pepper to taste. Simmer for 1 minute.

Fold crepes into triangles and place one on each of 4 warmed plates. Place a scallop on each crêpe and top with a foie gras slice. Spoon cherries and sauce over each serving. Garnish with drops of truffle oil.

Serves 4

Foie gras, a true luxury food, is the enlarged liver of a goose or duck that has been force-fed for 6 weeks to 5 months. With a literal French translation of "fat liver," it is no wonder that these livers may weigh as much as 3 pounds. This expensive delicacy may be marinated in a mixture made with seasonings and port or Madeira wine before being cooked to yield a flavor that is wonderfully rich.

Porcini Crêpes

Dried porcini mushrooms are a great substitute when fresh are not available.

¼ cup water
¼ cup milk
1 large egg
½ cup flour
½ ounce dry porcini mushroom, ground to powder
¼ teaspoon salt
1½ teaspoons melted butter

Mix ingredients in a blender. Refrigerate for 1 hour.

Heat an 8-inch nonstick pan over medium-high heat. Brush lightly with additional melted butter. Ladle 3 tablespoons batter into center of pan. Twirl pan to allow batter to spread evenly over pan. Cook for about 30 seconds or until edges are brown and underside is golden. Flip with fingers or a spatula and cook for 1 minute. Slide crêpe onto plate. Repeat until all batter is used, stacking finished crêpes between wax paper or off center for easy separation.

Yields 4 to 6 crêpes

Also called cèpes, porcini mushrooms have fat stems, a meaty texture, and a pungent, earthy flavor. Although you can sometimes find them fresh in specialty markets, the dried form of this mushroom is more readily available. Reconstituted dried porcini can be substituted for cultivated mushrooms and can be added to soups, stews, stuffings, salads, and sauces.

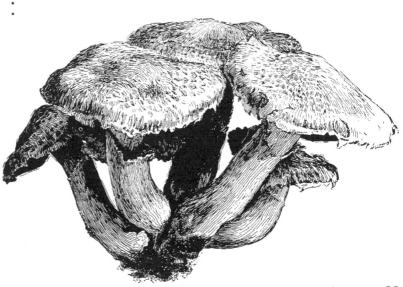

from the cooking school at la
campagne ~ from the cooking
school at la campagne ~ from the
cooking school at la campagne ~
from the cooking school at la
campagne ~ from the cooking
school at la campagne ~ from the
cooking school at la campagne ~
from the cooking school at la
campagne ~ from the cooking
school at la campagne ~ from the
cooking school at la campagne ~
from the cooking school at la
campagne ~ from the cooking
school at la campagne ~ from the
cooking school at la campagne ~
from the cooking school at la
campagne ~ from the cooking
school at la campagne ~ from the

salads

Fresh Herb Salad with Truffled Goat Cheese

After visiting a goat farm and creamery in Burgundy, we were treated to this lovely salad so that we could sample the freshly made herb wrapped chèvre.

¼ pound mixed baby greens (mâche, mizuna, lolla rosa)
¼ pound assorted fresh herbs (basil, sorrel, et al.)
1 shallot, minced
1 teaspoon Dijon mustard
¼ cup sherry vinegar
⅓ cup extra virgin olive oil
Salt and pepper
10 ounces soft goat cheese (also called chèvre)
1 ounce canned truffles, drained and finely chopped

Wash, dry, and mix greens and herbs together. In a separate bowl, whisk together shallot, mustard, and vinegar. Whisk in oil in a slow, steady stream. Season with salt and pepper.

Roll goat cheese into 12 balls. Roll balls in chopped truffles. Toss greens with dressing and divide among 4 chilled plates. Serve each salad with 3 truffled goat cheese balls.

Serves 4

The highly nutritious, rare, and expensive truffle is cultivated under the earth. Hence, farmers require the trained noses of dogs and pigs for assistance when harvesting. Once sniffed out, the truffle's peculiar, wrinkled appearance disguises a truly potent flavor that has been enjoyed for centuries.

Herb Salad with Nasturtium and Sherry Vinaigrette

Edible flowers such as peppery nasturtiums, pansies, marigolds, and rose petals are now readily available in food centers. They add a splash of color and a festive touch to any salad presentation.

2 ounces flat-leaf parsley, stemmed, rinsed, and dried

2 ounces chives, minced

2 ounces fresh mint, stemmed, rinsed, and dried

2 ounces fresh basil, stemmed, rinsed, and dried

2 ounces sorrel, stemmed, rinsed, dried, and cut into large chiffonade

Sherry Vinaigrette (see recipe)

4 nasturtium blossoms, stemmed

Combine herbs in a large bowl. Gently toss with vinaigrette. Arrange on 4 chilled plates and top with nasturtium petals.

Serves 4

chiffonade

[shihf-uh-NAHD]

French phrase that means "made of rags." In culinary terms it refers to herbs or leafy vegetables cut into fine shreds.

Sherry Vinaigrette

1 teaspoon sherry vinegar

1 teaspoon red wine vinegar

1 tablespoon olive oil

Salt and pepper

Whisk together vinegars, oil, and salt and pepper to taste in a stainless steel bowl.

Mâche and Roquefort in Vanilla-Lavender Vinaigrette

Lavender is very easy to grow and makes a lovely, aromatic accent for any garden. That's why we have over 100 lavender bushes growing on our property. The fragrance recalls wonderful memories and meals of Provence.

4 bunches mâche

2 heads Belgian endive

Vanilla-Lavender Vinaigrette (see recipe)

2 tablespoons chopped walnuts

2 tablespoons crumbled Roquefort cheese

Divide mâche among 4 chilled plates and place in center of plates. Arrange endive in a star pattern around mâche. Drizzle with vinaigrette. Garnish with walnuts and Roquefort.

Serves 4

Vanilla-Lavender Vinaigrette

1 cup white wine vinegar

½ teaspoon dried lavender

½ vanilla bean, split and cut into 1-inch pieces

1 shallot, minced

½ cup olive oil

Salt and pepper

Combine vinegar, lavender, and vanilla bean in a bottle or jar with a lid. Allow flavors to blend for at least 2 days.

In a mixing bowl, combine ¼ cup flavored vinegar and shallot. Whisk in olive oil. Season to taste with salt and pepper. (Reserve remaining lavender vinegar for future use.)

Balsamic vinegar and olive oil have become salad dressing staples, but there are a countless variety of vinegars and oils available in gourmet stores and many supermarkets. Experiment!

Although an abundance of truffle varieties exists, there are only three edible types. The most popular variety is the black truffle hailing largely from the Périgord region of France. This ebony colored fungus is generally used to flavor cooked dishes that include eggs, sauces, or chicken. From the Piedmont region of Italy, the white truffle boasts a raw pungent odor and mild flavor. It is delicious as a garnish or. when added at the last moment to many cooked dishes. The extremely rare summer truffle resembles the white truffle and can be used in similar ways as both the white and black varieties.

Mâche and Baby Artichokes in Truffle Vinaigrette

The best truffles we've ever seen were in the back room of a small tabac in St. Remy. But buyer beware!

4 small artichokes, trimmed, blanched, and thinly sliced
½ pound mâche
1 medium ripe tomato, peeled, seeded, and chopped
Truffle Vinaigrette (see recipe)

Arrange sliced artichokes on 4 chilled salad plates. Top with mâche and chopped tomato. Drizzle vinaigrette over each salad and garnish with reserved truffle slices.

Serves 4

Truffle Vinaigrette

1 small shallot, minced
⅓ pound fresh truffles, chopped (Reserve a few slices for garnish.)
¼ cup sherry vinegar
½ cup olive oil
Salt and freshly ground pepper

Whisk together shallot, truffles, vinegar, and oil in a mixing bowl. Season to taste with salt and pepper.

Caesar Salad

To ensure a perfect salad, be sure to use the best ingredients and don't dress the romaine until ready to serve.

3 large egg yolks
3 whole anchovy fillets
4 cloves garlic, peeled
2 teaspoons fresh lemon juice
1½ cups olive oil
1 teaspoon Worcestershire sauce
3 dashes Tabasco sauce
Black pepper
2 large heads romaine, washed and well dried
½ cup grated locatelli Romano cheese
Croutons (Recipe appears on page 292.)

Place yolks, anchovies, garlic, and lemon juice in a food processor or blender and puree. With motor running, add oil in a slow, steady stream. Blend in Worcestershire, Tabasco, and pepper to taste.

Tear romaine into bite-size pieces. Place in a large mixing bowl. Thoroughly toss romaine with the dressing and cheese. Divide salad among 4 plates. Top with croutons. Dust with additional fresh ground pepper to taste.

Serves 4

Commonly found in the popular canned, salted, and filleted form, anchovies may also be found as a paste, smoked or fresh. The unopened canned fillet can be stored at room temperature for up to 1 year. Because of its saltiness, the canned anchovy is classically used in Caesar salad but is otherwise used scantily in other preparations.

Arugula with Goat Cheese and Sugar Sautéed Onions

1 teaspoon butter

½ pint pearl onions

1 teaspoon sugar

1 log goat cheese (7 ounces)

1 bunch fresh thyme, stemmed and chopped

1 egg, beaten

½ cup breadcrumbs

6 ounces arugula or young spinach, cleaned

½ cup chopped pecans

Red Wine Vinaigrette (see recipe)

Melt butter in a skillet over medium heat. Add pearl onions and sugar and sauté until brown, 5 to 10 minutes. Reserve.

Preheat oven to 450°. Cut goat cheese log into 4 equal disks and sprinkle with thyme. Dip disks in egg wash; then in breadcrumbs. Bake on a lightly greased baking sheet for 4 minutes. Remove from oven and allow to cool for 1 to 2 minutes.

Divide arugula between 4 plates. Top arugula with sautéed pearl onions and pecans. Drizzle vinaigrette on each salad and garnish with a cheese crouton.

Serves 4

Arugula, also called rocket, roquette, and rucola, has a peppery, slightly bitter taste with nutty undertones. Look for bright green, fresh looking leaves. Wash leaves thoroughly before using. Store in refrigerator, tightly wrapped in plastic, for no more than 2 days.

Red Wine Vinaigrette

2 tablespoons red wine vinegar

1 teaspoon balsamic vinegar

6 tablespoons olive oil or walnut oil

1 teaspoon sesame oil

Salt

Combine vinegars in a mixing bowl. Whisk in oils in a slow, steady stream. Season to taste with salt.

Arugula and Penne Pasta Salad

Keep some extra Tomato Dressing in your refrigerator. You'll find fresh taste is a welcome addition to pasta salads, marinated fish salads, and grilled fish or poultry.

1 pound dry penne pasta
Tomato Dressing (see recipe)
2 bunches arugula, washed
Grated Parmesan cheese

Cook pasta according to directions on box. Refrigerate pasta. When cool, toss pasta with tomato dressing in a large bowl. Divide arugula among chilled plates. Top with pasta salad and sprinkle with cheese.

Serves 4 to 6

Tomato Dressing

3 tomatoes, peeled and seeded
1 teaspoon chopped garlic
2 teaspoons chopped shallot
½ cup balsamic vinegar or sherry vinegar
1½ cups good olive oil
Salt and pepper

Combine tomatoes, garlic, shallot, and vinegar in a mixing bowl. Whisk in olive oil in a steady stream. Season to taste with salt and pepper.

Oils to try

Olive oils – extra virgin, virgin

Nut oils – almond, hazelnut, sesame, peanut, walnut

Herb oils – basil, tarragon, lavender

Flavored oils – garlic, peppercorn

Lite – sunflower, safflower, grapeseed

Salad of Fennel, Orange, and Olives

This festive, colorful recipe celebrates the spirit and long sunny days in the south of France.

½ head fennel bulbs, cored and sliced
1 orange, peeled and sliced
½ small red onion, peeled and sliced
Kosher salt
Freshly ground black pepper
3 tablespoons extra virgin olive oil
1 small head romaine, cored, washed, and well dried
12 cured olives, pitted and chopped
Red pepper flakes, optional

Combine fennel, orange, and onion in a wooden bowl. Season to taste with salt and pepper. Sprinkle with oil and toss.

Divide romaine leaves among 4 plates. Top with fennel mixture. Garnish with olives. Sprinkle with pepper flakes if desired.

Serves 4

Fennel is a plant with bright green foliage that has been grown since ancient times and thought by the Greeks to give strength to those who ate it.

Farmstand Salad

*A rainbow of assorted roasted vegetables create an
eye-catching main course salad.*

1 cup great Northern white beans, soaked overnight
2 zucchini, cut into ½-inch-thick slices
2 eggplants, cut into ½-inch-thick rounds
2 yellow peppers, stemmed, quartered, and seeded
2 red peppers, stemmed, quartered, and seeded
1 red onion, cut into 1-inch-thick slices
Salt and pepper
1½ cups olive oil
1 can (16 ounces) firm artichoke hearts
2 tomatoes, peeled and diced
1 teaspoon chopped garlic
1 cup chopped assorted fresh herbs (basil, sorrel, et al.)
⅓ cup balsamic vinegar
Parmesan cheese, optional

Drain beans and put into a stockpot. Cover beans with
clean water and add salt. Bring to a boil and cook for 25
minutes or until tender. Drain and reserve.

Preheat oven to 350°. Season zucchini, eggplants,
peppers, and onion with salt and pepper and place in a
large roasting pan. Drizzle with ½ cup olive oil and toss to
lightly coat. Roast, stirring occasionally, until vegetables are
soft and lightly charred. Add artichokes and cook for 5
minutes. Allow vegetables to cool slightly. Remove skins from
peppers. Chop vegetables into bite-size pieces.

Cook tomatoes and garlic in remaining olive oil for 10
minutes. Remove from heat and allow to cool. When cooled,
whisk in herbs and vinegar. Mix beans with half the dressing and place beans in the middle of a platter. Place chopped
vegetables around beans. Sprinkle remaining dressing on
vegetables and dust with Parmesan cheese if desired.

Serves 6 to 8

A fruit often mistaken
for a vegetable, the
eggplant is a member
of the nightshade clan
and considered a
berry. The eggplant
originated over 5,000
years ago in India and
has since spread into
the Middle and Far
East and into northern
and southern
Mediterranean areas.
The most popular
type, the traditional
long, plum-colored
eggplant, can be
charbroiled, baked,
fried, roasted, etc.
Other varieties
include the long and
narrow Asian eggplant,
the small and round
Thai eggplant, and the
miniature Italian or
baby eggplant.

Ratatouille Salad

This classic recipe captures the taste of summertime in Provence, and, luckily, you can make it any time of year.

3 tablespoons olive oil
1 cup plus 1 tablespoon onion, diced
1 red bell pepper, diced
1 green bell pepper, diced
2 eggplants, peeled and diced
2 medium zucchini, diced
4 plum tomatoes, sliced
Basil-Anchovy Dressing (see recipe)

Heat olive oil in a large sauté pan over medium heat. Add 1 cup onion and peppers and cook for 2 minutes. Add eggplant and cook for 2 minutes. Add zucchini and cook for 2 minutes. When all vegetables are tender, remove vegetables from heat and allow to cool.

Place tomato slices around the edge of a serving platter. Sprinkle with remaining onion. Toss vegetables with dressing and place in center of platter. Serve at room temperature.

Serves 4

Zucchini is classified as a summer squash and sometimes referred to as baby squash. Like the eggplant, zucchini is a fruit that is used as a vegetable. Look for small zucchini that are brightly colored and smooth. Most zucchini are dark green, but there are also yellow and lime green Italian varieties. Just simply wash, dry, and trim the ends before cooking.

Basil-Anchovy Dressing

½

1 ounce anchovy fillet, crushed
2 tablespoons basil
1 tablespoon chopped capers
Juice of 1 lemon
½ head garlic, roasted and crushed
1½ cups olive oil
Salt and pepper

Combine first 5 ingredients in a food processor and puree. Add oil in a slow, steady stream. Puree again. Season to taste with salt and pepper.

Niçoise Salad

Ingredients such as fresh tuna, tomatoes, anchovies, and olives are the hallmarks of this classic salad. It is best enjoyed while sitting at a sidewalk cafe in Nice or in your own sunny kitchen.

1 head romaine lettuce, chopped or 4 cups mixed greens

2 stalks celery, sliced

1 small red onion, sliced

2 tuna steaks (8 ounces each), grilled and flaked or 1 can (16 ounces) tuna

3 hard-boiled eggs, quartered

½ cucumber, peeled and sliced

½ pound haricot verts (French green beans), snipped and blanched

6 ripe tomatoes, quartered

½ cup ripe niçoise olives

8 anchovy fillets, rinsed and dried

Niçoise Dressing (see recipe)

Toss greens, celery, and onion and divide among 6 chilled salad plates. Arrange tuna, egg, cucumber, haricot verts, tomatoes, olives, and anchovies neatly on top. Drizzle with dressing and serve.

Serves 6

Actually a native to the lower Americas, the French green bean goes by a number of other names, including string, haricot vert, dwarf, and Thai. The bean comes in a variety of shapes, sizes, and colors. Regardless of color, look for beans that are firm and crisp.

Niçoise Dressing

¼ cup extra virgin olive oil

3 tablespoons lemon juice

2 tablespoons chopped fresh basil

Salt and pepper

Whisk together oil, lemon juice, and basil in a mixing bowl. Season to taste with salt and pepper.

Fresh Seared Tuna Salad

We love the summer when the local fishermen bring us tuna from off the Jersey shore. It gives us ample opportunities to be creative with one of the sea's finest products.

1 pound fresh tuna loin, skinned and trimmed

3 tablespoons cracked black pepper

½ cup plus 2 tablespoons olive oil

2 tablespoons sherry vinegar

1 tablespoon Dijon mustard

2 tablespoons chopped shallot

1 tablespoon chopped fresh dill

Salt and pepper

¼ pound haricots verts (green beans), blanched and chilled

1 pound small new potatoes, quartered, boiled, and cooled

1 cup cherry tomatoes, halved

2 large hard-boiled eggs, peeled and quartered

Roll tuna in cracked pepper to coat. Heat 2 tablespoons olive oil in a sauté pan over medium-high heat. Add tuna and sear on all sides to desired doneness. Allow to cool.

Whisk together remaining oil, vinegar, mustard, shallot, and dill. Season to taste with salt and pepper. Toss the vegetables and eggs with vinaigrette, reserving 2 tablespoons for tuna.

Slice tuna into 4 portions. Place tuna in the center of a large platter. Arrange vegetables around tuna and top tuna with remaining dressing.

Serves 4

Stuffed Lobster Salad

4 gallons salted water

6 live Maine lobsters (1 pound each)

3 cups water or Chicken Stock (Recipe appears on page 278.)

1 cup medium grain couscous

½ small bulb fennel, cored and thinly sliced

½ hot house cucumber, peeled, seeded, and diced

1 large tomato, peeled, seeded, and diced

3 tablespoons extra virgin olive oil

1 teaspoon fresh lemon juice

¼ cup pitted and minced cured black olives

1 teaspoon chopped fresh oregano

4 basil leaves, cut into ribbons

Salt and pepper

4 bunches arugula, washed and dried

Bring water to boil in a pot large enough to hold lobsters. Plunge lobsters into pot head first and boil, covered, for 5 minutes. Plunge lobsters into ice water. Crack the claws and remove meat. Using a large, sharp knife, split lobsters down the middle. Reserve meat and discard corral and liver. Remove meat from the tails. Rinse and dry shells; then reserve. Dice meat.

Bring 1½ cups water or stock to a boil. Add couscous, stir, and remove pan from heat. Cover and let sit for 5 minutes. In a separate pan, bring remaining stock to a simmer and add fennel, cucumber, and tomatoes. Cook for 2 to 3 minutes. Drain. Fluff couscous with a fork. Fold in vegetables, oil, lemon juice, olives, and herbs. Add lobster meat and combine. Season to taste with salt and pepper.

Divide arugula among 6 chilled plates. Stuff lobster-couscous salad into reserved shells and serve atop arugula.

Serves 6

A traditional North African staple, couscous comes from semolina grains and may be used in a variety of dishes from porridge to bread pudding to salad to pasta. Look for couscous in Middle Eastern markets.

Lobster and Mango Salad

While traveling in Bar Harbor, Maine, we found this salad combination that is more than a few steps beyond your basic boiled with butter.

3½ quarts water
2 live Maine lobsters (1 pound each)
1 mango, peeled and diced
2 plum tomatoes, seeded and diced
1 shallot, finely diced
1 teaspoon Dijon mustard
3 tablespoons raspberry vinegar
6 tablespoons olive oil
Salt and pepper
1 bunch arugula, washed and dried

Bring water to a boil in a pot large enough to hold lobsters. Plunge lobsters into water head first, cover, and cook for 10 minutes. Remove lobsters from pot and plunge into ice water. Allow lobsters to cool. (May be refrigerated overnight.) Crack claws and remove meat. Using a large, sharp knife, split lobsters down the middle. Remove meat from tails. Discard stomach sacks. Rinse the 4 shell halves and reserve.

Dice lobster meat and toss with mango and tomatoes. In a separate bowl, whisk together shallot, mustard, vinegar, oil, and salt and pepper. Combine two-thirds dressing with lobster mixture. Toss together remaining dressing and arugula. Divide arugula among 4 chilled plates. Spoon lobster mixture into reserved shells and place on arugula.

Serves 4

Belgian Endive with Salmon and Blue Cheese in a Sugar Beet Vinaigrette

Our sweet beet vinegar comes from a small producer in Vermont. Known for its low acidity, you can actually drink it right from the bottle.

2 heads Belgian endive, stemmed and julienned
3 ounces good quality blue cheese (i.e., Roquefort)
Sugar Beet Vinaigrette (see recipe)
2 ounces cured or smoked salmon, thinly sliced
1 tomato, diced
2 tablespoons diced chives

Combine endive and blue cheese. Toss with vinaigrette. Divide among 4 chilled plates. Top with salmon slices and garnish with tomato and chives.

Serves 4

Sugar Beet Vinaigrette

½ cup olive oil
⅓ cup sugar beet vinegar or good quality white vinegar
1 teaspoon Dijon mustard
1 shallot, minced
Pinch of sugar
Salt and pepper

Whisk together oil, vinegar, mustard, shallot, sugar, and salt and pepper to taste in a mixing bowl.

Vinegars to try

Wine vinegars – red wine, white wine, sherry, champagne

Rice vinegars – varieties available from China, Japan, and other Asian countries

Fruit vinegars – peach, apple cider, raspberry, blueberry, blackberry

Herb vinegars – basil, thyme, chervil, mint, rosemary, tarragon, oregano, chive

Flavored – peppercorn, ginger, garlic

Roast Leg of Duck Salad with Goat Cheese and Raspberry Vinaigrette

Raspberry vinaigrette puts a new twist on a French favorite.

4 duck legs (thigh and drumstick), excess fat trimmed
Salt and pepper
4 ounces mesclun or lettuces of your choice
3 ounces goat cheese, crumbled
½ cup toasted walnuts
⅛ pint fresh raspberries
Raspberry Vinaigrette (see recipe)

Preheat oven to 450°. Place duck legs in a roasting pan. Sprinkle liberally with salt and pepper. Roast for 45 minutes or until leg and thigh separate easily at the joint.

Divide lettuce among 4 plates. Top each salad with a duck leg and one-quarter each crumbled goat cheese, walnuts, and raspberries. Drizzle with vinaigrette.

Serves 4

mesclun
[MEHS-klahn]

Mesclun is a mix of young salad greens. It will vary and may include arugula, mizuna, sorrel, radicchio, and Bibb.

Raspberry Vinaigrette

½ cup vegetable oil
¼ cup raspberry vinegar
1 teaspoon Dijon mustard
1 shallot, minced
⅛ pint fresh raspberries
Salt and pepper

Whisk together oil, vinegar, mustard, shallot, and raspberries in a mixing bowl. Season to taste with salt and pepper.

Grilled Chicken Salad with Roasted Tomato Vinaigrette

Oven roasting brings out the intensity of tomatoes even when they're not in season.

4 boneless chicken breasts (6 ounces each)
1 tablespoon olive oil
2 teaspoons chopped fresh thyme
1 teaspoon chopped fresh rosemary
Salt and pepper
1 pound mâche, stemmed
Roasted Tomato Vinaigrette (Recipe appears on page 59.)

Rub chicken breasts with olive oil. Sprinkle with chopped herbs and a little salt and pepper. Grill on a very hot preheated grill until juices run clear when pierced with a knife, about 4 minutes per side.

Divide mâche among 4 plates and top with a chicken breast. Drizzle with vinaigrette.

Serves 4

mâche
[MAHSH]

Also called field salad, field lettuce, lamb's lettuce, lamb's tongue, and corn salad, this delicate plant has a nutty taste. It can be used as a salad green or steamed and served as a vegetable. Although it can be expensive and difficult to find in markets, mâche can be easily grown in a sunny window garden and grows wild in American cornfields. Wash and dry well before using.

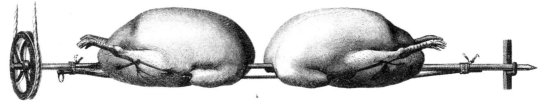

Roasted Tomato Vinaigrette

4 plum tomatoes, cut in half lengthwise
Salt and pepper
½ cup plus 2 tablespoons olive oil
¼ cup red wine vinegar
1 tablespoon Dijon mustard

Preheat oven to 375°. Place tomatoes, skin side down, on a baking sheet. Sprinkle with salt and pepper and drizzle with 2 tablespoons olive oil. Roast until well browned, about 30 to 40 minutes. Remove and cool.

Place cooled tomatoes in a blender with remaining olive oil, vinegar, mustard, and salt and pepper. Process until smooth. Adjust seasonings as needed.

Warm Squab Salad with Frisee

Ten years ago we tried to entice our guests to try squab but met with resistance. We even gave away samples! Now we can't keep enough of this delicious bird in the house.

1½ cups Chicken Stock (Recipe appears on page 278.)
3 tablespoons olive oil
2 squabs, halved and boned
½ cup white wine
2 tablespoons balsamic vinegar
2 plum tomatoes, chopped and seeded
2 teaspoons chopped and mixed fresh herbs (parsley, chives, basil, tarragon)
Salt and pepper
3 cups frisee
4 strips smoked bacon, diced and cooked until crisp
2 teaspoons chopped shallot

Heat chicken stock over medium heat until stock is reduced to ½ cup. Keep warm.

Heat 2 tablespoons olive oil in a sauté pan. Add squabs, skin side down, and sear for 2 minutes. Flip and sear for 2 minutes. Remove squabs from pan and set aside. Deglaze pan with reduced stock, wine, and vinegar. Whisk in remaining olive oil, tomatoes, and herbs. Season to taste with salt and pepper. Place frisee in a bowl and toss with warm dressing. Divide frisee among 4 plates. Top with squab. Garnish with bacon and shallot.

Serves 4

To deglaze a pan

After food (usually meat, fish, or vegetables) has been sautéed, remove it and any excess fat from pan. Add liquid such as wine, water, or stock to pan and heat. This is done to dissolve food particles and/or the caramelized drippings left in the pan. The resulting liquid is usually used as a base for a sauce.

Seared Tenderloin and Mizuna Salad with Ginger-Soy Vinaigrette

Be sure to use the best grade of beef available and cook the tenderloins as rare as you can stand.

1 beef tenderloin (8 to 10 ounces)
Salt and pepper
3 ounces mizuna
1 large carrot, julienned
1 English cucumber, julienned
Ginger-Soy Vinaigrette (see recipe)

Slice beef in half with the grain. Season with salt and pepper on all sides. Heat skillet over medium-high heat. Add tenderloins and sear on both sides until red juices start to bleed out. (This means the meat is medium rare.) Remove meat from pan and set aside to cool.

Divide mizuna among 4 plates and top with carrot and cucumber. Slice beef into ¼-inch slices and arrange around salads. Drizzle with vinaigrette.

Serves 4

Mizuna, an attractive salad green, originated in China, is widely used in Japan, and is the new darling of America's farmers' markets and specialty shops. Look for crisp, green leaves. Small, young leaves are especially nice in salads: just spin-dry like other salad greens and use immediately. Older leaves can be stir-fried with other leafy greens. Store mizuna in a plastic bag and refrigerate for no

Ginger-Soy Vinaigrette

½ cup peanut oil
1 teaspoon sesame oil
¼ cup rice wine vinegar
3 tablespoons soy sauce
1 small piece ginger, grated

Whisk together oils, vinegar, soy sauce, and ginger in a mixing bowl.

from the cooking school at la campagne ~ from the cooking school at la campagne ~ from the cooking school at la campagne ~ from the cooking school at la campagne ~ from the cooking school at la campagne ~ from the cooking school at la campagne ~ from the cooking school at la campagne ~ from the cooking school at la campagne ~ from the cooking school at la campagne ~ from the cooking school at la campagne ~ from the cooking school at la campagne ~ from the cooking school at la campagne ~ from the cooking school at la campagne ~ from the cooking school at la campagne ~ from the cooking school at la campagne ~ from the cooking school at la campagne ~ from the

soups
and stews

Golden Tomato and Ginger Soup

The lovely yellow color of this soup makes it perfect Indian summer fare.

2½ pounds yellow tomatoes (about 5 large), peeled
1 tablespoon butter
3 cloves garlic
1 small onion, very thinly sliced
2 tablespoons minced fresh ginger
2 cups Chicken Stock (Recipe appears on page 278.)
½ cup chopped fresh basil
½ teaspoon salt
½ teaspoon cumin
¼ teaspoon tumeric
⅛ teaspoon cayenne
Black pepper
4 slices country-style bread

Cut tomatoes in half and squeeze out seeds. Coarsely chop tomatoes. Set aside.

Melt butter in a heavy saucepan over medium heat. Mince 2 garlic cloves. Add minced garlic, onion, and ginger. Sauté until onion is translucent. Add tomatoes, stock, basil, and seasonings. Simmer 10 to 15 minutes.

Grill or brown bread under broiler. Rub bread with the remaining garlic clove. Put bread in bowls and ladle soup over top.

Serves 4

To peel a tomato

Cut an "X" in the bottom of tomato. Plunge tomato into boiling water. After 10 to 30 seconds (depending on tomato's age and ripeness), remove tomato with a slotted spoon. Immediately plunge tomato into ice water. Use a paring knife to easily slip off the skin.

Roasted Red Pepper and Tomato Soup

While you're roasting peppers for this recipe, consider roasting a few extra. They come in handy for many recipes and salad presentations.

¼ cup olive oil

1 medium onion, chopped

3 cloves garlic, minced

8 plum tomatoes, peeled and seeded

4 red peppers, roasted and skins removed

1 cup white wine

1 tablespoon fresh thyme

1 cup heavy cream

Salt and pepper

1 tablespoon chopped basil

Heat oil in a large saucepan over medium heat. Add onion and sauté for 3 to 4 minutes or until translucent. Add garlic and sauté for 1 minute. Add tomatoes, peppers, white wine, and thyme. Simmer for 20 minutes, stirring occasionally. Add the heavy cream and bring to a boil. Place in a food processor and puree. Season to taste with salt and pepper. Garnish with basil.

Serves 8

To roast peppers

Halve peppers and remove seeds. Place cut side down on an oiled baking sheet. Roast in a very hot oven or under broiler until evenly charred. Remove from oven and immediately cover with an inverted baking sheet or place in a brown paper bag. (This allows peppers to steam and makes them easier to peel.) Remove skin with fingers and/or a paring knife.

Sorrel Soup

Sorrel's trademark taste is elegantly tempered by the addition of rich cream.

1 tablespoon unsalted butter
¼ cup finely chopped scallions
½ pound sorrel, stemmed and chopped
5 cups Chicken Stock (Recipe appears on page 278.)
4 large egg yolks
2 cups cream
Nutmeg
Salt and pepper

Heat butter in a skillet. Add scallions and sauté until soft. Add sorrel and cook until just wilted. Set aside. Bring stock to a boil in a large saucepan. Whisk together yolks and cream in a large bowl. Whisk stock, 1 cup at a time, into yolk and cream mixture. Return soup to saucepan and heat gently over medium heat, stirring until slightly thickened. (Do not boil.) Remove pan from heat. Stir in sorrel and scallions. Season to taste with nutmeg and salt and pepper. Serve immediately.

Serves 8 to 10

Grown for centuries in Europe, Asia, North America, and Greenland, sorrel was used in ancient times to counteract overindulgence. Nowadays, this sour herb can be found fresh in limited quantities year-round. Sorrel has a bright green leaf that varies in shape from oval to arrowhead. The arrow-shaped garden sorrel is the most common. The more highly regarded French sorrel is not as sour while still offering the desired lemony zest.

Thyme-Scented Portabella and Lentil Soup

Hearty and very easy to prepare, serve this soup with good bread and a simple salad for a satisfying midwinter supper.

2 tablespoons vegetable oil

1 onion, diced

3 strips bacon, minced

2 portabella mushroom caps, sliced

1 teaspoon minced garlic

1 quart Chicken Stock (Recipe appears on page 278.)

1 cup French green lentils

2 teaspoons chopped fresh thyme

2 teaspoons chopped fresh parsley

Salt and pepper

Heat oil in a 2-quart saucepan over medium heat. Add onion and bacon and cook until bacon starts to crisp. Add mushroom slices and garlic and sauté for 1 minute. Add chicken stock, lentils, and herbs. Simmer until lentils are tender, about 20 to 25 minutes. Season with salt and pepper and serve.

Serves 4 to 6

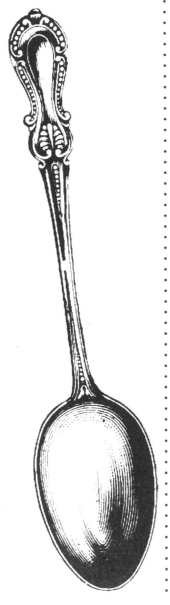

Potage Saint-Germain

This recipe came from one our chef's grandmom. Her advice?
Be sure to use a hearty, thick bacon so that you can really
enjoy the smoky flavor it imparts.

¾ cup butter

½ cup diced bacon

1 carrot, peeled and diced

1 onion, peeled and diced

1 large leek, washed and diced

Bouquet garni (See sidebar on page 78.)

1½ pounds split peas, rinsed twice

2½ quarts water

1 tablespoon salt

Croutons (Recipe appears on page 292.)

Chopped fresh parsley

Melt ½ cup butter in a large pot over medium heat. Add
bacon and vegetables and "sweat" for 5 minutes. Add
bouquet garni, split peas, water, and salt. Cook for 1½
hours. Process soup in a food processor or blender or with
an immersion blender until smooth. Return soup to pot and
bring to a boil. Add remaining butter. Serve hot with
croutons and fresh parsley.

Serves 8 to 10

sweat

to cook an item,
usually vegetables, in a
small amount of fat
until it softens and
releases moisture.

Pistou Soup

Italian ingredients have strongly influenced Provençal cooking. Such is the case with basil and the popular Provençal pesto called pistou. Centuries ago, it crept across the border into Nice and is now a staple throughout the region.

2 cups mixed dry beans

½ cup olive oil

1 cup diced celery

1 onion, diced

1 cup diced carrot

½ head garlic, chopped (about 2 tablespoons)

1 can (28 ounces) peeled tomatoes in juice

½ cup Pistou (Recipe appears on page 288.)

1 cup white wine

2 quarts Chicken Stock (Recipe appears on page 278.) or water

1 bay leaf

1 branch thyme

Salt and pepper

Grated Parmesan cheese

Cover beans with cold water and soak overnight. Drain, rinse, and reserve. Heat olive oil in a large skillet over medium heat. Add celery, onion, and carrot and cook for 5 to 10 minutes. Add garlic, tomatoes and juice, and pistou and cook for 10 minutes. Add reserved beans and wine and cook until liquid is reduced by half. Add stock, bay leaf, and thyme. Season to taste with salt and pepper. Cook for 1 hour. Serve sprinkled with grated cheese.

covered 7 1 hour

Serves 6 to 8

pistou
[pees-TOO]

A staple throughout Provence, pistou is the French version of Italy's pesto. Besides being a main ingredient in this classic hearty soup, pistou can be used as a spread on croutons and bread, tossed with pasta, or served with grilled meats and fish.

Onion Soup Gratinée

*Every chef has a favorite "secret" version of onion soup. This is mine. The **real** secret is to always make a double batch because everyone will want seconds.*

3 tablespoons unsalted butter

6 medium onions, peeled and thinly sliced

1 cup Burgundy wine

3 cups Beef or Chicken Stock (Recipes appear on page 279 and 278.)

½ teaspoon fresh thyme leaves

Salt and freshly ground pepper

4 slices French baguette (each 1 inch thick), toasted

½ pound Gruyère cheese, grated

Melt butter in a heavy-bottomed pan over low-medium heat. Add onions. Press a piece of buttered parchment or foil on top of onions. Cook gently over low-medium heat, occasionally lifting paper to stir, until golden brown. Remove paper. Add wine, stock, and thyme. Cover with lid and simmer for 20 to 30 minutes. Season to taste with salt and pepper.

Pour soup into 4 ovenproof bowls. Top soup with toasted bread and sprinkle generously with grated cheese. Place under broiler until cheese is brown on top.

Serves 4

Wild Mushroom Soup with Gruyère Croutons

We are lucky enough to be located near the self-proclaimed mushroom capital of the world, Kennett Square, Pennsylvania. This area, just outside Philadelphia, provides 25 percent of the entire mushroom crop of the United States. There's even a mushroom museum which inspired this soup — a true work of art.

4 tablespoons unsalted butter

¼ cup plus 2 teaspoons olive oil

10 shallots, chopped

2 pounds assorted wild mushrooms, cleaned, trimmed, and sliced

1 cup dry white wine

4 cups Chicken Stock (Recipe appears on page 278.)

½ cup heavy cream

Salt and pepper

6 slices baguette (each ½-inch wide)

¼ pound Gruyère cheese, grated

Combine butter and ¼ cup oil in a large pot over medium heat. Add shallots and sauté until soft but not brown. Add mushrooms and sauté until just softened. Add wine and simmer for 5 minutes. Add stock and cream and simmer for 10 minutes. Season to taste with salt and pepper.

Preheat oven to 350°. Arrange baguette slices on a baking sheet. Brush with remaining 2 teaspoons olive oil. Toast until light brown. Top with cheese and return to oven until cheese is slightly melted.

Ladle soup into 6 bowls and top each bowl with a crouton.

Serves 6

Mushrooms to try

Portabella – much like white mushrooms but more robust with a dense, firm texture

Hen-of-Woods – cooking brings out its rich, woodsy taste

Beech– a petite crisp mushroom with a zesty, nutty flavor

Shiitake – meaty texture and slightly smoky taste make it perfect for soups and stews

Consommé Clair

Consommés are clear soups made by simmering broth or stock with lean meat, egg whites, tomatoes, and aromatic vegetables. The finished product is full flavored with a rich body and deep color.

1 pound lean ground beef
3 to 5 cups water
1 carrot, finely chopped
1 stalk celery, finely chopped
1 onion, finely chopped
1 leek, washed and chopped
3 plum tomatoes, chopped
6 egg whites
3 quarts Chicken Stock (Recipe appears on page 278.)
Salt and pepper

Place beef in a bowl and cover with water. In a separate bowl, combine vegetables and egg whites. Pour stock into a large stockpot. Add ground beef and water and vegetable/egg white mixture. Stir constantly and bring mixture to a boil. Immediately reduce heat to low and stop stirring. A "raft" will form. Make a hole in the raft around the edge of the pot and skim if fat congeals. Simmer 45 minutes.

Consommé is finished when raft begins to sink. Season with salt and pepper. Drape a cheesecloth over a fine strainer and strain consommé into a separate pan. Reheat to serve.

Serves 12

Garnishes for consommé

julienned blanched vegetables

sliced wild mushrooms

diced garden vegetables such as fresh peas or tomatoes

strips of crêpes

Leek Soup with Foie Gras

*The addition of foie gras and duck fat make this low country
leek soup truly luxurious.*

2 leeks, washed and julienned

1 onion, diced

1 carrot, peeled and diced

2 cloves garlic, chopped

3 tablespoons duck fat

1 cup white wine

1 cup red wine vinegar

2 quarts Chicken Stock (Recipe appears on page 278.)

Salt and pepper

6 ounces foie gras, diced

Cook leeks, onion, carrot, and garlic in duck fat in a large
saucepan. Cook until released liquids totally evaporate.
Add wine and vinegar. Cook until liquid reduces by half.
Add chicken stock and salt and pepper and cook for 1 hour.
Just before serving, add diced foie gras to soup. Let infuse
for 2 minutes. Serve immediately.

Serves 8

Duck fat is available
at some specialty
stores and through
mail order catalogs.

Cream of Asparagus Soup

We make this soup every spring when the young asparagus spears just hit the farmers' market. Garnish with lightly toasted sesame seeds, fresh made croutons, or sautéed morels.

4 tablespoons butter

1 onion, diced

1 leek, washed and chopped

2 stalks celery, chopped

2 quarts Chicken Stock (Recipe appears on page 278.)

3 medium Idaho potatoes, peeled and chopped

1 bay leaf

2 bunches asparagus, trimmed, chopped, tips reserved

1½ cups heavy cream

Salt and pepper

Melt butter in a 4-quart saucepan over medium heat. Add onion, leek, and celery. Cook until tender but not browned. Add stock, potatoes, and bay leaf. Bring to a boil. Reduce to a simmer and cook until potatoes are tender. Add chopped asparagus and simmer for 5 minutes. Remove from heat and puree in a blender or food processor until smooth. Strain soup and return to saucepan. Add cream and asparagus tips. Simmer until tips are tender but still bright green. Season with salt and pepper and serve.

Serves 6 to 8

Cream of asparagus soup can also be served as a sauce over salmon, sea bass, and shrimp.

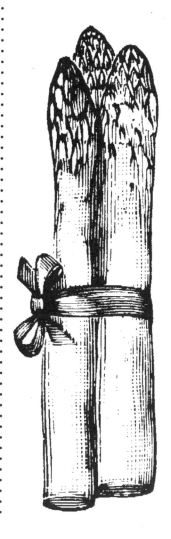

Fall Spiced Butternut Bisque

The flavor combination of nutmeg, ginger, and allspice just screams "fall." Your guests will scream for more.

3 tablespoons butter

1 onion, diced

1 teaspoon chopped garlic

3 medium butternut squash, peeled, seeded, and diced

1½ quarts Chicken Stock (Recipe appears on page 278.)

2 tablespoons ground ginger

1 tablespoon nutmeg

1 teaspoon allspice

Salt and pepper

½ cup heavy cream

1 tablespoon chopped fresh thyme

Melt butter in a 3-quart saucepan over medium heat. Add onion and sauté until translucent. Add garlic and sauté for 1 minute. Add squash and chicken stock and bring to a simmer. Add ginger, nutmeg, and allspice and continue to simmer until squash is soft. Transfer to a blender and blend until smooth. Season with salt and pepper. Add cream. Heat until just hot. (Do not boil.) Serve garnished with thyme.

Serves 8 to 10

Butternut is a winter squash as is acorn, Hubbard, spaghetti, and pumpkin. They are sweet, and most of the seeds are fleshy and can be roasted and used for garnish on any dish. Winter squash have a more pronounced flavor than summer squash like zucchini, pattypan, and crookneck.

Pumpkin Soup with Crème Fraîche

This is a great way to use the scooped out flesh of your Halloween jack-o-lantern. Or carefully remove the flesh and serve the soup in the hollowed out pumpkin. Serve with thick, chewy whole-grain bread and you're in for a real treat.

1 pound potatoes, peeled and quartered
2 pounds pumpkin, peeled and seeded
4 leeks, white part only, split
2 cups Chicken Stock (Recipe appears on page 278.) or water
½ cup heavy cream
Salt and pepper
Crème Fraîche (Recipe appears on page 289.)
1 tablespoon fresh chopped chives

Heat vegetables and stock in a large stockpot over medium-high heat. Cover and simmer for 30 minutes or until vegetables are very tender. Transfer to a food processor and puree. Return mixture to pot and add cream and salt and pepper to taste. Cook until heated through. Garnish with a generous dollop of crème fraîche and a sprinkle of chives.

Serves 6

Pumpkins were being grown by Native Americans as the first settlers landed in North America. A relative to the watermelon, pumpkins vary greatly in shape and size. Choose a pumpkin that is unblemished, heavy, and between 10 to 12 inches in diameter (think basketball). Look for fresh pumpkin in the fall and winter months and for canned pureed pumpkin in the off season. Fresh pumpkin can be stored in a cool, dry place for up to 6 months before it is boiled or baked.

Lobster Bisque

Use a nice drinking wine: the better the wine, the better the soup.

3½ quarts cold water

½ cup lemon juice

Bouquet garni (See sidebar on page 78.)

2 cups dry white wine

2 live Maine lobsters (1 pound each)

2 small onions, peeled and chopped

2 small carrots, peeled and chopped

5 cloves garlic

½ pound unsalted butter

1 cup flour

2 cups heavy cream

3 tablespoons brandy

Salt and pepper

Chive herb oil

The menu changes seasonally at La Campagne; but every time we try to take this silky soup off the menu, we get scads of special requests for it. Therefore, we've decided that lobster bisque is seasonless, timeless, and has a permanent place of honor on our menu.

Combine water, lemon juice, bouquet garni, and wine in a large stockpot. Bring to a boil. Plunge lobsters head first into water. Cook for 5 minutes. Remove lobster from stock and refrigerate to cool. Return water to a boil and cook until liquid reduces by half. Strain stock and set aside.

Once chilled, remove tails, claws, and knuckles from lobsters. Crack tails and remove tail meat. Crack claws and knuckles and remove meat. Dice lobster meat and set aside. Discard stomach sack from shell. Roughly chop shell and place in a food processor with onions, carrots, and garlic. Puree, adding 1 cup of stock.

Melt butter in a large, heavy-bottomed pot. Add contents of food processor and sauté over medium heat for 5 minutes. Sprinkle in flour and cook, stirring occasionally, for 10 minutes. Whisk in remaining stock and cream and bring to a simmer. Strain soup well. Return soup to pot and add brandy. Add reserved lobster meat. Season to taste with salt and pepper. Garnish with chive herb oil.

Serves 8

Provençal Fish Soup

In Provence a restaurant is judged by its fish soup.

5 pounds white fleshed fish, cut into steaks

¼ cup olive oil

10 cloves garlic

2 large onions, peeled and sliced

5 large plum tomatoes, chopped

1 pound potatoes, peeled and sliced

3 sprigs fennel, stalks and tops chopped

Bouquet garni (see sidebar)

1 piece (3 x 1-inch) orange zest

2 quarts Fish Bouillon (Recipe appears on page 280.) or
   clam juice

1 cup dry white wine

½ teaspoon saffron threads

2 tablespoons chopped flat-leaf parsley

16 Croutons (Recipe appears on page 292.)

1 cup Rouille (Recipe appears on page 289.)

Marinate fish steaks in oil and 4 cloves garlic for 1 hour. Remove fish from marinade. Pour marinade into a stockpot. Add remaining garlic, onions, tomatoes, potatoes, fennel, bouquet garni, and zest. Cook over medium heat, stirring often, for 10 minutes. Add bouillon or juice and bring to boil. Simmer 15 minutes.

In a small saucepan, warm white wine and saffron. Add to soup. Simmer 15 minutes or until all ingredients are tender. Pass soup through a food mill fitted with a medium-hole disk or process in a food processor until fairly smooth. Clean stockpot and return soup to it. Add fish and simmer, turning often, until tender. Remove fish from soup with a slotted spoon and discard skin and bones. Divide fish among 8 warmed serving bowls. Ladle soup over fish, sprinkle with parsley, and top with croutons. Serve rouille on the side.

Serves 8

bouquet garni
[boo-KAY gahr-NEE]

French phrase for a bunch of herbs (the classic trio being parsley, thyme, and bay leaf) that are either tied together or placed in a cheesecloth bag and used to flavor soups, stews, and broths. Tying or bagging the herbs allows for their easy removal before the dish is served.

Cucumber Vichyssoise with Tomato Cream

Our vegetable garden simply bursts with tomatoes and cucumbers so we created this light version of vichyssoise that substitutes cucumbers for the traditional leek and potato puree and is accented by a smooth swirl of tomato cream.

To make tomato concasse

Cut an "X" in the bottom of 3 plum tomatoes. Plunge tomatoes into boiling water. After 10 to 30 seconds (depending on tomatoes' age and ripeness), remove tomatoes with a slotted spoon and immediately plunge into ice water. Use a paring knife to easily slip off the skin. Halve each tomato crosswise at the widest point and gently squeeze out seeds. Coarsely dice. This will yield approximately ½ cup tomato concasse.

1 small Spanish onion, diced

1 sprig tarragon, stemmed

2 cups Chicken Stock (Recipe appears on page 278.)

2 large cucumbers, peeled, seeded, and chopped

1½ cups heavy cream

½ cup Tomato Concasse (see sidebar)

Salt and pepper

Combine onion, tarragon, and 2 tablespoons chicken stock in a saucepan. Cover and cook over low heat for 10 minutes. Add cucumbers and cook for 5 minutes. Add remaining stock and bring to a boil. Remove from heat.

Puree cucumbers and cooking liquid in a blender or food processor. Stir in 1 cup cream. Refrigerate until cold.

Sauté tomato concasse over medium heat until all liquid evaporates. Push through a food mill and stir in remaining cream. Chill.

Season soup with salt and pepper to taste. Serve chilled with a swirl of tomato cream.

Serves 4

Gazpacho

Gazpacho is perfect when you don't want to spend time in a hot kitchen. Serve in chilled bowls for a professional touch.

1 onion, quartered

3 cloves garlic

3 ripe tomatoes, peeled, quartered, and seeded

2 cucumbers, peeled and roughly chopped

1 green pepper, stemmed, quartered, and seeded

½ cup red wine vinegar

½ cup olive oil

2 cups tomato juice

1 teaspoon cumin

1 teaspoon chili powder

6 dashes Tabasco sauce

Salt and pepper

Chop onion and garlic in a food processor. Transfer to a large bowl. Working in batches, process remaining vegetables and transfer batches to the large bowl. Mix processed vegetables together. Add remaining ingredients and season to taste with salt and pepper. Cover and refrigerate for at least 4 hours before serving. Serve in chilled bowls.

Serves 6 to 8

Because colder foods tend to have less flavor than warmer foods, check the seasoning of a cold soup before you serve it. It might need an extra dash of salt and pepper.

Sour Cherry Soup

This soup was inspired by the many sour cherry trees we have on our property. Serve as a first course or even dessert.

3 cups dry white wine
½ cup sugar
1 pound sour cherries, pitted
2 tablespoons kirsch
Juice of 2 lemons
3 cups Crème Fraîche (Recipe appears on page 289.) or
  sour cream

Combine wine and sugar in a saucepan over medium heat and bring to a simmer. Add cherries and simmer for 2 to 3 minutes. Remove pan from heat and allow to cool.

Transfer mixture to a food processor or blender and puree. Press through a sieve or food mill. Whisk in kirsch, lemon juice, and 2 cups crème fraîche. Chill thoroughly. Ladle into chilled bowls and garnish with remaining crème fraîche.

Serves 8

Serve soup as a sauce over fruit salad or grilled chicken breasts.

Daube of Beef Provençal

This dish, served as an introduction to French cuisine, is very popular with the high school French classes that join us for lunch during the school year.

6 slices bacon, diced

1 large onion, diced

2 carrots, sliced

4 pounds lean beef, cut into 1-inch cubes

2 teaspoons chopped garlic

1 teaspoon chopped fresh thyme

1 teaspoon chopped fresh parsley

1 bay leaf

1 cup red wine

Zest of 1 orange

1½ cups Beef Stock (Recipe appears on page 279.)

½ cup pitted black olives

Salt and pepper

Preheat oven to 300°. Heat a large lidded pot or casserole dish over medium heat. Add bacon and cook for 2 minutes. Add onion and carrots and cook until lightly browned. Add cubed beef and stir frequently until browned. Add garlic and herbs and cook for 1 minute. Add red wine and zest and cook until liquid is reduced by half. Add beef stock; then cover and place in the oven. Cook for 2½ to 3 hours or until beef is very tender.

Take casserole from oven, remove lid, and skim off any scum that has risen to the top. Add olives and season with salt and pepper to taste. Replace lid and return to oven. Cook for another 30 minutes. Pour stew into serving bowls.

Serves 4 to 6

daube
[DOHB]

Sometimes called the mother of all stews, *daube* is a classic French dish of slowly braised beef, red wine, vegetables, and seasonings. Traditionally, *daube* was cooked in a *daubière*, a heavy casserole or pot with a concave lid. In the days of wood fires, the lid would be filled with water to help radiate heat around the stew. Although modern ovens make such a pot unnecessary, it is still the sentimental favorite and widely used in Provence. Thus, most any stew cooked in this pot is called a *daube*.

Blanquette of Veal

We serve our veal blanquette over rice pilaf for a hearty and satisfying supper. This recipe feeds a crowd so invite some friends over.

5 pounds veal cubes

1 onion, diced

2 carrots, diced

2 tablespoons fresh lemon juice

Bouquet garni (See sidebar on page 78.)

2 bay leaves

1 teaspoon black peppercorns

2 teaspoons salt

¼ cup flour

¼ cup butter

1 cup heavy cream

3 egg yolks

Pinch of nutmeg

Rice Pilaf (Recipe appears on page 178.)

Place veal, onion, carrots, lemon juice, bouquet garni, bay leaves, peppercorns, and salt in a large stockpot. Cover with cold water. Bring to a boil, reduce heat to low, and simmer for 1 hour, skimming often.

Cook flour and butter in a heavy-bottomed pot over medium heat. Stir constantly for 10 minutes or until roux is light brown.

In a separate pan, bring cream to a boil. Stir cream into roux. Whisk in egg yolks and season with nutmeg. Remove veal cubes from cooking liquid and reserve. Strain liquid and discard solids. Return liquid back to pot and stir in cream mixture. Cook for 10 minutes over medium heat. Season to taste with salt and pepper. Add veal to pot and stir to coat well. Serve stew over rice pilaf.

Serves 10 to 12

blanquette

[blahn-KEHT]

A blanquette, also called a fricassee, is a rich, creamy white stew. In this traditional French favorite, the meat is not cooked under pressure but is allowed to simmer in a liquid. The name comes from the word *blanc* which means "white" in French.

Bouillabaisse

It is difficult to find a restaurant in Marseilles that does NOT serve bouillabaisse. We serve ours with extra croutons so every last bit can be lapped up.

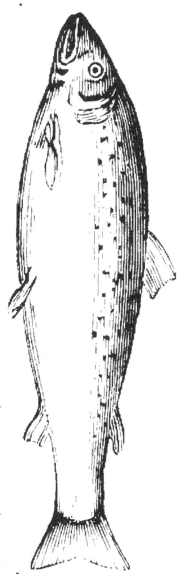

2 onions, sliced

8 plum tomatoes, sliced

1 bulb fennel, sliced

1 leek, sliced

8 cloves garlic, crushed

2½ pounds fish fillets (striped bass, snapper, perch, monkfish, or sole), cut into 2-inch strips

1 teaspoon crushed red pepper

½ teaspoon saffron

Zest of 1 orange

2 bay leaves

Salt and pepper

Olive oil

3 large potatoes, peeled and sliced ¼-inch thick

Fish Bouillon (Recipe appears on page 280.) or water

18 Garlic Croutons (Recipe appears on page 292.)

Rouille (Recipe appears on page 289.)

Place onions, tomatoes, fennel, leek, and garlic in a shallow braising pan or casserole. Cover with fish fillets. Sprinkle fish with crushed red pepper, saffron, orange zest, bay leaves, salt and pepper, and enough olive oil to moisten the entire dish. Marinate at room temperature for about 1 hour.

Place potatoes atop fillets. Add enough bouillon or water to come ½-inch below potatoes. Partially cover pot with lid and place over medium-high heat. Simmer for 15 to 20 minutes or until potatoes are tender.

Divide croutons among 6 soup bowls. Gently remove fish and potatoes from the pot and divide among bowls. Ladle in broth from pot and top with some rouille. Place remaining rouille in a dish and serve on the side.

Serves 6

Seafood Pot-Au-Feu

4 tablespoons olive oil

2 small leeks, white part only, chopped

1 stalk celery, chopped

⅓ cup chopped onion

1 tablespoon chopped shallot

2 tomatoes, peeled, seeded, and chopped

½ teaspoon fennel seed

1 bay leaf

4 cups Fish Bouillon (Recipe appears on page 280.) or equal
  parts clam juice, water, and white wine

1 cup dry white wine

4 tablespoons Beurre Manié (Recipe appears on page 287.)

3 pounds white fish (A combination of 3 fishes such as sole,
  halibut, flounder, haddock, monkfish, snapper, or bass is best.)

1 pound medium shrimp, shelled and deveined

2 dozen mussels, scrubbed and debearded

1 cup Crème Fraîche (Recipe appears on page 289.) or cream

2 tablespoons chopped fresh parsley

Salt and freshly ground pepper

Heat olive oil in a large pot over medium heat. Add leeks, celery, onion, shallot, tomatoes, fennel seed, and bay leaf. Cover, reduce heat to low, and cook for 15 minutes.

Meanwhile, combine bouillon and wine in a separate, smaller pot and bring to a boil. Reduce heat and whisk in beurre manié until the sauce is smooth and thickened. Simmer for 2 to 3 minutes and add to the vegetables. Bring to a boil, reduce heat, and simmer for 5 minutes. Cut fish into 3- to 4-ounce pieces, add to pot, and simmer for 5 minutes. Add shellfish and simmer for 5 minutes. Remove stew from heat. With a slotted spoon, transfer fish and shellfish to a warm serving tureen or dish and keep warm.

Stir crème fraîche and parsley into liquid. Season with salt and pepper. Pour sauce into tureen. Serve immediately.

Serves 6

pot-au-feu
[pot-toh-FEUH]

Literally "pot of fire" in French, pot-au-feu is a classic French stew of meat and vegetables slowly cooked in water. Our contemporary version contains a variety of white fish and shellfish.

from the cooking school at la campagne ~ from the cooking school at la campagne ~ from the cooking school at la campagne ~ from the cooking school at la campagne ~ from the cooking school at la campagne ~ from the cooking school at la campagne ~ from the cooking school at la campagne ~ from the cooking school at la campagne ~ from the cooking school at la campagne ~ from the cooking school at la campagne ~ from the cooking school at la campagne ~ from the cooking school at la campagne ~ from the

poultry

Chicken Tapenade

Olives, anchovies, and capers are the main ingredients in tapenade, Provence's olive spread, and bring an intriguing sharpness to chicken.

4 boneless chicken breasts (8 ounces each)

Flour

2 tablespoons olive oil

1 small onion, minced

2 teaspoons chopped garlic

1 small red pepper, finely diced

½ cup pitted and chopped black olives

4 anchovy fillets, minced

2 teaspoons chopped parsley

1 tablespoon capers, rinsed

1 teaspoon chopped fresh thyme

1 teaspoon crushed red pepper

¼ cup water

Salt and pepper

Dredge chicken in flour, shaking off excess. Heat oil in a large sauté pan over medium-high heat. Place chicken in pan and cook until golden on one side. Turn breasts and add onion, garlic, and red pepper. Cook for 2 minutes. Add remaining ingredients, except salt and pepper, and simmer until the liquid has evaporated and chicken is cooked through, about 5 to 8 minutes. Season to taste with salt and pepper and serve.

Serves 4

Originating in the ancient Fertile Crest before spreading throughout the Mediterranean, the black olive has been prepared much the same way for thousands of years. Also known as the Mission olive, black olives are ripe green olives that obtain their classic color and taste from curing and oxygenization. Traditionally used for their oils, black olives can also compliment a variety of dishes and offer the perfect saltiness to many drinks.

Cotelette Au Poulet, Ragoût Au Printemps

Chèvre-stuffed baked chicken is highlighted by a medley of springtime vegetables and fresh herbs.

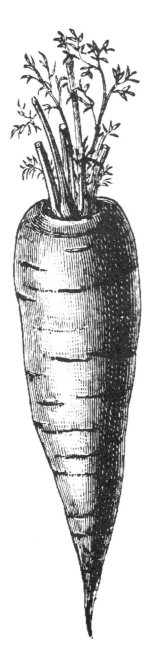

1 tablespoon chopped mixed fresh herbs
6 ounces chèvre cheese (goat cheese)
4 chicken breasts, skin and wing tip left on
Salt and pepper
4 tablespoons unsalted butter
½ pound small new potatoes, quartered
2 small turnips, quartered
8 baby carrots, peeled
4 small shallots, peeled
¼ pound asparagus, trimmed
3 ounces morels
½ cup dry white wine
½ teaspoon chopped fresh thyme leaves
1 teaspoon chopped fresh parsley
½ teaspoon chopped fresh mint

Preheat oven to 450°. Combine mixed herbs and chèvre. Stuff under chicken skin. Season chicken with salt and pepper. Bake for 12 to 18 minutes.

Meanwhile, melt 3 tablespoons butter in large, heavy-bottomed sauté pan over medium heat. Add potatoes, turnips, and carrots. Cover and cook for 5 to 7 minutes. Add shallots. Cover and cook for 3 to 4 minutes. Add asparagus, morels, wine, and remaining herbs. Simmer, stirring occasionally, until asparagus is tender. Stir in remaining butter. Season to taste with salt and pepper. Serve chicken over the ragoût.

Serves 4

Poulet Au Nid

Puff pastry lends a nice touch to this updated chicken pot pie — an elegant luncheon or dinner entree.

1 sheet frozen puff pastry, thawed
Cooking oil spray
1 small egg, lightly beaten
2 chicken breasts, skinned and boned
Salt and pepper
3 tablespoons olive oil
3 shallots, chopped
¼ pound mushrooms, sliced
½ cup dry white wine
½ cup heavy cream
1 sprig thyme, stemmed and chopped

Preheat oven according to directions on puff pastry package. Roll out puff pastry on a lightly floured work surface. Cut into 6-inch squares. Make a cut along the border of each square ½ inch in from the edge, leaving two of four opposite corners uncut. Fold the cut edges over each other. Lightly spray a cookie sheet with cooking spray. Place pastry on cookie sheet. Brush with egg wash. Bake according to package instructions.

Cut chicken into 1-inch pieces. Season with salt and pepper. Heat oil in a skillet. Add chicken and brown. Add shallots and mushrooms and sauté for 2 minutes. Add wine and simmer for 2 minutes. Add cream and thyme and simmer until sauce is a velvety consistency, about 4 minutes. Season with salt and pepper to taste. Cut tops out of pastry shells or press down the centers of the shells. Spoon chicken mixture into pastry shells and serve.

Serves 4

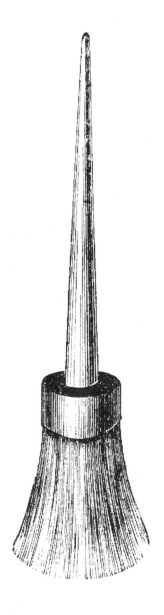

Duck à la Orange

We spice up this classic French dish with a shot of red currant jelly which reinforces the flavors of the other fruits.

1 duck (4 to 5 pounds)
Salt and pepper
¼ cup sugar
2 tablespoons water
3 tablespoons red wine vinegar
Zest and juice of 6 oranges
Zest and juice of 1 lemon
¼ cup white wine
2 tablespoons red currant jelly
1 teaspoon arrowroot
3 tablespoons Triple Sec

Preheat oven to 425°. Season duck with salt and pepper and place on a roasting rack in a roasting pan. Cook for 1 hour, basting regularly.

Dissolve sugar in water and bring to a boil. Stir often and cook until syrup turns a light caramel color. Add vinegar and citrus juices. Boil for 1 minute and remove from heat.

Remove duck from oven and keep warm on a serving plate. Skim fat from the roasting pan and deglaze with white wine. Transfer pan juices to a small saucepan and bring to a boil. Add currant jelly and caramel sauce and return to a boil. In a small bowl, blend arrowroot and Triple Sec. Add to the boiling sauce and cook until sauce is nap (thick enough to coat the back of a spoon). Add orange and lemon zests. Spoon sauce over duck.

Serves 2

zest
[ZEHST]

The outer portion of a citrus fruit's peel or rind. It is used to add color, texture, and flavor to various preparations. The zest consists of only the skin's brightly colored part, not the white pith which is bitter. To zest a fruit, use a paring knife, swivel-bladed peeler, or zester.

Roast Duck with Figs, Dates, Raisins, and Brandy

This recipe comes from the southwestern region of France where duck and goose are national icons.

½ pound EACH dried figs, dried dates, and raisins
2 cups red wine
3 cups Chicken Stock (Recipe appears on page 278.)
2 ducks (5 to 6 pounds each), rinsed and dried
Salt and pepper
2 large onions, quartered
2 oranges, quartered
4 bay leaves
6 tablespoons brandy
1 tablespoon butter, softened
1 tablespoon flour

Combine dried fruits, 1½ cups wine, and stock in a saucepan. Simmer for 10 minutes. Reserve.

Preheat oven to 450°. Trim excess fat from each duck cavity. Season inside and out with salt and pepper. Stuff each duck with equal amounts of onion, orange, and bay leaves. Prick duck skin all over with a fork. Place ducks on a roasting rack in a roasting pan. Roast for 30 minutes. Baste with fruit-wine mixture. Lower temperature to 325° and roast for 45 minutes or until meat thermometer inserted into legs reads 180°. Remove ducks from pan and reserve.

Skim fat from roasting juices. Add remaining wine and ½ cup fruit poaching liquid to pan. Bring to a boil and scrape up brown bits with a wooden spoon. Transfer to a saucepan. Add brandy and remaining poaching liquid. Simmer for 15 minutes. Mix together flour and butter and whisk into sauce to thicken. Simmer for 10 minutes and add poached fruit. Season to taste with salt and pepper. Bone duck and serve with sauce.

Serves 4 to 6

Joining the olive and the grape as one of the three basic foods of ancient Rome, the fig has long symbolized peace and prosperity. Spanish missionaries brought a variety of figs to California in the 1700s, including the popular Black Mission fig. Fresh figs can be found from June through October but will perish after 2 to 3 days even if refrigerated. They are available year-round candied, dried, concentrated, or baked. Figs are commonly used in making Italian appetizers, salads, tarts, and jams.

Duck Confit

1 cup coarse salt
2 tablespoons chopped garlic
2 teaspoons ground cloves
4 duck legs
1 quart duck fat

Mix salt, garlic, and ground cloves together. Rub duck legs with mixture and let cure overnight.

When ready to prepare confit, rinse off duck legs. Melt fat in a heavy-bottomed pan over medium heat. Add duck legs and gently cook (without boiling) for 1 hour or until skin is crispy and golden. Transfer legs to a shallow pan. Allow excess fat to cool and then pour fat over duck legs. Store in refrigerator until ready to use.

When ready to serve, preheat oven to 375°. Remove duck from pan and brush away excess fat. Place duck on a baking sheet and cook in oven until crispy.

confit
[kohn-FEE]

Confit, a specialty of Gascony, is one of the oldest methods of preserving meat. It involves cooking meat or poultry in its own fat and then packing it in a crock or pot and covering it with its own cooking fat. The cooking fat seals and protects the meat.

Duck with Sour Cherries

2 ducks (5 pounds each) or legs and breasts from 2 ducks
2 quarts plus 1 cup Demi-glace (Recipe appears on page 281.)
Salt and pepper
2 shallots, chopped
½ cup red wine vinegar
½ cup sugar
½ cup plus 1 tablespoon brandy
2 teaspoons cornstarch
1 cup pitted sour cherries

Using poultry shears or a sharp knife, cut along both sides of ducks' backbone. Remove backbones. Cut through the white cartilage of the breast bone until birds are halved. Cut through the loose skin between legs and breasts.

Place legs in a medium stockpot and cover with 2 quarts demi-glace. Simmer legs over medium heat, skimming often, until tender, approximately 45 minutes. Meanwhile, preheat oven to 450°. Trim breasts and place on a sheet pan. Season with salt and pepper and top with shallots. Roast for 10 minutes.

Combine vinegar and sugar in a saucepan and simmer over medium-high heat until mixture begins to caramelize and is mahogany brown in appearance. Reserve.

Place breasts, skin side down, in a heavy-bottomed skillet. Sear over low heat until very crisp. Remove breasts and drain off excess fat. Remove pan from heat and add ½ cup brandy. Carefully return pan to heat and flambé. When flames subside, add reserved caramel and 1 cup demi-glace. Bring to a simmer. Combine cornstarch and 1 tablespoon brandy in a small bowl. Stir mixture into simmering sauce. Strain. Add cherries. Season to taste with salt and pepper.

Place legs on a serving platter. Slice breasts lengthwise on a bias and arrange around legs. Spoon sauce and cherries over duck and serve.

Serves 4

Cassoulet

Although you need to plan ahead when making this recipe — it's a three day procedure — the melt in your mouth results are worth the effort.

1 duck (4 pounds), cut into 6 pieces

2 cups kosher salt

1 teaspoon cracked black pepper

2 bay leaves, crumbled

1 teaspoon dry thyme leaves

½ teaspoon juniper berries, optional

½ pound dried navy beans, soaked overnight in 6 cups water

½ pound bacon, diced

2 medium onions, diced

½ pound Italian rope sausage, cut into 2-inch pieces

1 pound tomatoes, peeled, seeded, and chopped

½ cup dry white wine

3 cloves garlic, chopped

1 tablespoon tomato paste

Salt and pepper

Cassoulet is a classic dish from the south of France. As with other traditional dishes, ingredients vary according to region and season, but the traditional ingredients include beans and meats that are simmered together.

Two days before serving, place duck pieces in a casserole dish. Combine kosher salt, pepper, bay leaves, thyme, and juniper berries in a bowl. Cover duck with mixture and refrigerate, turning pieces every 4 to 6 hours. When ready to continue preparation, remove duck from cure. Rinse off excess salt and discard salt cure.

Drain beans. Put 6 cups fresh water into a saucepan and add beans. Simmer over medium heat until tender, about 15 minutes. Meanwhile, in a separate pan, cook bacon over low heat until brown and crisp. Add onions and sauté until onions are translucent. Drain beans and reserve cooking liquid.

Preheat oven to 350°. Combine all ingredients, except cooking liquid, in a large casserole dish. Cover and bake for 50 to 60 minutes, adding reserved cooking liquid if needed.

Serves 6

Squab with Provençal Ragoût

At La Campagne squab is served rare. We find that it enhances both the flavor and texture of this bird.

2 plum tomatoes, quartered

½ small fennel bulb, cored and sliced

4 artichoke hearts, quartered

8 kalamata olives, pitted and chopped

4 cloves garlic, peeled

4 tablespoons olive oil

4 squabs, boned

Salt and pepper

½ cup dry white wine

½ cup Demi-glace (Recipe appears on page 281.)

1 tablespoon chopped fresh herbs (parsley, thyme, rosemary, et al.)

2 tablespoons unsalted butter, cut into ½-inch pieces

Preheat oven to 450°. Toss tomatoes, fennel, artichokes, olives, and garlic with 2 tablespoons oil. Set aside. Season squabs with salt and pepper. Heat remaining olive oil in a large ovenproof skillet over medium heat. Place squabs, skin side down, in skillet and sear until well browned. Turn and sear for 1 minute. Place vegetables in skillet with squabs. Place skillet in oven and roast for 8 minutes.

Transfer squabs to a serving platter and keep warm. Deglaze pan with wine and demi-glace. Stir in herbs. Stir in butter, one piece at a time. Season with salt and pepper. Serve squabs over ragoût.

Serves 4

ragoût
[ra-GOO]

Literally "to stimulate the appetite" in French, a ragoût is a thick, well-seasoned stew that can be made with or without vegetables.

Cornish Hens with Mustard and Rosemary

We use Dijon mustard, but you can experiment with any flavor or style you like. Browse the mustard aisle at your local specialty store — you'll be amazed at the varieties available.

4 tablespoons unsalted butter, softened

4 teaspoons stemmed and chopped fresh rosemary

2 teaspoons Dijon mustard

2 Cornish game hens (1½ pounds each)

Salt and pepper

1 cup Chicken Stock (Recipe appears on page 278.)

1 cup mayonnaise

3 tablespoons apricot preserves

Preheat oven to 450°. Combine butter, 2 teaspoons rosemary, and 1 teaspoon mustard in a bowl. Rub 1 tablespoon butter mixture under the skin of each hen. Season hens inside and out with salt and pepper. Put 1 teaspoon butter mixture in the cavity of each hen.

Place hens on a rack and set rack in a roasting pan. Pour ⅓ cup stock over hens. Dot each hen with equal amount of remaining butter mixture. Roast hens approximately 45 minutes, basting with remaining stock every 10 minutes. Hen is done when juices run clear after piercing thigh. Reserve ¼ cup pan juices. Allow birds to cool; then cut in half.

Mix together remaining rosemary and mustard, reserved pan juices, mayonnaise, and preserves. Cover and chill. Serve hens warm or at room temperature and top with apricot preserves.

Serves 4

Named after its city of origin, Dijon mustard is a combination of seasonings, black mustard seeds, white wine vinegar, and unfermented grape juice. Despite commercials advertising such, this mustard can be used in the kitchen for numerous dishes and should not be limited to spreading on your favorite processed luncheon meat.

Pheasant with Red Fruits

Pheasant is expensive but worth it. This recipe will be the crowning touch of any special celebration.

½ cup red wine vinegar

3 tablespoons sugar

1 cup red wine

2 tablespoons chopped shallot

1 pint mixed berries

4 tablespoons butter

2 pheasants (2 to 2½ pounds each), quartered

Salt and pepper

Combine vinegar and sugar in a saucepan over medium-high heat and cook until liquid reduces to a syrup. In a separate saucepan, combine red wine and shallots and cook until liquid is reduced by two-thirds. Add red wine to syrup and cook for 2 minutes. Strain liquid into a pot. Add berries and simmer for 5 minutes. Reserve.

Preheat oven to 425°. Melt butter in a skillet over medium-high heat. Season pheasant pieces with salt and pepper and add to pan. Pan sear on both sides until brown. Transfer pheasants to oven. Bake breasts for about 4 minutes or until medium. Bake legs for 10 minutes or until cooked through. Transfer pheasant pieces to a warm serving platter.

Deglaze pan with sauce. Serve sauce over pheasants.

Serves 4

Wild pheasants can be found roaming North America and Europe and have a gamey flavor and dark, lean meat. Farm raised birds are more delicate tasting and generally more moist and plump. Domestic pheasants are sold in three weight categories: young (1 pound); adult (about 2 pounds); and mature (3 to 4 pounds). We suggest you buy pheasant in the adult weight as they are more tender than mature birds and less expensive than the young ones.

Goose Stuffed with Chestnuts

Nothing is more festive or classic on a holiday table than a perfectly roasted goose with chestnut stuffing. Cheers!

1 goose (8 pounds)

1 stalk celery, diced

½ onion, diced

½ pint mushrooms, quartered

2 teaspoons butter

2 teaspoons jellied cranberry sauce

3 dinner club rolls, cubed and toasted

2½ cups Chicken Stock (Recipe appears on page 278.)

1 cup pureed chestnuts

½ cup chopped chestnuts

Salt and pepper

2 cups white wine

A Mediterranean native and said to have grown in abundance atop Mount Olympus, the chestnut is largely imported from Italy, although it is found throughout North America. Look for fresh imported chestnuts in the fall and winter months and canned or dried chestnuts year round. Be sure to remove the hard outer shell and inner skin before roasting over an open fire.

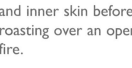

Clean goose of all excess fat and trim wings. Wash goose inside and out and pat completely dry.

Sauté celery, onion, and mushrooms in butter. When well sautéed, add cranberry sauce. In a large bowl, soak bread cubes in ½ cup stock. Add chestnut puree, chopped chestnuts, and sautéed mixture. Season to taste with salt and pepper. Check consistency. (One or 2 eggs can be added if you prefer a stiffer or richer stuffing.)

Preheat oven to 400°. Season goose inside and out with salt and pepper. Fill body cavity lightly. Fasten neck skin to back with a skewer. Tie or skewer legs to keep stuffing inside. Place goose in a roasting pan. Cook for 30 minutes. Remove goose from oven. Baste with pan juices and then remove fat from pan. Add white wine and remaining stock to pan. Reduce heat to 350° and return goose to oven. Cook for 45 to 60 minutes or until drumstick meat feels very soft when pressed between fingers. Let sit for 10 minutes; then carve and serve.

Serves 6 to 8

Morel Mushroom Stuffed Quail with Reduced Balsamic Demi-glace

These little birds are perfect for stylish luncheons or afternoon wedding receptions.

2 tablespoons oil

1 medium onion, diced

1 tablespoon chopped garlic

1 cup sliced morel mushrooms

1 cup dry red wine

1 tablespoon chopped fresh thyme

1 tablespoon chopped fresh tarragon

2 cups Croutons (Recipe appears on page 292.)

1 cup Chicken Stock (Recipe appears on page 278.)

Salt and pepper

8 semi-boneless quail

1½ cups balsamic vinegar

1 cup Demi-glace (Recipe appears on page 281.)

Heat oil in a large sauté pan. Sauté onion until translucent. Add garlic and mushrooms and sauté for 1 minute. Add red wine and herbs. Add croutons and chicken stock and cook until liquid is absorbed. Season with salt and pepper to taste. Remove from heat and cool.

Preheat oven to 375°. Wash and dry quail cavities. Lightly spoon stuffing into cavities. Fasten neck skins to backs with skewers. Tie or skewer legs to keep stuffing inside. Roast for 15 to 20 minutes or until a thermometer inserted into birds reads 140°.

Meanwhile, heat vinegar in a saucepan until thick and syrupy. Add demi-glace and reduce until sauce coats the back of a spoon. Season with salt and pepper and serve with birds.

Serves 4

Quail is a popular game bird that is indigenous to North America, Asia, Europe, and Australia. American quail is called various names such as bobwhite, partridge, and quail, depending on the region.

Quail Stuffed with Foie Gras and Figs in a Rhubarb-Kumquat Sauce

The acidity of the unusual combination of rhubarb and kumquats nicely complements and balances the richness of the foie gras.

8 quail, boned

8 ounces foie gras, cut into 8 pieces

8 figs, trimmed

Salt and pepper

4 tablespoons olive oil

8 ounces rhubarb, trimmed and cut into ½-inch pieces

8 kumquats, quartered

1 cup Chicken Stock (Recipe appears on page 278.)

½ cup sugar

½ cup red vinegar

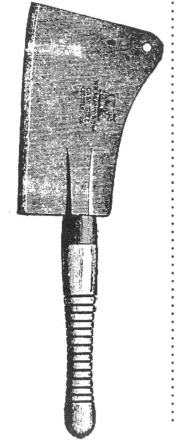

Wash and dry quail cavities. Stuff each quail with 1 piece foie gras and 1 fig. Fasten neck skins to backs with skewers. Season with salt and pepper.

Preheat oven to 450°. Heat oil in a large skillet over medium-high heat. Add quail and pan sear quail on all sides. Transfer quail to a roasting pan and bake for 8 to 10 minutes or until a thermometer inserted into birds reads 140°.

Meanwhile, combine rhubarb, kumquats, and chicken stock in a saucepan and simmer over medium-high heat until fruit is soft. In a separate pan, heat sugar and vinegar over medium-high heat and simmer until mixture is caramelized. Allow to cool slightly. Stir sugar mixture into fruit mixture. Season to taste with salt and pepper.

Serve 2 quail with rhubarb-kumquat sauce per person.

Serves 4

from the cooking school at la campagne ~ from the cooking school at la campagne ~ from the cooking school at la campagne ~ from the cooking school at la campagne ~ from the cooking school at la campagne ~ from the cooking school at la campagne ~ from the cooking school at la campagne ~ from the cooking school at la campagne ~ from the cooking school at la campagne ~ from the cooking school at la campagne ~ from the cooking school at la campagne ~ from the cooking school at la campagne ~ from the cooking school at la campagne ~ from the cooking school at la campagne ~ from the cooking school at la campagne ~ from the

meat
and game

Filet of Beef Niçoise

4 beef filet mignons (6 ounces each)

Salt and pepper

2 tablespoons olive oil

1 onion, finely diced

1 tablespoon chopped garlic

1 can (28 ounces) whole peeled plum tomatoes, drained, and chopped

½ cup pitted black olives

4 tablespoons fresh basil, cut into ribbons

Season steaks on both sides with salt and pepper. Heat olive oil in a sauté pan over medium-high heat. Add filets and sear each side until brown. Remove from pan and set aside. In the same pan, sauté onion and garlic until lightly browned. Add tomatoes and simmer for 15 to 20 minutes or until tomatoes are reduced and concentrated. Add olives and basil. Return steaks to the pan and simmer covered for about 5 minutes or until steaks reach desired doneness. Remove steaks from pan. Season sauce with salt and pepper and serve immediately on top of steaks.

Serves 4

à la niçoise
[nee-SWAHZ]

French for "as prepared in Nice," this term refers to the cuisine found in and around the French Riviera. Typical niçoise ingredients include tomatoes, black olives, garlic, and anchovies.

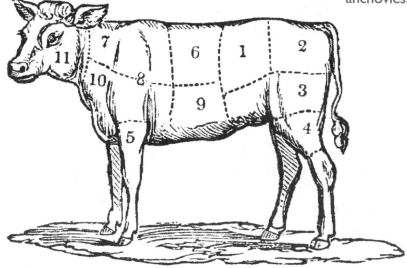

Boeuf Bourguignonne

This is the perfect midweek recipe — easy and affordable and the leftovers make for a fantastic lunch the next day. To extend the dish, serve with rice, egg noodles, or boiled potatoes.

¼ cup olive oil
2 pounds beef tenderloin tips
½ pound bacon, diced
1 medium onion, diced
½ pound wild mushrooms, sliced
Flour
½ cup Burgundy wine
1 cup Beef Stock (Recipe appears on page 279.)
Salt and pepper
½ teaspoon fresh thyme leaves
1 tablespoon chopped fresh parsley

Although this recipe and tradition call for Burgundy wine, a full-bodied red wine can be substituted in a pinch.

Heat oil in a heavy-based frying pan over medium flame. Add beef and brown. Remove beef from pan with a slotted spoon and reserve. Add bacon to pan and brown. Add onions and cook until soft. Add mushrooms and cook until soft. Remove bacon and vegetables from pan and reserve.

Sprinkle in just enough flour to absorb the pan juices and cook for 5 minutes, stirring often. Deglaze pan with wine and stock. Return beef, bacon, and vegetables to pan and simmer over low heat for 5 to 10 minutes. Season to taste with salt and pepper. Stir in fresh herbs and serve.

Serves 4

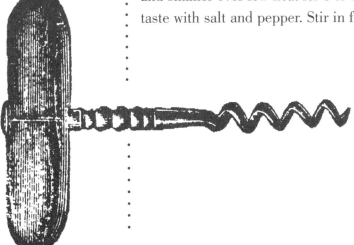

Heart-Shaped Beef Wellington with Béarnaise Sauce

A Valentine's Day favorite at La Campagne and a truly romantic meal any time of the year.

½ cup cleaned spinach leaves
¼ cup mixed mushrooms
Salt and pepper
3 tablespoons heavy cream
2 beef fillets (8 ounces each)
½ sheet frozen puff pastry, thawed
1 egg, beaten
Béarnaise Sauce (Recipe appears on page 284.)

Cook spinach in boiling water for 3 to 5 minutes. Drain and set aside. Sauté mushrooms in a nonstick skillet for 5 or 6 minutes. Season with salt and pepper. Add spinach and cream to mushrooms and cook until dry. In a separate pan, sear tenderloins until no juices run out.

Preheat oven to 425°F. Roll out puff pastry on a lightly floured surface. Cut pastry in half. Using a paring knife, cut out a heart shape from each pastry half. Place meat in the center of one heart and top with vegetable mixture. Place remaining pastry heart over vegetables and seal edges. Decorate with pastry scraps as desired. Brush with egg wash. Place on a baking sheet and bake for 15 to 20 minutes or until meat has an internal temperature of 130°.

Cut in half and serve with warm béarnaise sauce

Serves 2

Ossobuco Milanese

While traveling in Milan, we stayed at a family owned inn. They were kind enough to share their hospitality and this fantastic recipe. The secret is the intense demi-glace.

6 veal shank pieces with bone (each 1 inch thick)

½ cup all-purpose flour

½ cup Clarified Butter (Recipe appears on page 287.)

1½ cups diced onions

3 cloves garlic, crushed

¼ cup tomato paste

6 tomatoes, peeled, seeded, and chopped

2 cups dry white wine

1 quart Demi-glace (Recipe appears on page 281.)

5 sprigs thyme

2 bay leaves

Salt and pepper

Gremolada (Recipe appears on page 292.)

Dredge veal shanks in flour. Heat butter in a large sauté pan over medium heat. Brown shanks on all sides. Remove from pan and set aside. Add onion and cook until lightly browned. Add garlic and tomato paste. Cook until paste is lightly browned. Add tomatoes and white wine. Cook until liquid is reduced by half. Add demi-glace, thyme, and bay leaves and bring to a simmer. Add veal and braise slowly for 60 minutes until meat is fork tender. Remove veal shanks and keep warm.

Strain sauce, extracting as much liquid as possible. Return sauce to pan and bring to a boil. Cook until sauce reduces and coats the back of a spoon. Season to taste with salt and pepper.

Serve shanks topped with sauce and garnished with gremolada.

Serves 6

gremolada
[greh-moh-LAH-dah]

This classic garnish made of minced parsley, lemon peel, and garlic is traditionally sprinkled over ossobuco. Use it to add fresh flavor to fish, chicken, and vegetables.

Provençal Stuffed Pork Tenderloin

This is a festive way to dress up tenderloin for an autumn meal or any time. Thinly slice leftovers for sandwiches.

Roasted Provençal Vegetables (Recipe appears on page 205.)
1 center-cut pork tenderloin (3 pounds), trimmed of all fat
Salt and pepper
2 tablespoons olive oil
Roasted Red Pepper Coulis (Recipe appears on page 290.)

Place roasted vegetables on a sheet of plastic wrap, roll it up like a log, and tie the ends. Freeze until fully frozen or overnight.

Preheat oven to 450°. Cut pork lengthwise three-quarters through so it opens like a book. (You can also have your butcher butterfly it.) Season with salt and pepper. Remove plastic from frozen vegetables and place vegetables in the center of tenderloin. Wrap pork around vegetables and tie with butcher's twine. Heat oil in a skillet on medium-high. Brown rolled pork on all sides and transfer to a roasting pan. Roast for 15 to 20 minutes. Slice and serve with roasted red pepper coulis.

Serves 4 to 6

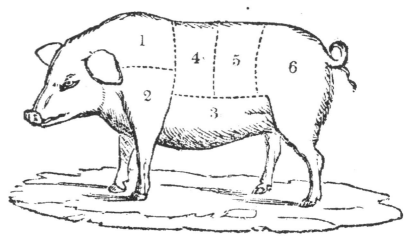

Rack of Lamb with Caramelized Shallot Crust

There is something undeniably elegant and just slightly indulgent about a rack of lamb, but that doesn't mean it should be reserved for special occasions. Indulge! (This recipe was Bill Boyer's favorite!)

1 tablespoon olive oil

4 tablespoons minced shallots

4 tablespoons balsamic vinegar

½ cup breadcrumbs

1 teaspoon chopped fresh thyme

1 teaspoon chopped fresh rosemary

Salt and pepper

1 tablespoon Dijon mustard

1 rack of lamb (8 bones), trimmed and frenched

Preheat oven to 425°. Heat oil in a sauté pan over medium heat. Add shallots and sauté until golden brown, about 5 minutes. Add vinegar and cook until liquid is reduced by half. Remove pan from heat. Stir in breadcrumbs, herbs, and salt and pepper to form a paste. Coat back of rack with Dijon mustard; then with breadcrumb mixture, pressing down to cover.

Bake for 20 to 25 minutes or until a thermometer inserted into center of rack reads 125°. Remove rack from oven and allow lamb to rest for 5 to 10 minutes before slicing.

Serves 2

The combination of caramelized shallots and tangy mustard give this dish a sweet and piquant crust. Choose dry-skinned shallots that are firm with no sign of wrinkling or sprouting. Refrigerate fresh shallots for up to 1 week. Store dry shallots in a cool, dry, well-ventilated place for up to 1 month.

Grilled Butterflied Leg of Lamb with Sour Cherries

Each June we hold a series of al fresco classes in our garden. While attendees sip wine under cherry trees, our chefs teach cooking and grilling secrets that will guide them through a summer of outdoor entertaining. This recipe is a favorite.

5 cloves garlic, minced

3 tablespoons anchovy paste

½ cup chopped fresh parsley

2 tablespoons Herbes de Provence (Recipe appears on page 292.)

2 teaspoons freshly ground black pepper

½ cup olive oil

1¾ cups Burgundy wine

1 leg of lamb (6 to 7 pounds), boned and butterflied

5 sprigs fresh rosemary

2 medium red onions, julienned

2 pounds sour cherries, pitted

½ cup golden raisins

2½ tablespoons honey

½ cup chopped fresh mint

Salt and pepper

Sour cherries such as Montmorency, Morello, and Early Richmond are smaller, softer, and rounder than sweet cherries. They are perfect for pies, jams, soups, and as compliments to meats and game. Look for firm cherries with a nice sheen.

In a blender or food processor, combine garlic, anchovy paste, parsley, herbes de Provence, pepper, and ¼ cup oil. Puree until smooth. With motor running, add 1¼ cups wine.

Arrange lamb in a large glass dish and cover with marinade. Dot with rosemary and cover. Marinate in refrigerator for at least 6 hours, turning several times.

Grill 4 inches above heat, 15 to 20 minutes per side for medium-rare. Baste with any extra marinade. Meanwhile, heat remaining oil in a saucepan. Sauté onions until lightly caramelized. Stir in cherries, raisins, honey, and remaining wine. Simmer for 10 minutes. Stir in mint. Season with salt and pepper.

Carve lamb into thin slices and serve with cherry sauce.

Serves 10

Roast Leg of Lamb with Spring Herbs

We grow over 15 varieties of herbs at La Campagne. They add texture, color, and fragrance to our garden and our menu.

1 leg of lamb (4 to 5 pounds), boned and trimmed
8 cloves garlic, sliced in half lengthwise
2 bay leaves
1 teaspoon fennel seeds
1 teaspoon lavender flowers
3 tablespoons chopped fresh parsley
2 tablespoons chopped fresh thyme
2 tablespoons chopped fresh basil
1 tablespoon chopped fresh rosemary
½ cup olive oil
Salt and pepper

Preheat oven to 400°. Place leg of lamb on a rack in a roasting pan, cut side down. Using a paring knife, make slits in the top and sides of leg. Insert garlic slivers into slits. Place dry herbs in a spice mill or mortar and pestle and grind together. Combine dried herbs, fresh herbs, oil, and salt and pepper to taste to form a paste.

Rub paste over entire leg and roast for 40 to 50 minutes or until an inserted meat thermometer reads 125° to 130°. Turn off oven and open door a crack. Allow lamb to rest in oven for about 10 minutes. Remove and serve with defatted pan juices.

Serves 8

Lamb is naturally enhanced by the flavors of rosemary, thyme, garlic, and olive oil. We serve this springtime roast with Garlic Mashed Potatoes, Ratatouille Vegetables, or Provençal Gratin.

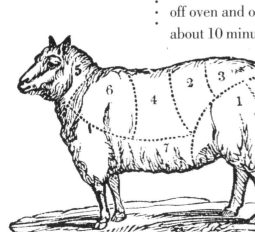

Lamb Shanks Braised in White Wine and Herbs

6 lamb shanks (8 to 9 ounces each)

½ cup flour

¼ cup olive oil

1½ cups onions, finely diced

6 cloves garlic, minced

2 ounces prosciutto, diced small

1 tablespoon tomato paste

2 cups white wine

1½ cups fresh tomatoes, peeled, seeded, and chopped

3 cups Demi-glace (Recipe appears on page 281.)

1 teaspoon grated lemon peel

½ teaspoon cayenne pepper

1 rosemary sprig, stemmed

1 oregano sprig

1 bay leaf

Salt and pepper

Braising is a cooking method in which the main item, usually meat, is browned in fat, then simmered in liquid in a tightly covered pot. The long, slow cooking process tenderizes the meat and enhances its flavors.

Dredge lamb shanks in flour. Heat oil in a 6-quart heavy-duty shallow braising pan over medium heat. Sear shanks on all sides. Remove from pan and keep warm. Add onions to pan and cook until lightly browned. Add garlic, prosciutto, and tomato paste and continue to cook for several minutes. Add wine. Cook until liquid reduces to 1 cup. Stir in remaining ingredients. Simmer for several minutes.

Reduce heat to medium-low. Add seared lamb shanks to sauce and cover. Braise very slowly for about 1¼ hours until meat pulls easily from the bone. When meat is fork tender, remove from sauce and keep warm.

Strain sauce through a fine mesh sieve. Return to heat and cook until sauce is reduced and coats the back of a spoon. Place shanks in pan, coat with sauce, and serve.

Serves 6

Sautéed Sweetbreads in Shiitake Cream Sauce

Madeira wine, mushrooms, and cream create a rich sauce that naturally enhances the taste and texture of sweetbreads.

2 pounds sweetbreads, trimmed of fat

½ cup dry white wine

2 quarts water

Juice of 2 lemons

1 teaspoon black peppercorns

Flour for dredging

Salt and pepper

4 tablespoons Clarified Butter (Recipe appears on page 287.)

2 large shallots, chopped

½ pound shiitake mushrooms, stems removed

½ cup Madeira wine or dry Marsala wine

¾ cup heavy cream

Combine sweetbreads, white wine, water, lemon juice, and peppercorns in a saucepan and slowly bring to a boil. Once boiling point is reached, reduce heat and poach for 5 minutes. Drain and rinse under running cold water. Place sweetbreads between 2 flat sheet pans. Set a 4-pound weight over the top pan. Refrigerate for 2 hours.

Slice sweetbreads into ½-inch medallions. Season flour with salt and pepper. Lightly dredge sweetbreads in seasoned flour, tapping off excess. Heat butter in a large sauté pan over medium-high heat. Brown sweetbreads on both sides. Remove from pan and set aside.

Add shallots and sauté for 2 minutes. Add wine and mushrooms and simmer for 2 minutes. Add cream and reduce until sauce coats the back of a spoon. Return sweetbreads to pan, coat with sauce, and serve.

Serves 4

Sweetbreads are the thymus glands of young animals. The meat is rich with a delicate flavor. Sweetbreads are available fresh or frozen. To prepare sweetbreads for cooking, first remove all traces of blood — soak them in cool water for 4 hours, changing the water as soon as it begins to turn pink — and then remove the membrane.

Seared Sweetbreads with Sherry Balsamic Reduction

We serve sweetbreads as a special and always sell out.

2 pounds veal sweetbreads

1 cup milk

1 cup flour

1 tablespoon vegetable oil

2 shallots, minced

1 teaspoon chopped garlic

¼ cup dry sherry

¼ cup balsamic vinegar

½ cup Demi-glace (Recipe appears on page 281.)

2 tablespoons butter

Salt and pepper

1 tablespoon chopped parsley

Trim sweetbreads of all membranes and large veins. Poach sweetbreads in boiling salted water for 4 to 5 minutes. Remove and cool. Slice cooled sweetbreads into medallions, cover with milk, and soak overnight.

Remove sweetbreads from milk and pat dry with paper towel. Dredge sweetbreads in flour, shaking off excess. Heat oil in a pan over medium-high heat. Add sweetbreads and sauté for 2 to 3 minutes per side or until crispy and golden brown. Remove from pan, reserve, and keep warm.

In the same pan, cook shallots and garlic until lightly browned. Deglaze with sherry and vinegar and cook until liquid is reduced by half. Add demi-glace. Cook and reduce until sauce is thick enough to coat the back of a spoon. Swirl in butter and season to taste with salt and pepper. Divide sweetbreads among 4 warmed plates, top with sauce, and garnish with parsley.

Serves 4

True sherry comes from only one place: the city of Jerez de la Frontera. Sherry-type wines, however, are produced in the United States, South Africa, and Australia. With true sherry, different types and qualities of wine are determined by the type of Spanish soil used to cultivate the grapes. Fino is a dry, pale wine while amontillado is a slightly darker, sweeter, and less dry variety. The wine of bullfighters, manzanilla is very dry and offers a subtle shadow of saltiness.

Braised Rabbit with Garlic and Basil

We often buy our rabbits at Philadelphia's two food meccas: The Reading Terminal Market and The Italian Market.

6 plump, fresh whole heads garlic

Flour for dredging

Salt and pepper

2 rabbits (about 1½ pounds each), cut into serving pieces

3 tablespoons olive oil

Bouquet garni (See sidebar on page 78.)

1 cup dry white wine

½ cup chopped fresh basil leaves

Trim and discard top third of each head garlic. Set heads aside. Season flour with salt and pepper. Lightly dredge rabbit pieces in flour, shaking off excess.

Heat oil in a large lidded sauté pan over medium-high heat. Add rabbit and brown on both sides. Remove browned rabbit. Place garlic, cut side down, in the remaining fat and cook for 2 to 3 minutes. Return rabbit to pan. Add bouquet garni and white wine. Cover and simmer for 1 hour.

Arrange rabbit and garlic on a warm platter. Remove bouquet garni. Add basil to cooking liquid and spoon over rabbit.

Serves 4

Americans are a bit squeamish about eating rabbit. Not so in France where rabbits are plentiful and ways of preparing them are innumerable. In the north, rabbit dishes often include juniper berries and mushrooms, while in the south, dried fruits are added to the hare stew pot. In Provence, rabbit pieces are sautéed in olive oil with garlic, onions, and tomatoes. Rabbit is not so easy to find in America; but frozen rabbit is available, and butchers will order it upon request.

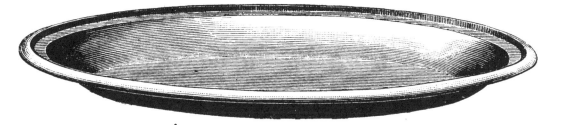

Herb Roasted Loin of Venison with Currant Sage Sauce

Fresh herbs highlight the natural floral accents found in venison.

1 tablespoon plus 2 teaspoons chopped fresh sage

2 tablespoons chopped fresh thyme

1 tablespoon chopped fresh rosemary

2 tablespoons chopped fresh parsley

2 tablespoons kosher salt

1 tablespoon ground black pepper

4 tablespoons vegetable oil

1 venison loin (2 pounds)

1 cup red wine

1 cup red currant jelly

1 cup Demi-glace (Recipes appears on pages 281.)

Salt and pepper

Preheat oven to 375°. Blend 2 teaspoons sage, herbs, salt, pepper, and 2 tablespoons oil into a paste. Rub paste on outside of venison loin. Heat remaining oil in a sauté pan over medium-high heat. When oil is smoking hot, add venison and sear loin on all sides. Transfer to a roasting rack in a roasting pan. Roast for 20 to 30 minutes or until an inserted meat thermometer reads 120°. Remove and allow meat to rest for 5 to 10 minutes before slicing.

Meanwhile, cook wine in a saucepan over medium heat until reduced to approximately ¼ cup. Add currant jelly and demi-glace. Cook until sauce reduces, thickens, and coats the back of a spoon. Add remaining 1 tablespoon sage. Season with salt and pepper. Serve with sliced venison.

Serves 4 to 6

In medieval times, a spit-roasted deer was often the centerpiece for lavish buffets. Venison, with its very lean, flavorful meat, is popular in modern times as well. Although grassy (herbal overtones are often present), the taste of both farm-raised and wild venison will vary according to environmental and dietary conditions.

Venison with Apple, Leek, and Rutabaga Compote

1½ pounds venison, trimmed of fat

Salt and pepper

4 tablespoons olive oil

1 leek, diced

2 Granny Smith apples, peeled, cored, and diced

1 teaspoon mustard seed, toasted

¼ cup maple syrup

1 medium rutabaga, peeled and cubed

2 shallots, minced

½ cup Demi-glace or Chicken Stock (Recipes appear on pages 281 and 278.)

½ cup balsamic vinegar

2 tablespoons unsalted butter, cubed

The clean delicate flavor of venison is nicely complimented by the slightly savory caramelized apples.

Preheat oven to 450°F. Season venison with salt and pepper. Heat 2 tablespoons olive oil in a heavy skillet over medium-high heat. Sear venison on all sides. Roast venison for 20 to 30 minutes or to desired doneness. (A meat thermometer inserted into tenderloin should read at least 130°. Rare to medium-rare is highly recommended!) Transfer meat to a platter, cover with foil, and let rest for 15 minutes.

In the same skillet, add remaining olive oil. Sauté leek until softened. Add apples, mustard seed, and syrup and cook until apples are lightly caramelized. Meanwhile, cook rutabaga in boiling water until just tender, about 10 minutes. Strain and add to apple mixture. Season to taste with salt and pepper.

In a small saucepan, combine shallots, demi-glace or stock, and vinegar. Cook over medium heat until liquid is reduced in volume by half. Once reduced, bring mixture to a simmer and stir in butter, one piece at a time. Slice venison. Divide apple compote among 4 warm serving plates. Arrange venison on top of compote and drizzle with sauce.

Serves 4

from the cooking school at la campagne ~ from the cooking school at la campagne ~ from the cooking school at la campagne ~ from the cooking school at la campagne ~ from the cooking school at la campagne ~ from the cooking school at la campagne ~ from the cooking school at la campagne ~ from the cooking school at la campagne ~ from the cooking school at la campagne ~ from the cooking school at la campagne ~ from the cooking school at la campagne ~ from the cooking school at la campagne ~ from the cooking school at la campagne ~ from the

fish

Poached Salmon with Cucumber Dill Cream

Poached salmon is a staple at Washington A-list parties and certainly a favorite at La Campagne.

1 cup white wine

½ cup water

Juice of 1 lemon

1 teaspoon peppercorns

1 bay leaf

1 sprig thyme

Pinch of salt

4 salmon fillets (6 ounces each)

1 small cucumber, peeled, seeded, and diced

1 cup Béchamel Sauce (Recipe appears on page 283.)

½ bunch fresh dill, chopped

Salt and pepper

Combine wine, water, lemon juice, peppercorns, bay leaf, thyme, and pinch of salt in a 12-inch sauté pan over high heat. Bring to a simmer; then immediately reduce heat to medium. Place fillets in pan. If necessary, add additional water to cover fish. Poach for 8 to 10 minutes or until salmon flakes easily. Turn heat off and keep fish in pan until ready to serve.

Pour 1 cup poaching liquid through a strainer and then into a 1-quart saucepan. Simmer until liquid is reduced by half. Add cucumber and béchamel sauce. Return to a simmer. Add dill and season with salt and pepper. Simmer for 1 minute.

Remove fish from pan with a slotted spatula and place on platter. Serve topped with sauce.

Serves 4

Some say salmon is the most beautiful fish in the world. Choose fillets or steaks that are orange to red orange in color and contain some fat (the white lines in the meat) but not too much. Whole fishes should be shiny with nice silver appearances. If very fresh, salmon can be eaten raw; otherwise, sauté, steam, poach, roast, bake, grill, or stew to medium rare or medium. If poaching and serving cold, cook all the way through.

Salmon Roulade with Roasted Pepper, Goat Cheese, and Swiss Chard

This novel presentation is perfect for parties. The roulade can be made in advance and the end result is glamorous. You'll find that goat cheese and Swiss chard perfectly complement the taste of Atlantic salmon.

1 bunch red Swiss chard, lightly blanched and coarse stems removed

½ pound goat cheese, softened

1 roasted red pepper, stemmed, peeled, and seeded

1 roasted yellow pepper, stemmed, peeled, and seeded

1 salmon fillet (2 pounds), boned and skinned

Salt and freshly ground pepper

Roughly chop chard and mix with goat cheese. Refrigerate until firm.

Place salmon fillet, trimmed side down, on a cutting board. Using a sharp knife, make an incision in fish, not cutting all the way through, so that fillet will open like a book. Gently open fillet and place on a large sheet of plastic wrap. Spread cheese mixture evenly over "butterflied" fillet. Starting at the thinner end, roll fish up, jelly-roll style, into a roulade. Wrap with plastic wrap and refrigerate for at least 1 hour.

Preheat oven to 400°. Unwrap and slice roulade crosswise into 1½-inch-thick slices. Bake for 10 to 12 minutes or until a thermometer inserted in the middle reads 140°.

Serves 4

roulade
[roo-LAHD]

A thin piece of meat or fish filled with a savory stuffing, rolled up, and baked or braised.

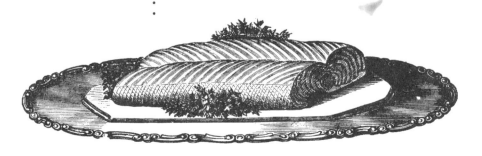

Porcini-Crusted Salmon with Roasted Garlic Ragoût

Dried porcini not only protects the tenderness of the fillets, it adds a wonderful earthy nuance.

1 ounce dried porcini mushrooms

4 salmon fillets (6 to 8 ounces each), skinned and boned

Salt and pepper

2 tablespoons olive oil

½ cup white wine

½ cup Chicken Stock (Recipe appears on page 278.)

4 plum tomatoes, stemmed and quartered

4 artichoke hearts, halved

8 cloves garlic

½ teaspoon chopped fresh thyme

½ teaspoon chopped fresh chives

Preheat oven to 450°. Grind mushrooms to a fine powder in a blender or with a mortar and pestle. Season salmon with salt and pepper; then dredge in mushroom powder.

Heat oil in a large sauté pan over high heat. Add salmon and sear for 2 minutes on each side. Add remaining ingredients. Place in oven and cook for 8 to 10 minutes. Season to taste with salt and pepper. Place salmon in the center of 4 warmed plates. Arrange vegetables around salmon and nap with broth.

Serves 4

Lavender and Mustard Seed-Crusted Salmon

The over 100 lavender bushes that are spread throughout our property are constant reminders of our trips to Provence.

3 tablespoons olive oil

1 red pepper, stemmed, seeded, and diced

2 medium red onions, peeled and diced

¼ cup dry white wine

1 tablespoon fresh lemon juice

1 tablespoon maple syrup

1 tablespoon honey

1 cup balsamic vinegar

3 tablespoons mustard seeds

2 teaspoons dried lavender blossoms

4 salmon fillets (6 ounces each), boned and skinned

Salt and freshly ground pepper

Fresh lavender is stronger than dried lavender. When dried, it has a more pronounced herbal character than when fresh and may remind you of thyme or marjoram. It works well in combination with other dried herbs and spices in both savory and sweet dishes. It is just as versatile in the garden, acting as both a decorative shrub and a usable crop.

Heat 1 tablespoon olive oil in a sauté pan over medium heat. Add red pepper and onions and cook for 15 minutes, stirring often. Add wine, lemon juice, maple syrup, and honey. Simmer for 5 minutes. Season to taste with salt and pepper. Reserve and keep warm.

Heat balsamic vinegar in a saucepan over medium heat until liquid reduces to 2 tablespoons and is syrupy.

Preheat oven to 450°. Combine mustard seeds and lavender in a shallow baking dish. Season fillets with salt and pepper and dredge in seed-lavender mixture. Heat remaining oil in a nonstick sauté pan over medium-high heat. Add fillets and sear for 1 minute. Turn fillets and sear for 2 minutes. Transfer to oven and bake for 3 to 8 minutes or to desired doneness.

Arrange fillets on 4 warm plates. Top with red onion marmalade. Sprinkle with balsamic syrup.

Serves 4

Wild Striped Bass Niçoise

1 cup dry white wine

2 large shallots, peeled and chopped

1 bay leaf

1 cup Fish Bouillon (Recipe appears on page 280.)

2 cups tomato juice

¼ teaspoon saffron threads

12 cloves garlic, peeled

3 tablespoons olive oil

Salt and pepper

12 niçoise or kalamata olives, pitted and sliced

1 cup chopped fresh basil leaves

4 wild striped bass fillets (8 ounces each), skin on and boned

Yellow Pepper Rouille (Recipe appears on page 289.)

Preheat oven to 350°. Combine wine, shallots, and bay leaf in a saucepan. Simmer over medium heat until liquid volume is reduced by half. Add bouillon and tomato juice. Return to a simmer and allow liquid to reduce in volume by half. Soften saffron threads in 2 tablespoons warm water. Arrange garlic in a small roasting pan and coat with 1 tablespoon oil. Season with salt and pepper.

Cover with foil and roast in oven for 25 to 30 minutes or until lightly browned and semi-soft. Add garlic to sauce. Stir in olives, saffron and its liquid, and basil. Season to taste.

Increase oven temperature to 450°. Season bass with salt and pepper. Heat remaining oil in a large, heavy skillet over medium-high heat. Sear bass, skin side down, for 1 minute in hot oil. Turn and sear 1 minute. Transfer to oven and roast for 5 to 12 minutes. (This depends on the thickness of the fillets and the desired doneness.) Spoon sauce onto 4 warm plates. Place bass on sauce and top with yellow pepper rouille.

Serves 4

Although wild striped bass is not available in New Jersey, we enjoy the farm raised variety at La Campagne and its wild cousin when we dine in many of our neighboring states.

Citrus Striped Bass

The acidity of the fruit juices brings out the freshness of the bass and makes for a very refreshing summer entree.

¼ cup olive oil

2 pounds striped bass fillets

3 cloves garlic, chopped

2 shallots, chopped

4 tablespoons rice wine vinegar

2 tablespoons soy sauce

Juice of 2 oranges

Juice of 1 lemon

Juice of 1 lime

1 piece ginger (3 inches), peeled and minced

1 tablespoon cornstarch

¼ cup water

4 tablespoons unsalted butter, cut into ½-inch pieces

4 scallions, cut into ½-inch pieces

2 tablespoons dried onion flakes

Cilantro leaves

Heat olive oil in a heavy skillet over medium heat. Add fillets, skin side down, and sear for 2 minutes per side. Remove from pan and set aside. Add garlic and shallots to pan and sauté for 1 minute. Add vinegar, soy sauce, citrus juices, and ginger and bring to a simmer. Combine cornstarch and water and add to skillet, stirring to thoroughly incorporate. Return fish to skillet and simmer for 2 minutes. Stir in butter. Top fillets with sauce and garnish with scallions, onion flakes, and cilantro leaves.

Serves 4

Chilean Sea Bass with Herb Crust and Black Trumpet Mushroom

Once called Patagonian Toothfish, a name change has turned Chilean sea bass into a very popular fish. We like it for its firm, bright white meat and ability to accommodate many different flavors and seasonal accents.

4 Chilean sea bass fillets (8 ounces each), boned

Salt and pepper

½ cup mixed stemmed and chopped fresh thyme and rosemary

3 tablespoons olive oil

6 shallots, sliced

1 cup dry white wine

1 cup Fish Bouillon (Recipe appears on page 280.) or clam juice

¼ pound black trumpet mushrooms, cleaned and sliced

1 plum tomato, seeded and diced

1 clove garlic, minced

1 tablespoon chopped flat-leaf parsley

2 tablespoons unsalted butter

Season sea bass on both sides with salt and pepper. Place herbs in a shallow bowl. Dredge fillets in herbs. Set aside.

Heat 2 tablespoons oil in a sauté pan. Add shallots and sauté until soft. Add wine and bouillon and cook until liquid volume is reduced by half. Stir in mushrooms, tomato, garlic, and parsley and cook for 1 to 2 minutes. Stir in butter until smooth. Season with salt and pepper and reserve.

Preheat oven to 450°. Heat remaining oil in a separate skillet over high heat. Add fillets and sear, about 2 minutes per side. Transfer to a roasting pan and bake until fish flakes easily, about 8 minutes. Transfer fish to a heated serving platter and top with reserved sauce.

Serves 4

Black trumpet mushrooms are named for their distinctive trumpet shape. They have thin dark skin and a lovely buttery flavor. You can buy them midsummer through midfall at specialty markets.

Sea Bass Provençale with Saffron Butter Sauce

Saffron-infused butter lends intense color and flavor to any member of the white fish family.

2 tablespoons olive oil

4 scallions, thinly sliced

2 cloves garlic, finely chopped

1 shallot, chopped

1 pound ripe tomatoes, peeled, seeded, and diced

4 ounces dry white wine

Salt and freshly ground pepper

½ teaspoon saffron threads

4 tablespoons butter, diced

2 tablespoons chopped basil

4 sea bass fillets

8 cured olives, pitted and sliced

4 fresh basil leaves, cut into ribbons

Heat olive oil in a large saucepan over medium heat. Add scallions, garlic, and shallot and sauté until soft. Add tomatoes and wine and simmer for 5 minutes. Season with salt and pepper.

Strain tomatoes into a saucepan and set tomato mixture aside. Heat juice from tomatoes over medium heat. Add saffron threads and cook until liquid is reduced by half. Whisk in diced butter. Stir in chopped basil and keep warm.

Preheat oven to 450°. Season fillets with salt and pepper and place on an oiled baking sheet. Roast for 5 minutes.

Arrange tomato mixture in the center of a heated service platter. Place fish fillets on top, pressing down lightly to expose a little tomato mixture. Spoon saffron butter sauce around fish. Garnish with chopped olives and basil leaves.

Serves 4

Saffron is the world's most expensive spice and for good reason. It is the stigma of a certain variety of crocus. Each flower yields only three stigmas and it takes over 14,000 of these stigmas to produce an ounce of saffron. Luckily only a few strands are needed to impart great taste and visual appeal.

Pan Seared Tuna with Ginger-Carrot Beurre Blanc

We serve our sushi grade tuna rare at La Campagne and you should too. You'll love the moist, sweet, red meat. We promise.

2 teaspoons plus 2 tablespoons unsalted butter

2 medium carrots, peeled and diced

3 tablespoons honey

1 tablespoon grated fresh ginger

¼ cup white wine

1 cup Chicken Stock (Recipe appears on page 278.)

1 cup heavy cream

Salt and pepper

4 sushi grade yellowfin tuna steaks (about 6 ounces each)

1 teaspoon oil

Heat 2 teaspoons butter in a heavy saucepan over medium heat. Add carrots and sauté until tender, about 4 minutes. Add honey and ginger and cook for 1 minute. Add wine and cook until liquid is reduced by half. Add chicken stock and cook until liquid is reduced to ¼ cup. Add cream and cook until mixture is thick and will coat the back of a spoon.

Transfer mixture to a blender and process smooth. Return mixture to pan and bring to a simmer. Swirl in remaining butter. Season to taste with salt and pepper. Reserve.

Season tuna steaks with salt and pepper. Heat oil in a large sauté pan over high heat. When oil is smoking, add steaks. Cook for 2 minutes on each side or to desired doneness. Serve steaks napped with sauce.

Serves 4

Translated as "white butter," beurre blanc is a lukewarm sauce traditionally served over French fish dishes. This rich sauce is a mixture of butter, vinegar, white wine, and shallots. Some important keys to making a beurre blanc sauce include fresh, room temperature butter; very finely chopped shallots; and you've got to whisk, whisk, whisk.

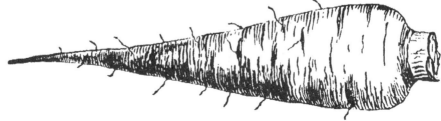

Pepper-Crusted Tuna with Ginger Glaze

Slightly hot with a hint of sweetness, this is a quick dish from pan to plate, but the memory will linger.

½ cup white wine

½ cup Fish Bouillon (Recipe appears on page 280.) or clam juice

¼ cup soy sauce

½ teaspoon sesame oil

1 small carrot, peeled and thinly sliced

1 piece fresh ginger (½ inch), peeled and thinly sliced

4 tablespoons cold unsalted butter

1 tablespoon cracked black peppercorns

4 sushi grade tuna fillets (6 to 8 ounces each)

2 tablespoons olive oil

2 teaspoons sesame seeds, lightly toasted

Combine wine, bouillon, soy sauce, sesame oil, carrot, and ginger in a saucepan over medium heat. Cook until liquid reduces to ½ cup. Stir in butter. Reserve and keep warm.

Place peppercorns in a shallow bowl. Roll tuna fillets in peppercorns to coat. Heat olive oil in a heavy skillet over high heat. When smoking, add fillets and pan sear on all sides to desired doneness. (Best served rare!) Place fillets on a serving plate. Sprinkle with sesame seeds and serve with glaze.

Serves 4

To toast sesame seeds

Cook in a nonstick skillet over medium heat. Stir constantly for 2 to 3 minutes or until lightly browned.

Potato-Crusted Hamachi with Orange Beurre Blanc

We coat the tuna in the potato crust to seal in moisture and flavor. A confetti of carrot and leek form a colorful base.

4 fillets hamachi (Pacific yellowtail tuna) or other fillet fish such as snapper or mahi mahi

1 egg yolk, beaten

½ pound potatoes, peeled and sliced into thin rounds

2 tablespoons Clarified Butter (Recipe appears on page 287.)

1 small carrot, julienned

½ leek, julienned

Orange Beurre Blanc (Recipe appears on page 286.)

Brush fish with egg yolk. Layer potato slices on top of each fillet to form "scales." Season with salt and pepper. Heat clarified butter in a nonstick pan over medium-high heat. Add fish and gently sauté each side until golden brown and cooked through. (If fish is thick, finish cooking in a 350° oven.) Remove fish from pan. Add leek and carrot strips and sauté for about 2 to 4 minutes.

Place leek and carrot strips in the center of a serving plate, top with fish, and pour orange beurre blanc around fillets.

Serves 4

All grades of yellowfin tuna — sushi grade, sushi-like grade, and no grade — can be eaten raw but must be very fresh. Otherwise, cook tuna to rare or medium rare, searing all sides of the tuna. If overcooked, the meat loses its fat and becomes dry.

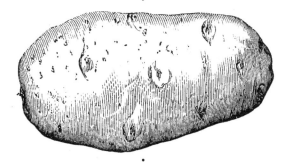

Prosciutto-Crusted Monkfish with Madeira Balsamic Syrup

Prosciutto, Madeira wine, and balsamic vinegar add smoke and sharpness to this Spanish-inspired dish.

4 monkfish fillets (6 ounces each), trimmed
8 thin slices prosciutto
2 tablespoons oil
¼ cup Madeira wine
½ cup balsamic vinegar
2 tablespoons butter
Salt and pepper

Preheat oven to 350°. Wrap each monkfish fillet with 2 pieces prosciutto. Heat oil in a nonstick skillet over high heat until smoking. Place fillets in pan and sear on all sides until prosciutto is crisp. Transfer to a baking pan and bake for 10 to 12 minutes.

Meanwhile, in same skillet, cook wine and vinegar over medium heat until liquid is reduced to ½ cup. Swirl in butter. Season to taste with salt and pepper. Spoon sauce over fish and serve.

Serves 4

Monkfish is also known as lotte, sea devil, and goosefish. Called "poor man's lobster," it has firm, white flesh and a sweet, mild flavor.

Pan Seared Arctic Char with White Asparagus and Red Butter Sauce

When white asparagus is in season, there is nothing better. If you see it in the market, don't hesitate to snap it up.

½ pound white asparagus
½ cup clam juice
1 bay leaf
½ teaspoon chopped garlic
2 shallots, chopped
2 cups red wine
8 tablespoons butter
Salt and pepper
4 arctic char fillets (6 ounces each), skin on
1 small bunch parsley, chopped finely

Remove the woody portions of asparagus by bending stalks gently until they snap. Peel stalks from blossom to end. Bring a pot of salted water to a boil. Cook asparagus in water until well done, about 5 to 8 minutes. Set aside and keep warm.

Place clam juice, bay leaf, garlic, and shallots in a saucepan over medium heat. Heat until liquid is reduced by half. Add red wine and reduce until sauce thickens. Gradually add 6 tablespoons butter, stirring gently with a whisk. Season with salt and pepper. Keep warm but do not overheat.

Melt remaining butter in a skillet over medium-high heat. Add fish, skin side down, and pan sear until crispy. Turn and cook until other side is crispy. Place fish on a serving plate and surround with asparagus. Cover fish with sauce and garnish with parsley.

Serves 4

White asparagus should be peeled and cooked until well done or it will taste bitter.

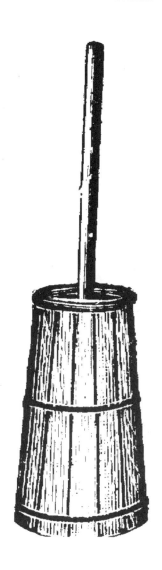

Hazelnut-Crusted Pompano with Swiss Chard

1 small beet, about the size of a tennis ball

1 cup plus 3 tablespoons olive oil

12 large shallots, peeled

4 pompano fillets (6 ounces each)

Salt and pepper

1 cup peeled and chopped hazelnuts

2 cloves garlic, chopped

1 pound Swiss chard, stems removed

¼ cup dry white wine

¼ cup Chicken Stock (Recipe appears on page 278.)

¼ cup balsamic vinegar

Preheat oven to 350°. Wash beet and place in a small ovenproof dish. Roast until it can be easily pierced with a paring knife, 30 to 40 minutes. Peel skin. Place beet and 1 cup olive oil in a blender. Puree until smooth and set aside.

Preheat oven to 450°. Rub shallots with 1 tablespoon oil. Arrange in a single layer in a baking dish. Cover with foil and roast in oven for 20 minutes or until tender.

Season pompano with salt and pepper. Place hazelnuts in a shallow dish and roll fillets in nuts to coat. Heat remaining oil in a large sauté pan over high heat. Add fillets and brown for 2 minutes per side. Remove from pan and transfer to a warm platter. Add garlic to same pan and lower heat. Add chard, season with salt and pepper, and cook until wilted. Remove chard from pan and keep warm. Add wine, stock, and vinegar to pan. Simmer until liquid is reduced by half. Season with salt and pepper.

Divide chard among 4 plates and place pompano on chard. Top each fillet with 2 shallots. Spoon sauce over fish and drizzle everything with beet oil.

Serves 4

To skin hazelnuts

Preheat oven to 400°. Place hazelnuts on a foil-lined bake sheet and bake for 5 minutes or until lightly browned under the skin. Wrap them in a dish towel and allow them to cool for a few minutes. Keep nuts in the towel and rub until the skins loosen and flake off. (Don't worry if all the skin doesn't come off — most will.)

South by Southwest Red Snapper

This is a superb combination of a fish from the American South and a presentation from the southwest of France.

4 red snapper fillets (6 ounces each)

1 cup white wine

1 cup Fish Bouillon (Recipe appears on page 280.)

Pinch of cayenne pepper

Salt and pepper

1¼ cups heavy cream

Pinch of saffron

4 tablespoons butter

4 plum tomatoes, peeled, seeded, and diced

1 leek, white part only, julienned

Preheat oven to 350°. Place fillets in a buttered ovenproof dish. Pour in wine and bouillon. Sprinkle with pinch of cayenne and salt and pepper. Bake for 10 to 15 minutes or until fish starts to flake. Transfer fillets and a few tablespoons of pan juices to a heated serving dish. Pour remaining pan juices into a 1-quart sauté pan. Cook over medium heat until liquid volume is reduced by half. Add heavy cream and saffron and continue to reduce liquid slowly.

In a separate pan, heat 2 tablespoons butter. Add tomatoes and leek and cook until very soft, almost a puree. Add the stock mixture and cook until sauce is smooth and will coat the back of a spoon. Stir in remaining 2 tablespoons butter. Season to taste with salt and pepper. Serve sauce over fillets.

Serves 4

Red snapper is an expensive but outstanding fish with firm, easy to handle meat. Very low in fat, it is a favorite with people who are watching their diets. Buy a medium size fillet for the best yield. Red snapper can be sautéed, roasted, baked, or even steamed.

Tomato Confit Poached Halibut with Tarragon Broth

This dish makes good use of end of the season tomatoes. Although halibut can be sautéed, we think poaching produces a better texture.

6 plum tomatoes, quartered, seeds and membranes removed

Salt and pepper

2 tablespoons olive oil

4 halibut fillets (6 ounces each)

1 cup Fish Bouillon (Recipe appears on page 280.) or water

¼ cup white wine

3 tablespoons anisette or Pernod

3 tablespoons tarragon

1 bay leaf

2 tablespoons butter

Preheat oven to 375°. Place tomatoes on a baking sheet. Sprinkle tomatoes with salt and pepper and olive oil and bake for 30 minutes or until firm. Place tomatoes and remaining ingredients, except butter, in a large saucepan over low heat. Cover and cook for 8 to 10 minutes or until fish flakes easily. Remove fish and bay leaf and reserve. Continue cooking liquid until reduced to ¾ cup. Swirl in butter. Season to taste with salt and pepper. Serve broth over fish.

Serves 4

A traditional French cuisine favorite, tarragon is most known for its use in béarnaise sauce. The fourth of the four *fines herbs* (the others being chervil, parsley, and chives), tarragon is a member of the daisy family. Russian tarragon offers little to no taste whereas French tarragon, when not used sparingly, can dominate the taste of any dish. Tarragon can be found fresh throughout the summer and dried, powdered, or as an oil or vinegar year-round.

Skate Wing with Citrus Brown Butter and Shallot Confit

This is a classic presentation of a much misunderstood fish. Its lovely "feathers" add real style and surprise to the serving plate.

2 skate wings, boned
Salt and pepper
5 tablespoons unsalted butter, cut into small pieces
½ cup dry white wine
1 orange, peeled and sectioned
1 lemon, peeled and sectioned
1 lime, peeled and sectioned
1 tablespoon chopped flat-leaf parsley
Shallot Confit (Recipe appears on page 291.)

Season skate with salt and pepper. Melt 3 tablespoons butter in a large sauté pan over medium-high heat. When butter just begins to turn brown, add skate and brown on both sides. Add white wine and fruits with juices. Simmer until skate is tender, about 8 to 10 minutes. Remove skate from pan and transfer to a warm serving plate.

Stir in remaining butter and parsley. Season to taste with salt and pepper. Spoon sauce over skate and top with shallot confit.

Serves 4

Skatefish (also called skate wings or just skate) is rich in magnesium, iron, and calcium. It has a firm, rich texture and holds up well to grilling.

Mahi Mahi in Potato Crust with Morels

This is a big seller on Father's Day. Dads love the uniquely crusted fillets and the nutty, earthy base that the morel mushrooms form. You will too.

Mahi mahi is a very tasty, white fleshed fish that holds up well during cooking and serving. Not as fatty as tuna or salmon, mahi mahi is great on the barbeque and in salads.

1 ounce dry morel mushrooms

2 cups warm water

1 shallot, minced

½ cup dry white wine

1 sprig fresh thyme, stemmed

2 tablespoons unsalted butter

6 mahi mahi fillets (6 ounces each), skin on

Salt and freshly ground pepper

3 eggs

1 cup instant potato flakes

½ cup olive oil

Soak morels in warm water for 10 minutes or until soft. Strain mushroom liquid into a saucepan through a coffee filter or fine sieve. Add shallot and wine. Cook until liquid reduces to ¾ cup. Add thyme and morels. Stir in butter.

Preheat oven to 400°. Season fillets with salt and pepper. Beat eggs in a shallow bowl. Dip fish fillets in egg and then dredge lightly in potato flakes. Heat olive oil in a skillet over medium heat. Add fish and cook for 2 minutes per side. Finish cooking fish in oven until it flakes easily, about 4 to 5 minutes.

Divide mushrooms between 6 warmed plates. Place fish on mushrooms.

Serves 6

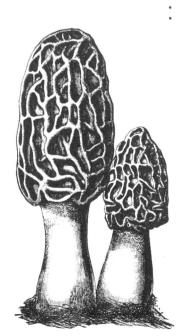

Dover Sole Provençal

This dish is one of the most popular at La Campagne.
Filleted tableside, it is both elegant and entertaining.

4 whole Dover sole (1 to 1½ pounds each), skinned and
  trimmed
Salt and pepper
2 tablespoons olive oil
3 tablespoons unsalted butter
1 cup dry white wine
2 cloves garlic, chopped
1 teaspoon capers, rinsed and drained
2 tablespoons chopped tomato
4 tablespoons lemon juice
1 tablespoon chopped fresh flat-leaf parsley

Preheat oven to 450°. Season sole with salt and pepper.

Heat oil and 1 tablespoon butter in a large sauté pan
over high heat. Add sole and brown on both sides. Transfer
to a baking pan and roast for 10 minutes.

Remove from oven. Bone sole by running a spoon down
the middle of the length of the fish, carefully lifting off and
transferring fillets to a warm serving platter.

Deglaze sauté pan with wine. Add garlic, capers, tomato,
and lemon juice. Simmer for 1 minute. Stir in parsley and
remaining butter. Season to taste with salt and pepper.
Spoon sauce over sole.

Serves 6 to 8

Parsley has been the essential herb of European cooking since the classical times. Rich in vitamin C, the flat or Italian parsley has more flavor than the curly parsley. Stalks and leaves can be used in stocks and soups, in butter sauces and stuffings, and as garnishes.

Use our three point appraisal system.

Sight: The fish or shellfish should look fresh, not discolored or "soft." Fresh fish will have a natural shine and be firm. When buying a whole fish, check to see that the eyes are out and bright, not sunken or cloudy; the fish is firm; and the gills are red.

Feel: The flesh should be firm and resilient or springy to the touch. It should be moist but not slimly (with the exception of trout or salmon, which produce a natural covering which indicates freshness).

Smell: Fish should not have a "fishy" odor. It should smell sweet and clean like the sea.

Trust your own instincts. If the fish doesn't appeal to you, don't buy it — we don't.

Trout in Puff Pastry

Get creative when forming the scales and fish features. You'll have fun and your guests will smile.

1 sheet frozen puff pastry, thawed

1 brook trout (8 to 12 ounces)

1 egg, beaten

2 tablespoons olive oil

Salt and pepper

Chive Beurre Blanc (Recipe appears on page 286.)

Cut pastry sheet in half widthwise. Roll puff pastry out to ⅛-inch thick on a lightly floured work surface.

Preheat oven to 400°. Wash and dry trout. Place fish on a piece of parchment paper and trace around it. Leave a ½-inch border and cut out fish template. Place template on pastry and cut out 2 "pastry fish." Brush pastry with egg. Rub trout with olive oil and season with salt and pepper and place on one piece of pastry. Cover with second piece of pastry and crimp the sides all the way around. Use a paring knife or butter knife to carve out scales on the pastry fish. Use scrap dough to form a mouth and eyes for the fish. Brush carefully with egg. Bake in oven for 15 to 20 minutes until golden brown and an inserted meat thermometer reads 170°. Serve with chive beurre blanc.

Serves 2

Whole Grilled Fish with Sauce Vierge

Don't be intimidated by whole fish. Filleting is a simple skill to master, and you'll look like a culinary genius at your next dinner party.

2 heads garlic, unpeeled

4 ripe plum tomatoes, peeled and chopped

½ cup fresh basil leaf chiffonade

1½ cups extra virgin olive oil

Kosher salt and pepper to taste

4 whole fish (1½ pounds each) such as bass or snapper, scaled and gutted

2 fresh bulbs fennel, halved, cored, and sliced 1-inch thick, fronds reserved

1 to 2 tablespoons olive oil

Wrap garlic in foil and place over hot coals for approximately 15 minutes or until softened. Remove garlic from foil and when cool enough to handle, squeeze cloves from the skins. Place garlic in a small saucepan with tomatoes, basil, and oil. Set aside.

Season fish inside and out. Place a few fennel fronds in the cavities. Brush outside of fish with oil. Set grill tray 6 inches from hot coals. Lay fennel on grill to form a bed for fish. Place fish on fennel and grill for 7 to 8 minutes per side. Warm sauce while fish is cooking.

Place whole fish on a large dinner plate. Accompany plate with a bowl of warmed sauce for spooning over fish.

Serves 4

To fillet a fish

Using a large serving spoon, make a lengthwise cut down the back of the fish, just above the backbone. Gently loosen the fish from the bones. Transfer the top half of the fish to a platter using the spoon and a large serving fork. Using the side of the spoon, make a lengthwise cut down the back of the fish below the backbone. Slide the spoon under the backbone and lift and discard the backbone, frame, and head. Lift the bottom section of the fish to a serving platter. Cut fillets into individual portions.

Salt-Crusted Whole Roasted Fish

Coarse salt forms an excellent protective crust that seals in the juices of the tender fish.

1 whole fish (2 pounds) such as sea bass or red snapper, gutted, not scaled, head on, gills removed, tail and fins trimmed

1 tablespoon salt

3 bay leaves

7 to 8 cups (approximately 4 pounds) coarse sea salt or kosher salt

Extra virgin olive oil

1 lemon, sectioned

Preheat oven to 450°. Rinse fish thoroughly and pat dry. Season cavity with salt and bay leaves. Spread 1 cup sea salt on the bottom of a baking dish. Place fish on top and pour remaining salt over fish to cover it completely.

Roast fish for 20 minutes (10 minutes per pound). Remove fish from oven and allow it to sit for 5 minutes. Remove from pan and brush away salt. Gently scrape away skin and discard. Remove and discard bay leaves. Fillet fish. Drizzle fillets with olive oil and garnish with lemon.

Serves 4

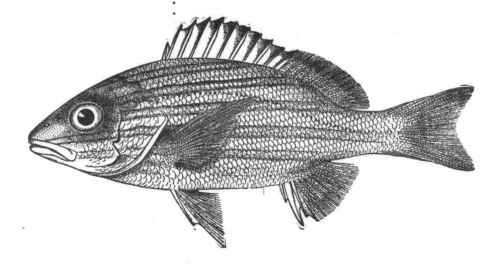

from the cooking school at la campagne ~ from the cooking school at la campagne ~ from the cooking school at la campagne ~ from the cooking school at la campagne ~ from the cooking school at la campagne ~ from the cooking school at la campagne ~ from the cooking school at la campagne ~ from the cooking school at la campagne ~ from the cooking school at la campagne ~ from the cooking school at la campagne ~ from the cooking school at la campagne ~ from the cooking school at la campagne ~ from the cooking school at la campagne ~ from the cooking school at la campagne ~ from the

shellfish

Crab Cakes

We update classic Chesapeake Bay style crab cakes with the addition of Japanese breadcrumbs which give the cakes an unusually crisp crust.

1 pound jumbo lump crabmeat, picked clean

1 tablespoon diced red bell pepper

1 tablespoon diced green bell pepper

½ cup diced scallions

1 teaspoon minced garlic

1 large egg, lightly beaten

¼ cup mayonnaise

1 tablespoon Dijon mustard

¼ cup chopped fresh parsley

Salt and pepper

1½ cups panko (Japanese breadcrumbs)

¼ cup Clarified Butter (Recipe appears on page 287.)

Combine the first 9 ingredients and 2 tablespoons breadcrumbs. Refrigerate for 1 hour. Form crab mixture into 8 cakes. Coat cakes in remaining breadcrumbs. Heat butter in a large skillet over medium heat. Add crab cakes and brown 5 minutes per side. Serve immediately.

Serves 4

Panko are the breadcrumbs used in Japanese cooking. The coarse texture ensures a crunchy crust. They are available at Asian markets and some specialty stores.

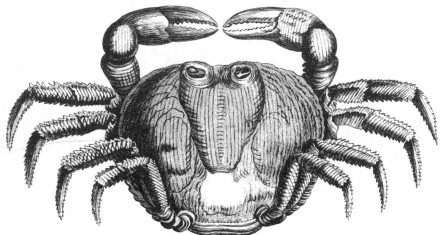

Crab Galette
with Chive Beurre Blanc

The addition of pureed shrimp make this dish especially flavorful and rich.

1 tablespoon unsalted butter

1 bunch scallions, thinly sliced

14 ounces large shrimp, peeled and deveined

2 large eggs

2 cups heavy cream

2 tablespoons Dijon mustard

1 tablespoon Worcestershire sauce

1 tablespoon Tabasco sauce

1 pound jumbo lump crabmeat, shelled

Vegetable oil

Chive Beurre Blanc (Recipe appears on page 286.)

Heat butter over medium heat. Add scallions and sauté until soft, about 3 to 5 minutes. Set aside. Puree shrimp in a food processor. Scrape down the sides of the bowl with a rubber spatula and add eggs. Process for 2 minutes. With motor running, add cream in a slow, steady stream. Transfer contents to a bowl and fold in cooked scallions, mustard, Worcestershire, Tabasco, and crabmeat.

Preheat oven to 400°. Heat a large nonstick skillet over medium-high heat. Add enough oil to coat pan. Spoon batter into hot pan and press down to form a circle. When bottom of galette is brown, flip and brown other side. Place pan in oven and bake for 5 to 8 minutes or until springy to the touch.

Cut galette into wedges and top with chive beurre blanc.

Serves 6 to 8

galette

[gah-LEHT]

A galette is a sweet or savory French tart that may or may not have a crust.

Soft-shell Crabs with Roasted Garlic and Tomato Risotto

Soft-shell crabs are our favorite harbinger of spring. Because they are so versatile and popular, we serve soft-shells as a special almost every night they're in season and never run out of ways to prepare them.

8 large live soft-shell crabs
Flour
4 tablespoons olive oil
½ cup dry white wine
3 tablespoons butter
Roasted Garlic and Tomato Risotto (Recipe appears on page 175.)
3 tablespoons chopped fresh parsley

Rinse crabs under cold running water. Cut or snip off heads, right behind eyes. Lift pointed cap on belly (mantle) and remove any gills and matter found below. Push on shell to extract any remaining yellow or green matter. Bend back apron (or tail flap) and twist to remove it and the intestinal vein at the same time. Wash crabs and pat dry.

Preheat oven to 450°. Dredge crabs in flour. Heat oil in a skillet over medium-high heat. Add crabs and sauté about 3 minutes per side. Place in oven for 5 minutes. Transfer crabs to a plate and keep warm.

Deglaze pan with wine. Whisk in butter. Place crabs on risotto and nap with pan sauce. Garnish with chopped parsley.

Serves 4

Garlic rumors

Aristophanes claimed it gave courage.

Mohammed said it eased pain.

Pliny used it to battle consumption.

We can *confirm* it lends a wonderful flavor to dishes and is a staple in our kitchen.

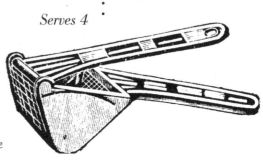

Shrimp, Zucchini, and Tomato Misto

This is fun party food that can be served as a passed hors d'
oeuvre, first course, or entree, but we like it best when
presented as a hearty snack. Have some good beer nearby
and invite some friends over.

Pomace oil

2 eggs

2 tablespoons cold water

2 cups plus 4 tablespoons flour

Salt and pepper

2 pounds shrimp, peeled and deveined

2 medium zucchini, sliced into ovals

3 plum tomatoes, quartered and membrane removed

12 basil leaves

1 lemon

Fill a heavy sauté pan ¾-inch deep with oil. Heat oil to 325°.

Mix together eggs, water, and 2 cups flour to make a smooth, fairly thin batter. (Add more water if needed.) Season with salt and pepper.

Dredge shrimp, zucchini, and tomatoes in flour, tapping off excess. Working in batches, dip shrimp and vegetables into batter. Add to pan and fry until golden. Remove from oil, drain on paper towel, and reserve. Add basil to oil and fry until crispy. Remove from oil and drain.

Arrange fried shrimp and vegetables on a serving platter and top with basil leaves. Squeeze lemon over platter and serve immediately.

Serves 4

misto
[MEES-toh]

The Italian word for "mixture," misto refers to a dish that includes pieces of meat, fish, vegetables, or cheese that are dipped in batter and fried.

Roasted Lobster with Vanilla-Ginger Butter and Mango Compote

The perfect aphrodisiac for any season, we created this recipe for a Valentine's Day dinner at the James Beard House in New York City.

4 lobsters (1¼ pounds each)
Salt and pepper
½ vanilla bean, split and scraped
2 teaspoons grated ginger
1 cup white wine
Zest and juice of 1 orange
10 tablespoons butter
Mango Compote (Recipe appears on page 298.)

Bring a large pot of salted water to a boil. Plunge lobsters into pot head first and cook for 10 minutes. Remove and cool.

Preheat oven to 400°. When lobsters are cool enough to handle, split in half lengthwise and remove the sac from the head. Do not remove the coral and tomalley. Crack the claws with the back of a heavy bladed knife. Place lobsters in a baking pan. Sprinkle with salt and pepper. Cut 2 tablespoons butter into small pieces and place on lobsters. Roast in oven for 5 to 7 minutes or until hot.

Combine vanilla bean, ginger, wine, and orange zest and juice in a saucepan over high heat and bring to a boil. Reduce heat and simmer until liquid is reduced to ½ cup. Swirl in remaining butter, 1 tablespoon at a time, until sauce is emulsified. Season with salt and pepper. Pour sauce over lobsters and top with mango compote.

Serves 4

Clams, mussels, oysters, crabs, and lobsters should always be purchased live. These shellfish deteriorate quickly when dead.

Lobster Pernod

Pernod is a popular French liqueur. The anise-licorice flavor enhances all shellfish.

4 female Maine lobsters (1½ pounds each)

4 tablespoons olive oil

½ cup Pernod or anise-flavored liqueur

1 pound wild mushrooms (shiitake, crimini, et al.), sliced

6 shallots, chopped

2 tablespoons lemon juice

2 cups heavy cream

Salt and pepper

¼ cup fresh basil leaf, cut into ribbons

4 tablespoons chopped fresh parsley

In bistros, the waiter will pour some yellow-colored Pernod in a glass and give you a water pitcher. You add as much water as you want and watch as it turns whitish and cloudy. Drink and repeat. Be careful — it packs a punch!

Using a French knife, cut through thorax and head of the live lobsters. Cut off tails and claws. Remove tail shells. Cut each tail into 4 medallions and reserve. Crack the shells of claws. Split bodies lengthwise. Remove and discard sand sacs behind eyes. Remove and reserve tomalleys (livers) and any roe.

Heat oil in a large braising pan over medium-high heat. Add lobster bodies, claws, and tails and sauté until shells turn red. Remove pan from heat and add Pernod. Return pan to flame and carefully ignite Pernod, shaking pan until flames subside. Add medallions, tomalleys and any roe, mushrooms, shallots, lemon juice, and cream. Season with salt and pepper. Cover and simmer for 10 minutes. Stir in basil.

Arrange lobster bodies on warm serving platters. Fill body cavities with mushroom mixture. Arrange tail and claw pieces around stuffed bodies. Garnish generously with chopped parsley.

Serves 4

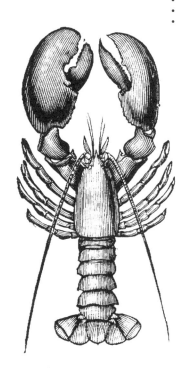

Mussels in Fennel Saffron Cream

We tried this dish at a seaside restaurant in Juan les Pins and loved it. The chef wouldn't give us the recipe, but a local fisherman knew how to prepare it and was all to happy to share.

1 tablespoon butter
½ bulb fennel, diced
1 teaspoon chopped garlic
1 teaspoon saffron threads
3 pounds mussels, cleaned and debearded
¼ cup white wine
1 cup cream
Salt and pepper

Heat butter in a large lidded saucepan over medium heat. Add fennel and cook, stirring frequently, until well caramelized. Add garlic and saffron and cook for 1 minute. Add mussels, wine, and cream. Cover and simmer for 5 to 7 minutes until all mussels are open. Season with salt and pepper and serve.

Serves 6

One of the leanest foods of the sea, mussels offer a delicious meat that is tougher but sweeter than its clam cousin.

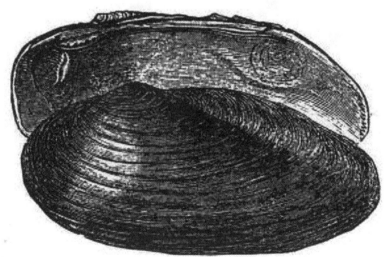

Mussels with Tomato, Cilantro, and Lime

Serve this dish with a strong German beer and enjoy.

1 tablespoon olive oil

2 teaspoons chopped garlic

3 pounds mussels, cleaned and debearded

½ cup white wine

½ cup Chicken Stock (Recipe appears on page 278.)

Juice of 2 limes

3 tablespoons rice wine vinegar

4 plum tomatoes, seeded and diced

½ bunch cilantro, chopped

Salt and pepper

Heat oil in a large lidded saucepan over medium heat. Add garlic and sauté until light brown. Add mussels, wine, and chicken stock. Cover and cook for 4 to 5 minutes until all mussels are open. Add remaining ingredients, stirring well until heated through. Season to taste with salt and pepper and serve.

Serves 6

We prefer farm-raised mussels to wild ones as they give the broth a cleaner taste and tend to be less sandy.

Seared Scallops in Curry Beurre Blanc

Beware of scallops that are stark white in color. This means they have been soaked in water to increase their weight. Look for sea scallops that are pale beige or creamy pink.

1½ pounds sea scallops, muscles removed

Salt and pepper

2 tablespoons vegetable oil

2 medium carrots, cut into matchsticks

1 leek, finely julienned

1 stalk celery, julienned

2 teaspoons chopped shallot

1 teaspoon chopped garlic

1 tablespoon curry powder

¼ cup white wine

1 cup heavy cream

2 tablespoons butter

Season scallops with salt and pepper. Heat oil in a sauté pan over high heat. When oil is smoking, add scallops. Sear for 2 minutes on each side. Remove scallops from pan and reserve in a warm place.

Add carrots, leek, celery, shallot, and garlic to pan and sauté for 1 minute. Add curry, wine, and cream. Cook until mixture reduces and will coat the back of a spoon. Swirl in butter. Season to taste with salt and pepper. Pour sauce into a serving dish and top with scallops.

Serves 4

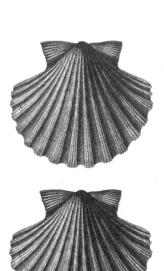

Diver Scallops with French Lentils and Balsamic

Prepare this hearty dish for your seafaring friends.

1 cup balsamic vinegar

6 tablespoons olive oil

3 shallots, chopped

2 cloves garlic, chopped

½ cup green French lentils, washed

1½ cups Chicken Stock (Recipe appears on page 278.)

1 sprig fresh thyme, stemmed and chopped

½ cup dry white wine

2 Roma tomatoes, peeled, seeded, and diced

12 large diver (dry) sea scallops

Salt and pepper

6 tablespoons unsalted butter, cubed

Place balsamic vinegar in a small saucepan over medium heat. Cook until liquid reduces to 1 tablespoon. (Be careful. Do not let vinegar burn.) Remove from heat and set aside.

Heat 4 tablespoons oil in a saucepan over medium-high heat. Add shallots and sauté until soft. Add garlic and sauté for 1 minute. Add lentils and stock and simmer for 30 minutes or until lentils are soft. (Add more stock if lentils are too firm.) Stir in thyme and wine. Add tomatoes and season to taste with salt and pepper. Keep warm.

Season scallops with salt and pepper. Heat remaining oil in a nonstick pan over high heat. Add scallops and sear until caramelized on both sides. Stir butter into lentils.

Divide lentils among 4 plates. Top each plate with 3 scallops and drizzle with balsamic reduction.

Serves 4

The tiny lentil bean has long been used as a meat substitute for the large vegetarian population in India and around the world. Lentils offer a strong protein base for many of the spicy dishes and soups in which they are used. Brown lentils, the most popular, should be soaked in luke warm water for 30 minutes before cooking. Red, orange, and green varieties are also available but are harder to come by.

from the cooking school at la campagne ~ from the cooking school at la campagne ~ from the cooking school at la campagne ~ from the cooking school at la campagne ~ from the cooking school at la campagne ~ from the cooking school at la campagne ~ from the cooking school at la campagne ~ from the cooking school at la campagne ~ **from the cooking school at la campagne** ~ from the cooking school at la campagne ~ from the cooking school at la campagne ~ from the cooking school at la campagne ~ from the cooking school at la campagne ~ from the cooking school at la campagne ~ from the

La Campagne

cuisine rapide

Simple Green Salad

What is more sophisticated than a simple green salad?

2 heads Bibb lettuce, stemmed and cleaned
2 heads Belgian endive, halved and cored
2 ripe tomatoes, sliced
½ cup olive oil
¼ cup of good red wine vinegar
1 tablespoon Dijon mustard
Salt and freshly ground pepper

Arrange lettuces and tomato slices on a plate. Whisk together oil, vinegar, and mustard. Season with salt and pepper and drizzle over salad.

Serves 4

Belgian endive (aka Flemish witloof) is blanched chicory. It was discovered by accident less than 200 years ago by a monsieur from Brussels who was attempting to maintain a chicory supply for his winter coffee. The result of his experiments — small shoots of tightly packed leaves that were far less bitter than traditionally grown chicory. Varieties include the classic whiteleaf, radicchio red, and sugarloaf (a romaine lettuce look alike).

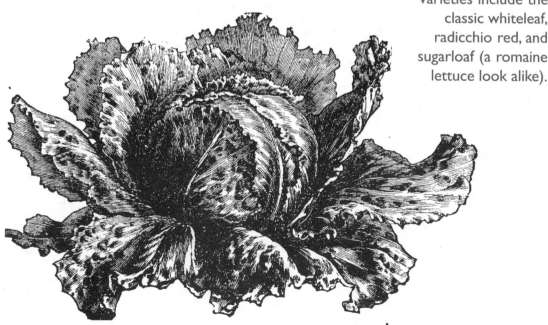

Weekday Fish Soup

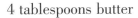

This is a great dinner soup with plenty of protein and vegetables. Even on a hot day it's hard to pass up. To save time, store bought fish stock may be used. Watch the salt!

4 tablespoons butter

1 shallot, diced

3 plum tomatoes, seeded and diced

1 teaspoon dry thyme

½ teaspoon crushed red pepper

2 cups chopped Swiss chard

Juice of 1 lemon

2 cups chopped spinach

5 cups Fish Bouillon (Recipe appears on page 280.)

1½ pounds assorted firm fish fillets (monkfish, snapper, sea bass, etc.), diced

Croutons (Recipe appears on page 292.)

Heat butter in a 4-quart saucepan over medium heat. Add shallot, tomatoes, thyme, and crushed red pepper and sauté for 1 minute. Add Swiss chard and lemon and cook until chard is wilted. Add spinach and cook until wilted. Add fish bouillon and bring to a boil. Add fish fillets and simmer until tender, about 5 to 10 minutes. Season with salt and pepper. Ladle into bowls and top with croutons.

Serves 4 to 6

Wild Mushroom and Chicken Sauté

This is a Cooking School favorite because it's quick and versatile and tastes great. Serve over a bed of wild rice or pasta.

1 cup flour
4 boneless chicken breasts (6 to 8 ounces each), pounded
2 tablespoons butter
1 tablespoon oil
1 shallot, minced
1 tablespoon chopped garlic
2 cups wild mushrooms (shiitake, chanterelle, etc.), sliced
1 cup sherry or Madeira wine
1 cup Chicken Velouté (Recipe appears on page 282.)
Salt and pepper

Place flour in a shallow bowl. Dredge chicken in flour and shake off excess.

Heat butter and oil in a large sauté pan over high heat until butter begins to foam. Add chicken to pan and sauté for 3 minutes. Turn chicken and add shallot, garlic, and mushrooms and sauté for 3 minutes. Remove chicken from pan and keep warm. Add wine to pan and cook until liquid is reduced by half. Add velouté. Simmer for 2 minutes. Season with salt and pepper. Serve chicken topped with sauce.

Serves 4

velouté
[veh-loo-TAY]

Velouté is a stock-based white sauce made from chicken or veal stock or fish fumet and white roux. Considered one of the "mother sauces," it is used as a base for many other sauces.

Herb Roasted Chicken

When a quick meal is needed, busy cooks often reach for chicken breasts and often find themselves at a loss for a "new" way to serve them. This recipe takes less than 20 minutes to prepare, and because the amount and variety of herbs used can be adjusted, it always tastes new.

1 small sprig rosemary

2 sprigs thyme

6 leaves basil

¼ bunch Italian parsley

4 boneless chicken breasts, skin on

Salt and pepper

3 tablespoons olive oil

Caper Oil, optional (see recipe)

Preheat oven to 400°. Roughly chop herbs, combine, and stuff under chicken skin. Season chicken with salt and pepper.

Heat oil in a large skillet over medium-high heat. Add breasts and sear both sides until brown. Transfer to a baking sheet and bake for 7 to 10 minutes or until juices run clear when chicken is pierced. Serve as is or with caper oil.

Serves 6 to 8

Caper Oil

Native to flower buds found in the Mediterranean, capers are picked, sun-dried, and pickled, usually in vinegar brine. Be sure to rinse away the excess salt before using capers in a wide range of sauces, soups, and meat or veggie dishes.

1 cup olive oil

½ cup white wine

Juice of 1 lemon

2 tablespoons rinsed, drained, and chopped capers

2 tablespoons chopped parsley

1 tablespoon chopped basil

1 teaspoon freshly ground black pepper

1 teaspoon chopped garlic

1 teaspoon salt

Combine all ingredients and mix well.

Breast of Duck Au Poivre

*We love the mild kick that peppercorns give this dish.
Experiment with black, red, pink, or white peppercorns. Each
will impart a unique bite and contrast.*

2 duck breasts

2 tablespoons chopped shallot

½ cup brandy

1 tablespoon green peppercorns

1 cup Chicken Stock (Recipe appears on page 278.)

2 cups heavy cream

Trim duck breasts of excess fat. Place skin side down in a
large sauté pan. Cook over low heat until most of the fat is
rendered and the skin is very crisp. Remove excess fat as it
accumulates in the pan. Turn breasts over and sear for 1
minute. Remove breasts from pan.

Add shallot and sauté for 1 minute. Add brandy and
flambé until alcohol is cooked off. Add peppercorns, stock,
and cream. Simmer until sauce is thick enough to coat the
back of a spoon. Season to taste with salt and pepper.

Slice duck and serve with sauce.

Serves 4

A single breast fillet of chicken is called a supreme in French and a cutlet in English. In the same manner, a single breast fillet of a larger Muscovy or Moulard duck is called a magret. Muscovy and Moulard ducks can be found at butcher shops and specialty food stores.

Tenderloin with Roquefort Sauce

Sir Isaac Newton said that nature is pleased with simplicity.
He must have been referring to this dish —
simple to prepare and simply delicious.

4 filet mignons (6 ounces each)

Salt and pepper

6 tablespoons butter

3 shallots, chopped

1 ounce brandy

1 cup cream

4 ounces Roquefort cheese

Be sure to cook your steaks "bleu," the traditional French term meaning very rare.

Season steaks with salt and pepper. Melt butter in a skillet over medium-high heat. Add steaks and pan sear until steaks are medium rare. Transfer steaks to a serving plate and reserve. Remove fat from pan.

Add shallots to pan and cook until soft. Add brandy and cook until alcohol evaporates. Add cream and bring to a boil. Stir in cheese. Turn off heat and add juices from the serving plate. Serve sauce over steaks.

Serves 4

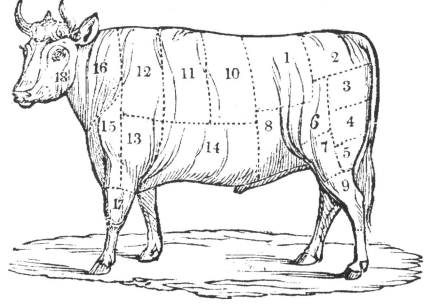

Rabbit Loin with Mushroom Broth and Truffles

Rabbit loins are a small but wonderful taste sensation and are perfectly complemented by winter truffles.

2 ounces dry porcini mushrooms
2 cups warm water
8 boneless rabbit loins
Salt and pepper
1 tablespoon olive oil
½ cup dry white wine
1 tablespoon unsalted butter
1 sprig fresh thyme, stemmed
1 small fresh black truffle, very thinly sliced

Soak mushrooms in water for 1 hour. Drain and reserve soaking water. Season rabbit loins with salt and pepper. Heat oil in a sauté pan over medium heat. Sear loins for 2 to 3 minutes. Add wine and porcini soaking liquid. Cook until liquid is reduced to ½ cup. Stir in butter and thyme. Slice loins. Pour sauce over loins and garnish with truffles.

Serves 4

Each year we buy our truffles from a mysterious traveling truffle salesman. Do you know the truffle man?

Lemon-Steamed Arctic Char with Cucumber Aïoli

1 cup white wine
1 cup Fish Bouillon (Recipe appears on page 280.)
Juice of 1 lemon
Salt and pepper
4 arctic char fillets (6 ounces each)
Cucumber Aïoli, optional (see recipe)

Combine wine, bouillon, lemon juice, and pinch of salt and pepper in a sauté pan and bring to a boil. Reduce heat to medium-low. Add fillets, cover, and cook until fish flakes easily, about 6 to 8 minutes. Remove with a slotted spoon or spatula to a serving platter and top with cucumber aïoli if desired.

Serves 4

Poaching or steaming are healthy, quick, and no mess ways to prepare almost any white fish.

Cucumber Aïoli

2 eggs
1 tablespoon Dijon mustard
4 cloves garlic
½ bunch chives, chopped
1½ cups olive oil
1 cup English cucumber, peeled and diced
2 tablespoons red wine vinegar
Dash of Tabasco sauce
Salt and pepper

Place eggs, mustard, garlic, and chives in a blender and puree. With motor running, slowly drizzle in oil until a thick mayonnaise forms. Add cucumber and vinegar and blend until smooth. Season with Tabasco and salt and pepper to taste.

Red Snapper with Opal Basil Buerre Blanc

The deep purple color of opal basil provides striking contrast in the garden and in this recipe. We use it and sun-dried tomatoes to make a regal purple and red salsa.

½ cup white wine

½ cup white wine vinegar

3 tablespoons heavy cream

2 shallots, chopped

½ pound cold unsalted butter, chopped

Salt and freshly ground pepper

1 small bunch opal basil, stemmed and cut into ribbons

3 tablespoons olive oil

6 snapper fillets (4 ounces each), skin on

Combine wine, vinegar, cream, and shallots in a small saucepan over medium heat. Simmer until liquid is reduced to ¼ cup. Stir in butter, a few pieces at a time. Strain and season with salt and pepper. Stir in basil and keep warm.

Heat olive oil in a large skillet over medium-high heat. Add fillets, skin side down, and sear until just cooked through, about 2 to 4 minutes per side. Serve fish topped with sauce.

Serves 6

The sweet and spicy flavor of basil can work perfectly with pastas and pesto, soups and salads, breads and butters. This diverse herb is native to Asia, Africa, and Central and South America and can range in color from purple to shades of green. The bright green sweet basil variety is most common and of moderate size. The dark green lettuce leaf basil and purple dwarf (or bush) basil are larger and smaller respectively. A Provençal staple, the flavor of this herb in many dishes is not replaceable.

Red Snapper en Papillotes

Cooking in paper steams the fish and captures its moisture. You can prepare the packets ahead of time, which makes this a perfect dinner party recipe. And there's almost no clean up!

Clarified Butter (Recipe appears on page 287.) or vegetable cooking spray

½ bulb fennel, thinly sliced

4 snapper fillets (6 to 8 ounces each)

Salt and pepper

8 large shiitake mushrooms, stems removed

2 cloves garlic, minced

2 teaspoons fresh chopped herbs (thyme, parsley, chives)

¼ cup white wine

Preheat oven to 350°. Fold four 12 x 8-inch pieces parchment paper in half; then cut each into the shape of a heart. Lay "hearts" open on a work surface and brush with butter or oil.

Place fennel slices on the right side of each heart and top with a fillet. Season fish with salt and pepper and top each fillet with 2 mushroom caps. Sprinkle with garlic, herbs, and wine.

Fold the left side of heart over to cover contents and make small pleats in the paper to seal the two edges. Transfer to a baking sheet and bake for 15 to 20 minutes. Cut open packages at tableside and serve.

Serves 4

We often prefer steaming to boiling because the food's flavor, texture, shape, and nutrients are retained. This is especially true with fish.

Sole Meunière

French men live for sole meunière, the essence of simple (but sensational) peasant cooking.

1 whole Dover sole (1 to 1½ pounds)
Salt and pepper
Flour
½ cup unsalted butter
Juice of 1 lemon
2 tablespoons chopped fresh parsley

Trim away outer fins with a sharp knife and remove head (optional). Score the skin on each side just above the tail to loosen skin. Grip skin with fingers or pliers and firmly pull skin away from the body. Repeat on the other side.

Sprinkle both sides of sole with salt and pepper. Dredge in flour and shake off excess.

Melt butter in a 10-inch skillet over medium-high heat. Sauté sole for 4 minutes on each side. Remove sole from pan. Add lemon juice and parsley to pan and combine.

Bone sole by running a spoon down the middle of the length of the fish, carefully lifting off and transferring fillets to a warm serving platter. Spoon sauce over sole.

Serves 2

meunière
[muhn-YEHR]

Literally "miller's wife" in French, meunière refers to a simple cooking style where a food (usually fish) is seasoned, lightly dusted with flour, and sautéed in butter.

Mussels with Lemon Grass

48 mussels, scrubbed and beards removed

2 stalks lemon grass, thinly sliced

1 tablespoon chopped fresh cilantro

1 teaspoon chopped garlic

3 Serrano peppers, seeded and minced

½ cup dry white wine

2 tablespoons olive oil

2 tablespoons unsalted butter

Salt and pepper

Combine all ingredients in a large stockpot over medium-high heat. Cover and simmer until the mussels open. Discard any unopened mussels. Serve immediately.

Serves 4

The black shelled mussel has been a European favorite for many centuries. Today, the growing of mussels in Maine, California, and Washington have increased this mollusk's popularity in the United States. To avoid ingesting toxins sometimes associated with mussels, do not pick them yourself. Search out a reliable source for procurement.

Mussels in White Sauce

¼ cup olive oil

2 tablespoons chopped garlic

1 teaspoon crushed red pepper

1 cup white wine

1 cup Chicken Stock (Recipe appears on page 278.)

2 to 3 pounds mussels, cleaned and debearded

¼ cup chopped parsley

2 tablespoons butter

Salt and pepper

Heat oil in a large saucepan over medium-high heat. Add garlic and crushed pepper and cook until garlic is light brown. Add wine and stock and bring to a boil. Add mussels and parsley. Cook covered until mussels open, about 4 minutes. Stir in butter and season with salt and pepper. Serve in bowls with lots and lots of bread to soak up the sauce.

Serves 6 to 8

Chocolate Truffles

Offer these to last minute guests. These intense chocolate confections will disappear in no time which is fitting because they take almost no time to make.

¼ cup heavy cream
4 ounces semi-sweet chocolate, chopped
4 ounces bitter chocolate, chopped

Bring cream to a boil. Place semi-sweet chocolate pieces in a bowl. Pour boiling cream over chocolate and whisk until mixture hardens. Form the mixture into small balls using a melon baller. Melt bitter chocolate in a bowl over a double boiler. Dip balls in the melted bitter chocolate and refrigerate until ready to serve.

Yields 1 dozen

Chocolate Nut Truffles

5 ounces semi-sweet chocolate
2 tablespoons unsalted butter
4 ounces mixed nuts, lightly toasted
7 tablespoons confectioners' sugar
3 tablespoons cocoa powder

Melt chocolate and butter in a bowl over a double boiler. Transfer to a food processor, add nuts and sugar, and blend. Chill mixture. Form the mixture into small balls using a melon baller. Roll in cocoa powder and refrigerate until ready to serve.

Yields 1 dozen

To toast nuts

Preheat oven to 350°. Scatter nuts in a single layer on a baking sheet and bake until lightly colored and fragrant, about 5 to 10 minutes. Toasting intensifies nuts' natural flavors and also aids in the process of removing the outer papery skins of some nuts such as walnuts.

Poached Pears with Red Wine

French grandmothers know how to handle fresh fruit. Good pears and apples need only to be baked with red wine or cider and a luxurious color and taste will be the result. Grandmom knows best.

Low fat and low fuss, simply prepared fruit is always a midweek winner. Cut up fruit and arrange it in a bowl and you'll have a healthy and refreshing dessert with minimal effort.

1 small cinnamon stick

1 vanilla bean, split

Zest and juice of 1 orange

2 cups water

2 cups Burgundy wine

1 cup sugar

4 Anjou pears, peeled, cored, and halved

4 tablespoons unsalted butter, cut into ½-inch cubes

6 mint leaves, cut into ribbons

Combine cinnamon stick, vanilla bean, orange zest and juice, water, wine, and sugar in a saucepan over medium-high heat. Bring to a simmer. Add pear halves and cook until tender, about 8 to 10 minutes. Remove pears from pan with a slotted spoon and reserve.

Continue cooking poaching liquid until reduced to 1 cup. Return pears to saucepan. Add butter, one piece at a time, stirring to incorporate. Transfer pears to 4 serving plates, drizzle with syrup, and garnish with mint.

Serves 4

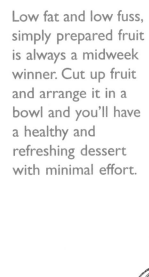

from the cooking school at la campagne ~ from the cooking school at la campagne ~ from the cooking school at la campagne ~ from the cooking school at la campagne ~ from the cooking school at la campagne ~ from the cooking school at la campagne ~ from the cooking school at la campagne ~ from the cooking school at la campagne ~ from the cooking school at la campagne ~ from the cooking school at la campagne ~ from the cooking school at la campagne ~ from the cooking school at la campagne ~ from the cooking school at la campagne ~ from the

La Campagne

risottos and a few pastas

White Wine Risotto

Our version of the classic risotto Milanese is a cheerful bright yellow thanks to the addition of saffron. Serve as an accompaniment to ossobuco or other roasted meats or poultry.

4 cups Chicken Stock (Recipe appears on page 278.)
Pinch of saffron threads
6 tablespoons butter
¼ cup finely diced onion
1½ cups Arborio rice
½ cup dry white wine
Pinch of white pepper
½ cup grated Parmesan cheese

Heat chicken stock in a saucepan over medium heat. Transfer ½ cup hot stock to a small bowl and add saffron. Reserve.

Heat 3 tablespoons butter in a large sauté pan over medium heat. Add onion and sauté until translucent. Add rice, stir to coat with butter, and cook for 2 minutes. Add wine and bring to a simmer, stirring until liquid is absorbed. Add ½ cup hot stock to rice, stirring often until liquid is absorbed. Add remaining stock (including saffron-infused stock), ½ cup at a time, stirring often until all stock is absorbed. Add pepper.

Remove from heat, cover, and let rest for 2 minutes. Stir in remaining butter and ¼ cup grated Parmesan. Transfer risotto to a serving dish and sprinkle with remaining cheese.

Serves 4 to 6

Risotto waits for no one. In fact, it makes *you* wait for it to reach perfection and then demands that you consume it immediately. But don't worry, you'll want to. Risotto is one of the most satisfying dishes to prepare and enjoy.

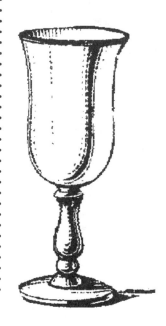

Truffled Risotto

Chef's secret: To amplify the flavor of this recipe, store your truffles with the rice for a few days. The truffle aroma will permeate the rice and the dish.

3 cups Chicken Stock (Recipe appears on page 278.)
¼ cup olive oil
1 small onion, chopped
½ cup Arborio rice
3 tablespoons butter
¼ cup heavy cream
2 ounces black truffles, chopped
Salt and freshly ground pepper
3 ounces Pecorino Romano, grated

Heat stock in a saucepan to a simmer. Meanwhile, heat oil in a heavy-bottomed saucepan over medium-high heat. Add onion and sauté until translucent. Add rice and stir until brown. Add ½ cup hot stock to rice, stirring often until liquid is absorbed. Add remaining stock, ½ cup at a time, stirring often until all stock is absorbed. Stir in butter, heavy cream, and truffles. Season to taste with salt and pepper. Stir in grated cheese.

Serves 4

Risotto is made by stirring hot stock into a rice mixture. Arborio, a short-grain Italian rice, is the only rice to use. Making a risotto is time consuming and labor intensive: the stock is added a half cup at a time, and the mixture must be stirred continuously until all the stock is absorbed. This stirring creates a friction which softens the outer hull of the rice grains. The result — a creamy, richly flavored, and highly satisfying meal —is well worth the effort.

Porcini Mushroom and Red Wine Risotto

Rich and rustic, warm and welcoming, this full-bodied risotto is hearty enough to be served as a main course for lunch or dinner and is particularly nice on a snowy winter's day.

4 cups Burgundy wine
½ ounce dried porcini mushrooms
1 cup warm water
1 cup Chicken Stock (Recipe appears on page 278.)
2 tablespoons unsalted butter
2 tablespoons olive oil
½ cup chopped onion
2 shallots, chopped
1 clove garlic, chopped
1 cup Arborio rice
Salt and pepper

Heat wine over medium-high heat until reduced to 1 cup. Soak mushrooms in warm water until soft. Strain and reserve soaking liquid.

Heat stock in a saucepan to a simmer. Heat butter and oil in a sauté pan. Add onion, shallots, and garlic and sauté for 1 minute. Add rice and cook for 2 minutes. Add wine reduction and bring to a simmer, stirring until it is absorbed into rice. Add porcini and strained soaking liquid. Cook, stirring until absorbed. Add ½ cup hot stock to rice, stirring often until liquid is absorbed. Add remaining stock, ½ cup at a time, stirring often until all stock is absorbed. Season with salt and pepper.

Serves 4 to 6

Arborio
[ar-BOH-ree-o]

Arborio is an Italian grown medium- to short-grain rice that is traditionally used for risotto. Arborio's oval shape, chewy texture, and increased starch help risotto achieve its desired texture and creaminess.

Roasted Garlic and Tomato Risotto

Do not fear if, at first glance, the garlic in this recipe seems overpowering. Slow roasting takes away the bite, leaving a nutty, mellow taste that is a perfect complement to the sweetness of the tomatoes.

Over the centuries, the uses of garlic have ranged from magical to medicinal. The Greeks cast spells with garlic while the Romans ate it for stamina. Need to ward off a vampire or get rid of a headache? Garlic should do the trick. The culinary uses of garlic are just as profound as they form the foundation from which an overabundance of flavors originate. With garlic, generally the larger the bulb, the milder the taste. First peel, then slice, chop, mince, or crush and enjoy the flavors (and powers) that garlic brings to each dish.

1 head garlic

4 tablespoons olive oil

5 tablespoons unsalted butter

1 medium onion, diced

1 cup Arborio rice

20 kalamata olives, pitted and chopped

4 Roma tomatoes, roasted

3 cups Chicken Stock (Recipe appears on page 278.)

½ cup dry white wine

1 tablespoon fresh thyme leaves

½ teaspoon chopped fresh rosemary

Salt and pepper

Preheat oven to 350°. Wrap garlic in aluminum foil and roast in oven for 40 minutes or until soft. Allow to cool slightly. Remove skin and set aside.

Heat oil and 2 tablespoons butter over medium heat. Add onion and sauté until translucent. Add rice and sauté for 5 minutes. Add garlic, olives, and tomatoes. In a separate saucepan, bring stock to a simmer. Add ½ cup hot stock to rice, stirring often until liquid is absorbed. Add remaining stock, ½ cup at a time, stirring until all stock is absorbed. Add wine and remaining butter. Stir in herbs. Season to taste with salt and pepper.

Serves 4

Lobster Risotto

How convenient that fall is peak lobster season for we feel the familiar craving for risotto as soon as the first crisp night of autumn sneaks up on us.

2 lobsters (1½ pounds each)
3 tablespoons olive oil
1 small onion, minced
1 bulb fennel, cored and diced
2 teaspoons chopped garlic
1 pound Arborio rice
½ cup white wine
1 quart Chicken Stock (Recipe appears on page 278.), heated
2 tablespoons chiffonade fresh basil
¼ cup heavy cream
2 tablespoons butter
3 plum tomatoes, seeded and diced
¼ cup grated Parmesan cheese
Salt and pepper

Bring a large pot of salted water to a boil. Plunge lobsters into pot head first and cook for 10 minutes. Remove and cool. When lobsters are cool enough to handle, split in half lengthwise and remove the sac from the head. Crack the claws with the back of a heavy bladed knife. Remove meat from claws and body. Dice meat and reserve.

Heat olive oil in a 2-quart saucepan over medium heat. Add onion and fennel and sauté until tender. Add garlic and cook for 1 minute. Add rice and stir for 30 seconds. Deglaze with white wine and add enough stock to cover contents. Cook, stirring often, until liquid is absorbed. Continue to add stock, 1 cup at a time, until all stock is absorbed. Fold in lobster meat and basil. Add cream, butter, tomatoes, and cheese and cook until fully incorporated. Season with salt and pepper and serve.

Serves 6

To mince an onion

Set the peeled onion on a cutting board. Use a sharp knife to cut the onion in half lengthwise. Set one half, cut side down, on the board and make a series of horizontal cuts from the shoot end to the root, but not through it. Turn the onion 90 degrees and make cuts through the onion to the board. Turn the onion back to its original position and slice across the onion from the shoot to the root, keeping the cuts close together. Repeat with the other half of the onion.

Shrimp and Shiitake Mushroom Risotto

Meaty shittakes and plump shrimp add great taste and texture to every bite of this risotto. Leftovers are especially good so consider making extra.

3 cups Chicken Stock (Recipe appears on page 278.)
2 tablespoons butter
½ medium onion, diced
1 teaspoon chopped garlic
1 cup Arborio rice
2 tablespoons olive oil
8 shrimp, peeled and deveined
1 cup stemmed and sliced shiitake mushrooms
½ cup grated Parmesan cheese
¼ cup heavy cream
1 tablespoon chopped fresh basil
Salt and pepper

Heat stock to simmer. Melt butter in a heavy-bottomed 2-quart saucepan on medium-high heat. Add onion and garlic and sauté for 1 minute. Add rice and enough hot stock to cover rice. Stir often until liquid is absorbed. Add remaining stock, ½ cup at a time, stirring often until all stock is absorbed.

While rice is cooking, heat olive oil in a sauté pan over medium-high heat. Add shrimp and mushrooms and sauté gently for about 5 minutes or until shrimp are firm. When all liquid in risotto is absorbed, add shrimp and mushrooms. Stir in cheese, cream, and basil and heat through. Season with salt and pepper to taste.

Serves 4

Hailing from Parma, Italy, Parmigiano-Reggiano is the very best Parmesan cheese. A small quantity of this expensive cheese offers a noticeably sharp, nutty flavor. Parmesan cheeses of lesser quality are made in Argentina, Australia, and the United States. The less pricey Asiago and Romano cheeses can also be used as adequate substitutes.

Herb Rice

Our herb combination is determined by what's growing in our garden. Explore, experiment, and enjoy!

2 tablespoons olive oil

1 cup chopped yellow onion

1 bay leaf

2 cups long-grain white rice

4 cups vegetable or Chicken Stock (Recipe appears on page 278.)

1 cup chopped fresh mixed herbs such as basil, thyme, parsley, rosemary, or marjoram

1 tablespoon lemon zest

1 teaspoon white pepper

Heat oil in a large saucepan over medium-high heat. Add onion and cook for 5 minutes or until soft. Add bay leaf and rice and stir to coat with oil. Slowly stir in stock. Bring to a boil and cover. Reduce heat to low and cook for 15 minutes. Stir in herbs, zest, and pepper. Fluff with fork and serve.

Serves 8

Rice Pilaf

2 tablespoons butter

1 small onion, diced

2 cups long-grain white rice

3 cups hot water

1 tablespoon dry thyme

2 teaspoons salt

Melt butter in a saucepan over medium-high heat. Add onion and cook for 2 minutes. Add rice and stir to coat with butter. Add hot water, thyme, and salt. Bring to a boil and cover. Reduce heat to medium and cook for 15 to 20 minutes or until all liquid is absorbed.

Serves 8

In past centuries, rosemary, meaning "dew of the sea," has been used to ward off evil (or a fever), sharpen the mind, and symbolize fidelity. Its resin scent makes it a wonderful addition to both potpourri and most white meats. Part of the mixture of Provençal herbs (herbs de Provence), this member of the mint family is also delicious when added to soups, breads, butters, and vinegars. The herb can be found as a leaf, fresh or dried, and in a powdered form.

Tomato, Basil, and Couscous Salad

The flavors of fresh sweet basil, sun-ripened tomatoes, and olive oil create a robust summer salad whether you are spending the season in South Jersey or the south of France.

2¼ cups Chicken Stock (Recipe appears on page 278.)
1 box (10 ounces) couscous
1 cup chopped scallions
1 cup seeded and chopped plum tomatoes
⅓ cup sliced fresh basil
½ cup olive oil
¼ cup balsamic vinegar
¼ teaspoon red pepper flakes
Salt and pepper

Bring stock to a boil in a saucepan. Add couscous. Remove from heat, cover, and let stand for 5 minutes. Transfer to a large bowl. Fluff with a fork and cool. Mix remaining ingredients into couscous. Season to taste with salt and pepper.

Serves 6

Scallions are onions grown from seed and harvested before their green shoots have matured and withered. Generally eaten raw or added near the end of the cooking process, they can range in taste from mildly delicate to peppery.

Potato Gnocchi

Gnocchi are very quick to make and cook. We find it's best to boil them in small batches to ensure they don't overcook. Sweet potatoes can be substituted for russet but you may want to reduce the number of eggs used.

1 pound russet potatoes, quartered
2 tablespoons butter, melted
2 egg yolks
½ cup all-purpose flour
½ cup semolina
Pinch of nutmeg
Pinch of salt and pepper
½ cup grated Parmesan cheese

Place potatoes in a pot and cover with cold salted water. Bring to a boil and simmer about 15 minutes. Drain and mash potatoes through a ricer while still hot. Add butter, egg yolks, flour, semolina, nutmeg, and salt and pepper. Mix ingredients together. Add more flour if necessary to make dough thick enough to work. Roll dough into finger-thick cylinders and cut crosswise into 1½-inch-long pieces. Press each gnocchi into the curve of a dinner fork. The outside surface should be ridged and the form should be curved so the center is thinner than the edges.

Bring a pot of salted water to a boil. Add gnocchi. When gnocchi begin to rise to the surface, remove with a slotted spoon. Toss with tomato sauce, butter, or Mushroom Ragoût (Recipe appears on page 194.) and top with grated Parmesan.

Serves 6

Native to northern Italy, gnocchi are dumplings made from flour, potatoes, or a combination of both. Eggs, cheese, and spinach are traditional additions to the gnocchi dough that can either be baked, boiled, or fried. Gnocchi ridges are the perfect receptacles for creamy sauces, but they are equally tasty when topped with just butter or pesto sauce.

Gnocchi au Gratin with Goat Cheese and Tomatoes

Potatoes always go well with dairy products and potato gnocchi are no exception. We love the richness that goat cheese adds and the color that the tomatoes and basil contribute. You'll love how quick and easy this recipe is.

Potato Gnocchi (Recipe appears on page 180.) or frozen
   gnocchi
2 cups diced tomatoes
⅔ cup goat cheese
2 tablespoons chopped basil
⅔ cup grated Parmesan cheese

Preheat oven to 450°. Toss cooked gnocchi with tomatoes, goat cheese, and basil. Place mixture in single-serving au gratin dishes or a shallow casserole. Sprinkle with Parmesan cheese and bake for 10 to 15 minutes until cheese has browned.

Serves 4 to 6

Also known as chèvre cheese, goat cheese is white with a taste that clearly distinguishes it from cheeses made with cow's milk. There are many varieties of goat cheese that, among other things, may differ in texture and shape. Some popular varieties hailing from regions in France include Banon, Montrachet, and Crottins.

Chicken and Spinach Tortellini with Sage Butter Sauce

Although this dish is a bit labor intensive, it's not difficult to master. After one or two twists you'll get the hang of it. And the sublime sage butter is very simple to make and tastes great over any kind of pasta.

1 pound chicken tenders
Salt and pepper
1 bag (10 ounces) spinach, cleaned, blanched, and chopped
1 teaspoon chopped garlic
1 tablespoon pine nuts, optional
¼ cup grated locatelli cheese
1 sheet (approximately 30 inches) fresh pasta
1 egg, beaten
Sage Butter Sauce (Recipe appears on page 282.)

Preheat oven to 350°. Season chicken tenders with salt and pepper. Place tenders and a little water in a baking pan. Roast tenders until fully cooked, about 10 minutes. Remove, cool, and dice. Combine chicken, spinach, garlic, pine nuts, cheese, and salt and pepper in a bowl.

Cut pasta into 2-inch squares. Place 1 tablespoon chicken mixture in the center of each square. Brush edges of pasta with egg and fold corner to corner to form a triangle. Press edges to seal. Twist the corners together to form a tortellini. Bring salted water to a boil and add tortellini. Simmer until al dente, about 3 to 5 minutes. Serve topped with sage butter sauce.

Serves 4 to 6

Spinach was first discovered in Persia, then in China and North America. The Moors brought it to medieval Spain where it became popular in monastic gardens. By the 16th century it was well known throughout Europe. Spinach is an excellent source of calcium, potassium, and iron. When eaten raw, it is also chock full of vitamins A, B, and C. Look for small, young, bright green leaves that have a crisp texture. Remove damaged or discolored leaves and trim off thick stems. Spinach leaves can be very gritty, so be sure to carefully wash them.

Fettucine with Roquefort, Lemon Zest, and Rosemary

Serve this unusual pasta dish as a pungent accompaniment to any meat, especially lamb. Reserved cooking water thins the sauce without adding extra fat.

3 tablespoons unsalted butter

3 tablespoons Roquefort cheese, room temperature

1 pound fettucine pasta

Grated zest of 1 lemon

1 tablespoon minced fresh rosemary

Freshly ground nutmeg

Salt and pepper

Mash together butter and cheese in a small bowl. Cook pasta in 6 quarts boiling salted water until al dente. Drain and reserve 1 cup cooking liquid. Place pasta in a warm serving bowl. Add cheese mixture and toss gently. Slowly add cooking liquid. Stir in lemon zest and rosemary. Add nutmeg and salt and pepper to taste.

Serves 4 to 6

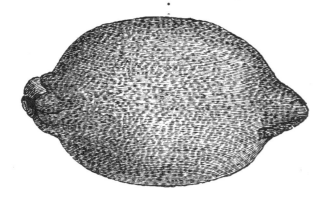

from the cooking school at la
campagne ~ from the cooking
school at la campagne ~ from the
cooking school at la campagne ~
from the cooking school at la
campagne ~ from the cooking
school at la campagne ~ from the
cooking school at la campagne ~
from the cooking school at la
campagne ~ from the cooking
school at la campagne ~ from the
cooking school at la campagne ~
from the cooking school at la
campagne ~ from the cooking
school at la campagne ~ from the
cooking school at la campagne ~
from the cooking school at la
campagne ~ from the cooking
school at la campagne ~ from the

vegetables

Marinated Artichokes

Add these garlic-infused artichokes to salads, pastas, and fish dishes. Or include them in an antipasto tray with crostini, olives, feta cheese, and roasted peppers. They can be served hot, cold, or at room temperature.

4 globe artichokes
Lemon juice
½ cup extra virgin olive oil
2 teaspoons chopped fresh garlic
2 teaspoons chopped fresh parsley
½ teaspoon crushed red pepper
Salt and pepper

Bring a pot of salted water to a boil and add a little lemon juice. Trim artichokes, immediately add to pot, and boil for about 10 minutes or until tender. Drain and cool. Combine oil, garlic, parsley, red pepper, and a little lemon juice in a large bowl. Add artichokes and toss with marinade. Season with salt and pepper and serve.

Serves 4

When boiling whole artichokes, check for doneness by pulling on the top of an interior leaf. If the leaf pulls away easily, it is done. If it needs more than a tug, then it needs more cooking time.

Gratin of Artichokes and Goat Cheese

Artichokes make the ingredients they are cooked with taste sweeter and magnify subtle flavors such as those found in goat cheeses.

A tender heart hides behind the bravado of the artichoke's spike shaped leaves. A member of the thistle family, the artichoke was grown for centuries in the Mediterranean and is now a product of California. Artichokes that are to be eaten raw should be smaller and less mature then those you wish to boil or steam. To eat an artichoke, pull off a leaf, dip it in butter or sauce, and pull it through your teeth to find the fleshy part of the leaf. When all the leaves have been removed, separate the artichoke heart from its haylike crown and enjoy this wonderful delicacy.

16 baby artichokes
2 quarts water
Juice of 2 lemons
1 tablespoon olive oil
4 cloves garlic, chopped
1 tablespoon chopped thyme
½ cup heavy cream
6 ounces goat cheese
Salt and pepper
2 tablespoons shredded Parmesan cheese
¼ cup homemade breadcrumbs

Cut off the tops and bottoms of artichokes, peel away the outer leaves, and cut in half. Soak artichokes in water and lemon juice in a large pot until ready to use. (This prevents browning.) In same water, simmer artichokes over medium heat until tender, about 15 minutes. Remove artichokes from hot water and plunge into ice water.

Heat olive oil in a medium skillet over medium heat. Add garlic and sauté for 3 to 5 minutes. Add thyme, heavy cream, goat cheese, and salt and pepper. Bring mixture to a simmer; then remove from heat.

Preheat oven to 350°. Arrange artichokes in an oven-proof dish. Pour cream mixture over artichokes. Sprinkle with Parmesan cheese and breadcrumbs and bake until browned, about 15 minutes.

Serves 8

White Asparagus in Puff Pastry

Exotic white asparagus atop a delicate crunch of puff pastry that's draped with creamy mousseline . . . is this heaven?

1 pound white asparagus
1 sheet puff pastry, thawed
1 egg, lightly beaten
Mousseline Sauce (Recipe appears on page 285.)
2 teaspoons chopped parsley

Remove the woody portions of asparagus by bending stalks gently until they snap. Peel stalks from blossom to end. Bring a pot of salted water to a boil. Cook asparagus in water until well done, about 5 to 8 minutes. Set aside and keep warm.

Preheat oven to 400°. Roll puff pastry out on a lightly floured work surface. Cut pastry into 4 even squares. Brush pastry squares with egg wash and bake for 10 minutes. Cut baked squares in half; set top halves aside. Place asparagus in the center of the 4 pastry bottom halves and top with sauce. Sprinkle on chopped parsley and cover with remaining pastry halves. Serve warm.

Serves 4

Asparagus is a member of the lily family. Green-stemmed asparagus is allowed to grow naturally into the light and is harvested when it is 6 inches tall. White asparagus is grown under mounds of dirt and cut just as the tips begin to show. Purple asparagus is cut when the stalks are about 1½ inches above the ground. Look for firm, straight spears with tight tips.

Asparagus in Vanilla Honey Sauce

Reminiscent of Old World cooking, this dish is warm and comforting. Serve it with simply prepared meat or fowl.

1 pound asparagus, washed and stemmed

2 egg yolks

1 tablespoon honey

1 cup heavy cream

¼ vanilla bean, split and scraped

Bring a pot of salted water to a boil. Add asparagus and cook for 4 to 5 minutes. Remove and keep warm. Combine egg yolks and honey in a mixing bowl. In a small saucepan, bring cream and vanilla to a boil. Temper yolks by whisking in a little hot cream. Pour yolks into saucepan with cream mixture. Gently heat mixture, stirring constantly, until sauce is thick enough to coat the back of a spoon. Strain sauce and serve over asparagus.

Serves 4

Few tastes are as sweet and natural as pure honey. This golden liquid, made by bees from flower nectar, has been enjoyed and praised by Provençals for years and used in the flavoring of nougats, breads, ice cream, and meats. Depending on where in you are in Provence, the honey made there will have its own distinctive flavor and consistently. Generally, the darker the honey, the stronger the taste. Enjoy the honey but respect the bee!

Broccoli Rabe with Toasted Garlic

Broccoli rabe is a wonderful leaf that is only made better by the Italian treatment of garlic and olive oil.

2 tablespoons olive oil
1 tablespoon chopped garlic
2 bunches broccoli rabe, washed and stemmed
½ cup Chicken Stock (Recipe appears on page 278.)
½ teaspoon crushed red pepper
Salt and pepper
1 lemon

Heat olive oil in a medium sauté pan over medium-high heat. Add garlic and cook until nut brown in color. Add broccoli rabe, chicken stock, and red pepper. Cover and simmer until broccoli rabe is tender but still firm, about 5 minutes. Season with salt and pepper and a squeeze of lemon.

Serves 4

Carrots Bercy

Bercy is a traditional French sauce.

2 pounds baby carrots with tops, peeled and blanched
3 tablespoons chopped fresh chives
2 tablespoons butter
3 tablespoons honey
¼ cup sparkling water (Perrier)
Salt and pepper

Melt butter in a sauté pan over medium heat. Add carrots and sauté for about 2 minutes. Add honey and chives and toss until well blended. Deglaze with sparkling water. Season with salt and pepper and serve.

Serves 4

A cousin of cabbage, broccoli rabe or rape falls somewhere between broccoli and greens. Having long been a Northern European tradition, rabe's bitter taste is most commonly associated with popular Italian cuisine. In recent years, this vegetable has become increasingly more popular in America. Look for broccoli rabe in produce markets from fall through spring.

Carrot Flan

Carrots and honey add natural sweetness to this rich baked side dish.

2 pounds carrots, peeled
½ cup heavy cream
2 eggs
2 egg yolks
1 teaspoon nutmeg
2 tablespoons honey
1 teaspoon salt
½ teaspoon pepper

Preheat oven to 300°. Boil carrots in water until soft, about 15 to 20 minutes. Transfer carrots to a blender or food processor. Add remaining ingredients and puree until smooth. Butter 4 ramekins or spray with nonstick spray and fill each with mixture. Bake in a water bath for 25 to 30 minutes or until a skewer inserted near the center of ramekins comes out clean. Unmold and serve.

Serves 4

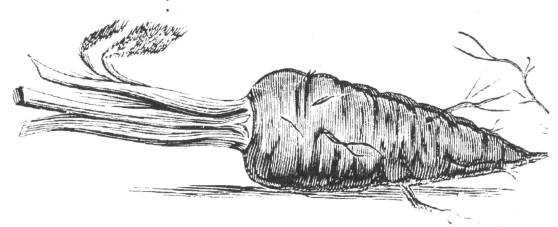

Fennel Flan

Travel to Provence in the winter and you'll see roadside fields bursting with bright yellow fennel flowers. This dish bursts as well with the pronounced anise flavor of fennel.

1 tablespoon olive oil
1 large bulb fennel, stalks removed, cored, and thinly sliced
1 cup water
2 eggs
2 egg yolks
6 tablespoons heavy cream
1 tablespoon fennel seeds
Salt and pepper

Preheat oven to 300°. Heat olive oil in a skillet over medium heat. Add fennel and sauté for 4 to 5 minutes or until caramelized. Add water and boil until most of the liquid is reduced. Transfer fennel to a blender or food processor. Add eggs, egg yolks, heavy cream, and fennel seeds and puree until smooth. Season with salt and pepper to taste.

Butter 4 ramekins or spray with nonstick spray and fill each with mixture. Bake in a water bath for 25 to 30 minutes or until a skewer inserted near the center of ramekins comes out clean. Unmold and serve.

Serves 4

Fennel has a strong aroma and slight licorice flavor that is sweeter and more subtle than anise. The seeds and leaves of common fennel are primarily used to sweeten and flavor salad and fish dishes. The raw stalks and bulbs of Florence fennel are desirable in salads and delicious when sautéed. Found from fall through spring, fresh fennel should first be rinsed under cold water and then dried thoroughly.

Grilled Figs with Goat Cheese and Mint

Stuffed grilled figs are a perfect accompaniment to grilled leg of lamb.

12 Black Mission figs
6 ounces goat cheese, softened
1 small sprig mint, stemmed and chopped
Coarse salt and black pepper

Slice figs in half lengthwise. Mix goat cheese with mint and salt and pepper to taste. Spoon dollops of cheese-mint mixture onto figs and refrigerate for 1 hour. Place on aluminum foil over hot grill. Grill until cheese softens.

Serves 12

Mint is a diverse herb with uses ranging from meats to desserts and from salads to vegetables. With over 25 true species, the herb is available year-round and can be found fresh, dried, or as an extract.

Mushroom Ragoût

This versatile dish can be tossed with gnocchi, pasta, egg noodles or vegetables; ladled over grilled bread or polenta; or served as a side dish. We like to eat it right out of the pan.

⅓ cup olive oil

1 cup diced red onions

6 cloves garlic, finely minced

1½ pounds assorted mushrooms, sliced

1 cup dry white wine

½ cup Marsala wine

1 cup sliced sun-dried tomatoes

½ cup Beef Stock (Recipe appears on page 279.)

2 tablespoons chopped parsley

1 tablespoon chopped rosemary

Salt and pepper

Heat olive oil in a skillet over medium heat. Add onions and garlic and sauté until onions are translucent. Add mushrooms and sauté until soft. Add wines and simmer for 5 minutes. Add sun-dried tomatoes and beef stock. Stir in parsley and rosemary. Season to taste with salt and pepper.

Serves 6

Keeping herbs fresh

Wrap fresh herbs loosely in a damp paper towel, seal in a plastic bag, and refrigerate. Or place a bunch of herbs in a vase and set in direct sunlight.

Glazed Pearl Onions with Currants and Almonds

This traditional holiday dish has a gentle crunch and smooth sweet finish.

1 pound pearl onions

¼ cup sherry vinegar

6 tablespoons water

2 tablespoons dried currants

2 tablespoons honey

1 tablespoon butter

½ teaspoon minced fresh thyme

⅓ cup slivered almonds, toasted

Drop onions into a pot of boiling water. Cook for 2 to 3 minutes to loosen skins. Remove from water. When cool, cut root end from onions and squeeze to remove skins. Place onions, vinegar, water, currants, honey, and butter in a saucepan over medium heat. Simmer for 45 minutes, stirring often. Stir in thyme and almonds.

Serves 4

Named after the Greek city of Corinth, currants are either dried fruit that resemble raisins or tiny berries similar to gooseberries. In the United States, true currants are rarely sold, and tiny, dried Zante grapes are substituted instead. However, red and white currants may be found from time to time at your local farmers' market.

Provençal Onion Tart

This is our version of the classic onion bread that is served on the streets of Nice.

3 tablespoons unsalted butter
1 pound yellow onions, peeled and sliced
1 tablespoon fresh thyme leaves
Freshly grated nutmeg to taste
Salt and pepper
4 large eggs
¼ cup milk
3 tablespoons heavy cream
8 whole anchovies, rinsed
8 black olives, pitted

Preheat oven to 425°. Grease a 10-inch round baking dish. Combine butter, onions, thyme, nutmeg, and salt and pepper in a large sauté pan over moderate heat. Cover and cook until onions are soft, about 8 minutes. Do not brown. Adjust seasonings as needed.

Whisk together eggs, milk, and cream in a small bowl. Transfer onions to prepared dish and smooth out with the back of a spoon to create an even layer. Pour egg mixture over onions. Arrange anchovies radiating from the center. Place olives in between anchovy "spokes." Bake about 30 minutes or until tart is firm to touch and golden.

Serves 4 to 6

Yellow onions, actually more golden-brown than yellow, are the backbone of our sauces and soups. They are our general all-purpose onion because they are neither too sweet nor too pungent and are readily available all year round.

Pommes Soufflés

Double frying puffs the potatoes; hence, the name "soufflé" potatoes. Eat them piping hot and enjoy!

2 pounds russet potatoes, peeled
2 quarts vegetable oil
Salt and pepper

Cut potatoes into ⅛-inch-thick rectangles. Rinse and pat dry. Divide the oil between two saucepans. Heat the oil in one pan to 210°; the other to 400°. Place potatoes into the 210° oil and cook until they begin to brown.

Remove potatoes with a strainer and transfer to second saucepan. Cook until potatoes are browned and puffy. Remove from pan and drain on paper towel. Sprinkle with salt and pepper and serve immediately.

Serves 6

Originating five millenniums ago in South America, the potato was not a main Irish staple until the 17th century. Presently, close to 400 varieties of potatoes are grown around the world.

Potatoes à la Normande

1¾ pounds russet potatoes, peeled and finely sliced
Salt and pepper
3 large leeks, cleaned and finely sliced
1 bunch parsley, washed and sliced
2 cups Chicken Stock (Recipe appears on page 278.)
3 ounces butter

Preheat oven to 400°. Butter a flameproof casserole dish. Spread half the potatoes in the dish and sprinkle with salt and pepper. Spread leeks and parsley on top and sprinkle with salt and pepper. Cover with remaining potatoes and season again. Add chicken stock to cover potatoes and dot with small pieces of butter. Cover and bake for 45 minutes or until potatoes are cooked.

Serves 6 to 8

Potato Morel Gratin

This upscale version of potatoes au gratin is best prepared in the spring when morels are fresh and abundant.

1¼ cups Chicken Stock (Recipe appears on page 278.)
1 teaspoon nutmeg
Salt and pepper
1¼ pounds potatoes, peeled and very thinly sliced
3 tablespoons butter
4 ounces Gruyère cheese, grated
1 cup sliced morel mushrooms

Preheat oven to 375°. Bring chicken stock to a boil over low heat. Add nutmeg and salt and pepper and remove from heat. Grease a 10 x 7-inch baking dish with ½ teaspoon butter. Spread a layer of potatoes over the bottom. Sprinkle with morels. Add a layer of cheese. Repeat. (Cheese should be the top layer.) Pour stock over potatoes and dot with remaining butter. Bake for 45 minutes and serve hot.

Serves 4 to 6

Found in your local specialty produce market in the spring, fresh morels hide a smoky, nutty flavor within their helical shape. Belonging to the same species as the truffle, this edible fungus is freshest when darker brown with a spongy texture. Imported canned and dried morels can be found year-round and, as with all types of morels, should be cleaned thoroughly under cold running water.

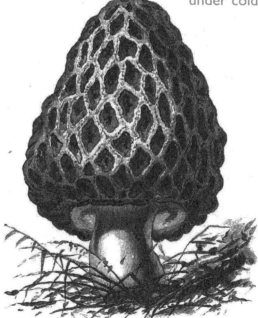

Garlic Mashed Potatoes

Creamy potatoes with a flavorful hint of garlic have been a La Campagne staple for years (yes, before they were trendy).

3 pounds russet potatoes, peeled
½ pound unsalted butter, softened
1 tablespoon chopped garlic
2 tablespoons chopped mixed fresh herbs
½ cup heavy cream
Salt and pepper

Place potatoes in a large pot and cover with cold water. Bring to a simmer, but do not allow water to boil. Cook until tender, about 40 minutes.

Meanwhile, combine butter, garlic, and herbs in a food processor. Blend until well mixed. Chill.

Strain cooked potatoes. Rice potatoes in a food mill or mash in a large bowl. Stir in garlic butter and cream. Season with salt and pepper.

Serves 8

Potato varieties can range in both starch and protein content. The traditional Idaho or russet potato is a floury type with a high starch, low moisture content making it ideal for baking or making French fries. Californian long white potatoes are similar in shape and content. Waxy potatoes such as the round white and red varieties are firmer, less starchy, and richer in protein. This makes them excellent for boiling and mashing. New potatoes are young potatoes of any variety. They can be cooked whole, are excellent boiled or roasted, and are best suited for salads.

Mashed Potatoes, Rutabega, and Parsnips with Caramelized Shallots

Root cellar madness! Take your time when you caramelize the shallots — the longer they cook, the sweeter they'll be.

3 pounds Idaho potatoes, peeled and cut into 1½-inch pieces
1½ pounds rutabega, peeled and cut into ½-inch pieces
1¼ pounds parsnips, peeled and cut into 1½-inch pieces
8 cloves garlic
¾ cup butter, softened
Salt and pepper
10 shallots, thinly sliced
1 sprig fresh thyme, stemmed

Combine vegetables and garlic in a large pot over medium heat. Cover with water and simmer until tender, about 30 minutes. Drain. Add ½ cup butter and mash. Season to taste with salt and pepper. Transfer mixture to a buttered 13 x 9 x 2-inch casserole dish.

Preheat oven to 375°. Melt remaining butter in a heavy skillet over medium-high heat. Add shallots and sauté until brown, about 5 minutes. Reduce heat to low and cook shallots, stirring, about 15 minutes or until caramelized. Stir in thyme and season to taste with salt and pepper. Top mashed vegetables with shallots. Bake 20 minutes.

Serves 10

Shallots are hollowed leaves that can grow up to a foot tall. A member of the onion family, shallots grow bunched together like garlic and have a distinctive taste somewhere between the onion and garlic. Shallots are commonly used in the making of sauces. In the spring, look for fresh shallots that are firm with crisp outer skins and no signs of green shoots.

Swiss Chard Gratin

A common green in French cookery, especially in Provençal dishes, Swiss chard is similar to spinach but a bit richer and heartier.

2 pounds Swiss chard, washed
4 tablespoons butter
2 teaspoons flour
1½ cups cream
Salt and pepper
1 egg yolk
4 tablespoons grated Parmesan cheese

Butter a gratin dish (a shallow oval baking dish) or a casserole dish. Separate chard leaves from stems. Cut stems into 2-inch sticks. Bring salted water to a boil in a medium saucepan. Boil stems (sticks) for 2 minutes; then add leaves and boil for an additional 1 minute. Remove and strain.

Preheat broiler. Melt butter in a sauté pan over medium heat. Add chard and sauté for 3 minutes. Add flour and stir to coat. Add cream and salt and pepper to taste and cook for 5 minutes until mixture reduces slightly. Stir in egg yolk. Pour mixture into prepared dish and sprinkle with grated cheese. Bake under broiler for 2 minutes.

Serves 6 to 8

Swiss chard is also called silver chard, silverbeet, and seakale. It is from the red beet family but is grown for its leaves — which taste a bit like spinach — rather than its root. Look for shiny, brightly-colored leaves and crisp spines. Swiss chard is rich in vitamins A and C.

Lavender-Scented Tomato Gratin with Goat Cheese

This dish is perfectly balanced and perfectly delicious. The acidity of the tomatoes heightens the perfume of the lavender while the richness of the goat cheese softens and carries its flavor.

1 pound Roma plum tomatoes, seeded and quartered

1 tablespoon extra virgin olive oil

2 cloves garlic, chopped

2 teaspoons dried lavender blossoms

2 sprigs fresh thyme, stemmed

1 sprig rosemary, stemmed and chopped

Salt and freshly ground pepper

8 ounces goat cheese

18 cured black olives, pitted and chopped

Preheat oven to 200°. Arrange tomatoes in a single layer on a baking sheet. Sprinkle with olive oil, garlic, lavender, half of herbs, and salt and pepper. Bake for 1½ to 2 hours or until tomatoes are very soft.

Crumble goat cheese and divide among 4 single-serving ovenproof baking dishes. Sprinkle with remaining herbs. Top with tomatoes and olives. Place dishes under broiler until cheese is just melted.

Serves 4

We host many wedding receptions at La Campagne. Because lavender is an aphrodisiac, traditionally denoting devotion, love, and romance, we present the bride with a sprig of lavender to tuck in her bouquet.

Root Vegetable Gratin

*The crispy crumb topping hides a creamy blend of rustic
ingredients. Serve this make-ahead dish with a simple
roasted chicken or as an item on a buffet table.*

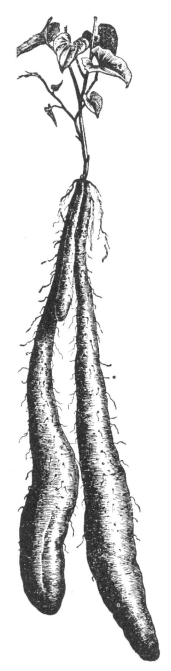

4 small eggplants, cut into ½-inch circles

4 small zucchini, cut into ½-inch circles

8 tomatoes, cored and sliced into ½-inch rounds

2 green peppers, stemmed, seeded, and cut into rings

2 red peppers, stemmed, seeded, and cut into rings

2 yellow peppers, stemmed, seeded, and cut into rings

½ cup olive oil

4 cloves garlic, finely chopped

4 tablespoons finely chopped parsley

4 tablespoons Herbes de Provençe (Recipe appears on page 292.)

Salt and pepper

2 tablespoons butter

4 tablespoons fresh breadcrumbs

Preheat oven to 450°. Arrange vegetables on sheet pans,
sprinkle with olive oil, garlic, parsley, herbs, and salt and
pepper. Roast vegetables in batches until just softened.

    Butter a gratin dish (a shallow oval baking dish) or a
casserole dish. Arrange roasted vegetables in dish, overlapping eggplant, zucchini, and tomatoes. Sprinkle with
breadcrumbs. Arrange peppers in a lattice over the vegetables. Brown under broiler and serve immediately.

Serves 4 to 6

Ratatouille Vegetables

This classic vegetable combination can be served hot or cold. Use leftovers as a topping for foccacia, a filling for lasagne, and an addition to chicken or beef soup.

2 tablespoons olive oil

2 onions, diced

2 green peppers, diced

1 large eggplant, diced

2 zucchini, quartered and sliced

6 tomatoes, diced

1 tablespoon chopped fresh parsley

1 tablespoon chopped fresh basil

1 tablespoon chopped garlic

Salt and pepper

Heat oil in a large sauté pan over high heat. When oil is smoking, add onions and peppers and sauté for 3 minutes or until tender but not browned. Transfer to a large bowl. Add eggplant to same pan and sauté for 3 minutes or until tender but not browned. Transfer to the bowl. Add zucchini to pan and cook until almost tender. Add garlic and cook until zucchini is tender but not browned. Transfer to the bowl. Add tomatoes and sauté for 1 minute. Transfer to the bowl. Add basil and parsley. Season with salt and pepper. Toss well and serve.

Serves 6

The ideal eggplant can be found at the end of summer and is firm, heavy, and smooth but supple. In general, the smaller the eggplant, the milder, more desirable the flavor. Salting is rarely necessary or beneficial.

Roasted Provençal Vegetables

Bold flavors and bright colors make this dish a favorite any time of year.

1 small carrot, peeled and cut into ¼-inch sticks

1 small zucchini, peeled and cut into ¼-inch sticks

1 red pepper, stemmed, seeded, and cut into strips

1 green pepper, stemmed, seeded, and cut into strips

1 yellow pepper, stemmed, seeded, and cut into strips

½ small eggplant, peeled and cut into ¼-inch strips

2 teaspoons Herbes de Provence (Recipe appears on page 292.)

2 cloves garlic, chopped

4 tablespoons olive oil

Preheat oven to 450°. Toss prepared vegetables, herbs, garlic, and olive oil in a large mixing bowl. Transfer to a baking sheet and roast until just softened, about 8 to 10 minutes. Remove from oven and allow to cool.

Serves 4 to 6

from the cooking school at la campagne ~ from the cooking school at la campagne ~ from the cooking school at la campagne ~ from the cooking school at la campagne ~ from the cooking school at la campagne ~ from the cooking school at la campagne ~ from the cooking school at la campagne ~ from the cooking school at la campagne ~ **from the cooking school at la campagne ~** from the cooking school at la campagne ~ from the cooking school at la campagne ~ from the cooking school at la campagne ~ from the cooking school at la campagne ~ from the cooking school at la campagne ~ from the cooking school at la campagne ~ from the

tarts, tortes, and more

Alsatian Apple Tart

*A classic dessert from the Alsace-Lorraine region of France,
this tart relies on a custard to bind the apples together,
giving it a richer texture than tart Tatin.*

10 ounces Pâte Sucrée (Recipe appears on page 297.), chilled
1 pound Granny Smith apples, peeled, cored, and sliced
4 egg yolks
⅓ cup sugar
½ teaspoon vanilla extract
¼ teaspoon cinnamon
¾ cup heavy cream

Preheat oven to 425°. Butter a 10-inch tart pan. Roll out
chilled dough on a lightly floured work surface until dough
is slightly larger than the inverted tart pan. Carefully fold
pastry in half, transfer to pan, and unfold. Press firmly into
bottom and up sides of pan. Prick bottom with a fork.

Arrange apple slices in an overlapping, circular fashion
in tart shell. Bake for 15 minutes.

Whisk together egg yolks, sugar, vanilla, and cinnamon
in a mixing bowl. Whisk in cream and pour mixture over
apples. Bake for 30 minutes. Serve warm.

Serves 6 to 8

Apple Walnut Strudel

Delicate layers of crispy phyllo dough, cinnamon spiked apples, and crunchy bits of walnut are complemented by the deep, rich caramel sauce. Although pecans can be substituted, we prefer the less rich walnuts when paired with caramel.

5 tablespoons butter

6 Granny Smith apples, peeled and diced

1 cup chopped toasted walnuts

1 cup sugar

1 teaspoon cinnamon

4 sheets phyllo dough

Heat 3 tablespoons butter in a large sauté pan. Add apples, walnuts, sugar, and cinnamon and cook until apples are tender and liquid is syrupy. Remove from heat and cool.

Preheat oven to 375°. Grease a baking sheet. Melt remaining butter. Lay out 1 sheet phyllo dough on a clean work surface. Brush with butter, cover with another sheet, and repeat until all sheets are layered. Place filling across the bottom of the sheets lengthwise, leaving a 1-inch margin on all sides. Fold side edges over filling and gently roll into a log. Place seam side down on a baking sheet. Bake for 35 minutes or until lightly browned and crisp. Slice and serve warm as is or with Caramel Sauce (see recipe).

Serves 4 to 6

Caramel Sauce

1 cup sugar

¼ cup water

1½ cups heavy cream

Heat water and sugar in a saucepan over high heat until mixture is caramel in color. Slowly add heavy cream, whisking until smooth. Remove and serve warm.

strudel
[STROOD-l]

Strudel is a pastry made up of many layers of very thin dough that are spread with a sweet or savory filling, then rolled up and baked. Paper-thin strudel dough is used traditionally, but phyllo dough is a suitable substitute. Strudel is very popular in Germany, Austria, and much of Europe with apple strudel being the universal favorite.

Sour Cherry Almond Tart

We serve this homespun tart in the summertime when our cherry trees start to bear their fruit. Be sure to use sour cherries and don't skimp on the heavy cream.

8 tablespoons unsalted butter, melted and cooled

¾ cup sugar

Pinch of salt

2 teaspoons vanilla extract

½ cup finely ground blanched almonds

1½ cups all-purpose flour

5 tablespoons heavy cream

1 egg, lightly beaten

1 tablespoon kirsch, optional

1 pound sour cherries, pitted

Preheat oven to 350°. Butter a 9-inch tart pan.

    Combine butter, ½ cup sugar, salt, 1 teaspoon vanilla, and 2 tablespoons almonds in a medium bowl. Add 1¼ cups flour and stir to form a smooth dough. Press dough firmly into bottom and up sides of pan. Prick bottom with a fork. Bake for 10 minutes or until pale brown.

    Combine cream, egg, and remaining vanilla in a small bowl. Whisk in remaining flour and sugar, 2 tablespoons almonds, and kirsch. Sprinkle 2 tablespoons almonds on the bottom of baked crust. Top with cherries. Pour in filling and top with remaining almonds. Bake for 40 minutes or until firm and golden brown.

Serves 8

A German creation, kirschwasser (kirsch for short) is a brandy made from the juice of black cherries.

Chocolate Strawberry Tart

Plump chocolate-covered strawberries inspired us to create this dessert, and just like a kid in a candy store, you won't want to stop at just one piece.

Baked Tart Shell (Recipe appears on page 296.)
1½ ounces bitter chocolate, melted
¼ cup strawberry jam, melted
1½ pints strawberries, hulled and halved

Brush bottom of shell with melted chocolate. Refrigerate until set. Brush chocolate with half of melted jam. Arrange strawberries, cut sides down, in an overlapping circular fashion in tart shell. Brush berries with remaining jam and refrigerate until set.

Serves 6 to 8

Raspberry Tart

This is a variation of a sensational tart we sampled at a brasserie in the town of Eze a few years ago. We make it every year to celebrate the beginning of the all-too-short raspberry season.

¾ cup sugar

1 cup flour

1 teaspoon baking powder

Zest of 1 lemon

1 cup half-and-half

¼ cup vegetable oil

2 large eggs

3 tablespoons unsalted butter, melted

2 cups raspberries, hulled

Baked Tart Shell (Recipe appears on page 296.), cooled

¼ cup confectioners' sugar

Combine sugar, flour, baking powder, and lemon zest in a bowl. Mix gently with an electric mixer on low. Add half-and-half and oil. Mix to blend. Add eggs and melted butter and mix until a smooth batter forms.

Preheat oven to 375°. Arrange raspberries in the bottom of prepared tart shell. Add batter to ¼ inch below rim. Bake for 35 minutes or until firm and brown. Sprinkle with confectioners' sugar. Cool and serve at room temperature.

Serves 6

The raspberry has thrived in North America for over a century. Whether eaten raw or within a dessert, sauce, or jam, this wild berry boasts an intense flavor that is unmistakable. While red is the most common type of raspberry, there are also black and golden varieties as well.

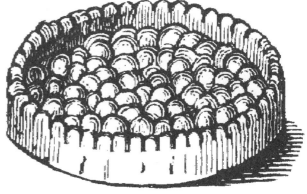

Rhubarb-Raspberry Galette

Many older cooks and gardeners refer to rhubarb as the "pie plant," and one bite of this rosy red pie will tell you why. Raw rhubarb is incredibly tart, but it swings into sweetness when cooked, making this rhubarb-raspberry combination the perfect balance of sweet and sour.

1½ pounds rhubarb, trimmed and peeled

1 cup raspberries

1¼ cups sugar

3 tablespoons flour

1 teaspoon cinnamon

Zest of 1 orange

Pâte Brisée (Recipe appears on page 296.)

1 egg, beaten

Cinnamon and sugar

Cut rhubarb into 1-inch long pieces. Toss rhubarb with raspberries, sugar, flour, cinnamon, and zest. Allow mixture to stand for 5 to 10 minutes or until moist.

Preheat oven to 375°. Roll out dough on a lightly floured work surface to a 14-inch disk. Transfer dough to a baking sheet. Spread filling in the center of dough, leaving a 2-inch margin. Brush margin with egg wash. Gently fold edge over fruit, pleating as you go. Brush entire galette with egg wash and sprinkle with cinnamon and sugar. Bake for 40 to 45 minutes.

Serves 6 to 8

Rhubarb is another one of those vegetables that is often mistaken for a fruit. The celerylike, tart stalks are juicy and are used to make pies and jams. Look for crisp, bright stalks that have blemish-free leaves.

Lemon Tart

Bright and beautiful, this tart recalls sunny days and warm summer evenings in Provence.

2 eggs
3 egg yolks
1 cup sugar
8 tablespoons unsalted butter, cut into 8 pieces
Grated zest of 2 lemons
½ cup lemon juice, strained
Lemon Pastry Shell (see recipe)

Combine eggs, egg yolks, and sugar in a bowl set over a double boiler. Whisk until thick and pale, about 8 to 10 minutes. Add butter, 1 tablespoon at a time. Add zest and lemon juice and whisk for 4 minutes. Pour into prepared shell and smooth with a spatula. Refrigerate until set.

Serves 6 to 8

Lemon Pastry Shell

Not just for lemon filling! Try it with most any fruit or custard.

8 tablespoons unsalted butter, melted and cooled
¼ teaspoon vanilla extract
Grated zest of 1 lemon
¼ cup confectioners' sugar
Pinch of salt
1¼ cups plus 1 tablespoon flour

Preheat oven to 350°. Butter a 9-inch fluted tart pan with removable bottom or a 9-inch springform pan. Combine melted butter, vanilla, zest, sugar, and salt in a bowl. Gradually add flour and knead to form a soft dough. Press dough evenly into bottom and up sides of pan. Bake for 12 to 15 minutes. Cool completely before filling.

Many recipes call for the "juice of 1 lemon" or "zest of 1 lemon." Just how much is that? Well, it depends on the size (and generosity) of the lemon, but generally you can extract ¼ cup of juice and 1 teaspoon of compacted, grated zest.

Strawberry Tart with Almond Cream

Escoffier loved Provençal strawberries so we are sure he'd approve of this beautiful tart.

One would not have to travel too far in western Provence to find an almond tree. In winter, the fruits of this tree bloom, and the soft shells are edible right from the stem. As the season progresses, the nuts harden and become an essential ingredient for Provençal desserts. The sweeter variety almonds are delicious eaten as is or cooked and can be found in a variety of forms, including whole, sliced, smoked, or in a paste. Bitter-flavored almonds are usually used in making extracts.

½ cup butter, softened
½ cup ground almonds
⅓ cup sugar
¼ cup flour
1 egg
Basic Tart Shell (Recipe appears on page 297.)
½ cup strawberry jam
2 pints strawberries, tops removed and sliced
Confectioners' sugar

Preheat oven to 350°. Combine butter, almonds, sugar, flour, and egg in a bowl and beat until smooth. Pour almond cream into prepared tart shell and spread smooth. Bake for 30 minutes until filling is golden brown. Remove and cool on a rack.

Remove tart from pan. Spread a thin layer of jam over tart. Arrange strawberries in a circle starting from the outside in until tart is completely covered. Sprinkle with confectioners' sugar.

Serves 6

Vanilla Gènoise

A classic sponge cake named after the city of Genoa where it was developed, gènoise is the "little black dress" of the cake world — dress it up with a variety of frostings, use it as a basis for anything from petit fours to Baked Alaska, or simply eat "as is" and enjoy.

6 eggs
1 cup sugar
1 teaspoon vanilla
1 teaspoon salt
1 cup flour, sifted

Preheat oven to 350°. Butter a 10-inch round cake pan. Dust the bottom and sides of pan with sugar, tapping out any excess.

Place eggs, sugar, vanilla, and salt in a mixing bowl on top of a double boiler. Heat over simmering water until mixture is warm to touch, about 110°. (Make sure the bowl does not touch the water.) Remove bowl from heat. Beat mixture with an electric beater on medium speed until cool. Batter will triple in volume and be thick and fluffy.

Carefully fold sifted flour into egg mixture in three additions until flour is just combined. (Do not overfold or the mixture will lose its volume.) Pour batter into prepared cake pan. Bake for 20 to 25 minutes until springy to touch.

Allow cake to cool completely. Run a knife around edges of pan to loosen cake. Cover with a serving plate and invert both pan and plate. Gently remove pan. Serve cake as is or frosted or use as a base for other dessert recipes.

Serves 8 to 10

Grown close to the equator on a vine, vanilla is a fruit that after hand pollination produces a bean which is then harvested and cured. The flavor these beans produce is called for in just about every pastry recipe. Its ability to compliment most any other flavor makes vanilla's uses infinite.

Chocolate Gènoise

When "plain Jane" vanilla won't do, consider this chocolate sponge cake. Alone, it is delicious. Dressed up with icing and fruits . . . dangerously decadent.

6 eggs

1 cup sugar

1 teaspoon vanilla

1 teaspoon salt

½ cup flour

½ cup cocoa powder

Preheat oven to 350°. Butter a 10-inch round cake pan. Dust the bottom and sides of pan with sugar, tapping out any excess.

Place eggs, sugar, vanilla, and salt in a mixing bowl on top of a double boiler. Heat over simmering water until mixture is warm to touch, about 110°. (Make sure the bowl does not touch the water.) Remove bowl from heat. Beat mixture with an electric beater on medium speed until cool. Batter will triple in volume and be thick and fluffy.

Sift together flour and cocoa. Carefully fold dry mixture into egg mixture in three additions until ingredients are just combined. (Do not overfold or the mixture will lose its volume.) Pour batter into prepared cake pan. Bake for 20 to 25 minutes until springy to touch.

Allow cake to cool completely. Run a knife around edges of pan to loosen cake. Cover with a serving plate and invert both pan and plate. Gently remove pan. Serve cake as is or frosted or use as a base for other dessert recipes.

Serves 8 to 10

Praline Mousse Cake

This cake was inspired by the famous praline shops of New Orleans' French Quarter. From the street you can watch candymakers guard the huge kettles that turn a humble sugar mixture into a legendary confection.

1½ cups unsalted butter, softened

1½ cups praline paste, available at gourmet stores (Peanut butter can be substituted.)

6 egg whites

¾ cup sugar

¾ cup water

¾ cup hazelnut liqueur

Vanilla Gènoise Cake, cut into three equal disks (Recipe appears on page 216.)

½ cup crushed praline candy

Beat butter until creamy. Add praline paste and mix well. Reserve.

Combine egg whites and sugar in a stainless steel mixing bowl. Heat over a double boiler, whipping periodically to prevent eggs from cooking, until a candy thermometer reads 140°. Remove from heat. Whip with electric mixer until mixture is cool and whites are stiff and glossy. Incorporate praline butter into egg whites and mix well.

Place water and liqueur in a saucepan and bring to a boil. Boil for about 3 minutes or until syrupy. Remove from heat.

Place a gènoise disk on a cake plate. Brush one-third hazelnut syrup over cake. Spread one-third mousse over cake. Repeat procedure with second and third disk. Refrigerate until set, about 2 hours, or up to 3 days. Sprinkle cake with crushed praline candy when ready to serve.

Serves 6 to 8

Praline is a brittle candy made of almonds, pecans, and other nuts and caramelized sugar. Eat it as a candy or crush it for use in a favorite dessert. Praline is also the name of a Louisiana candy-cookie .

Chocolate Raspberry Cake

Your dinner party will end on a high note when you serve this beautiful layer cake. A real plus when entertaining, the cake can be made ahead of time and refrigerated for up to 3 days.

2 pints raspberries, hulled

1 teaspoon unflavored powdered gelatin

1 tablespoon cold water

6 egg whites

¾ cup sugar

1 pint heavy cream, whipped

6 ounces raspberry liqueur

Chocolate Gènoise Cake, cut into three equal disks (Recipe appears on page 217.)

Ganache (Recipe appears on page 295.)

Puree raspberries in a food processor. Soften gelatin in cold water. Heat gelatin mixture and 1 cup puree in a saucepan over low heat until gelatin is smooth and combined. Remove from heat and cool to room temperature. Add remaining puree, mix thoroughly, and reserve.

Combine egg whites and sugar in a stainless steel mixing bowl. Heat over a double boiler, whipping periodically to prevent eggs from cooking, until a candy thermometer reads 140°. Remove from heat. Whip with electric mixer until mixture is cool and whites are stiff and glossy. Mix in puree. Fold whipped cream gently into mousse.

Place liqueur in a saucepan and bring to a boil. Boil for about 3 minutes or until syrupy. Remove from heat.

Place a gènoise disk on a cake plate. Brush one-third raspberry syrup over cake. Spread one-third mousse over cake. Repeat procedure with second and third disk. Refrigerate until set, about 1 to 2 hours. When ready to serve, evenly cover entire cake with warm ganache and refrigerate again until set.

Serves 6 to 8

Raspberries grown quickly and in abundance which makes them an ideal berry for your home garden. Easily separated at the root in the wild, a raspberry plant can be relocated and thrive with little effort. If you choose the more traditional route — the market — look for the plumpest, brightest berries available through summer and fall.

Chocolate Almond Torte

Our students love to share their family recipes such as this one. It was usually served on "special occasion Sundays" when aunts and uncles came over. It's so rich and dense — you won't want to wait for a special occasion (or even Sunday!) to make it.

6 ounces semi-sweet chocolate, chopped

1½ sticks unsalted butter

⅔ cup sugar

8 eggs, separated

½ cup plus 2 teaspoons chopped blanched almonds

1 teaspoon vanilla extract

Ganache (Recipe appears on page 295.)

Preheat oven to 350°. Butter a 10-inch round cake pan. Dust the bottom and sides of pan with sugar, tapping out excess.

Melt chocolate in a bowl set over a pan of simmering water. Set aside and allow to cool for 5 minutes.

Whip butter with ⅓ cup sugar in a mixer until very light. Beat in egg yolks and melted chocolate. In a separate bowl, whip egg whites until frothy. Gradually add remaining ⅓ cup sugar and whip until whites are stiff. Fold ½ cup almonds, vanilla, and one-third egg whites into chocolate mixture; then fold in remaining whites. Pour batter into pan and bake for 30 to 40 minutes. Cool completely and unmold.

Evenly spread entire cake with ganache and sprinkle with remaining chopped almonds.

Serves 6 to 8

To fold

Folding is a technique used to combine a light mixture (such as beaten egg whites) with a heavy mixture (such as custard). The heavy mixture must be at the bottom of the bowl. Using a large spatula, cut down through the center of the layers to the bottom, lifting both mixtures upward. As you fold, use the other hand to turn the bowl. Continue folding and turning until the light mixture is fully incorporated.

Cranberry Upside Down Cake

We serve this fun, fruity, fall cake on Black Friday, the day after Thanksgiving, when shoppers need all the sustenance (and sugar) they can get.

1 cup sugar

3½ cups fresh cranberries, sorted, washed, and drained

6 tablespoons butter, softened

1 large egg

1 teaspoon vanilla extract

1 teaspoon orange zest

1¼ cups flour

1½ teaspoons baking powder

¼ teaspoon salt

½ cup milk

⅓ cup red currant jelly

Preheat oven to 350°. Generously butter a 9-inch round cake pan. Sprinkle ½ cup sugar evenly over bottom of pan. Arrange cranberries in pan.

Cream butter and remaining sugar. Add egg, vanilla, and orange zest and beat. In a separate large bowl, sift together flour, baking powder, and salt. Fold flour mixture into butter mixture, alternating with milk, in three additions. Pour batter over cranberries. Bake for 1 hour (top will be brown).

Cool on a cake rack for 10 minutes. After 10 minutes, run a knife around the edges of pan to loosen cake. Cool for 10 minutes more. Loosen cake again, cover with a serving plate, and invert both pan and plate. Remove the pan.

Melt jelly in a small saucepan and brush over cake. Serve as is or with whipped cream or vanilla ice cream.

Serves 8

Profiteroles

The word profiterole translated loosely in French means a "small profit" or "gain." It refers to old-time restaurant chefs who would use leftover batter to make something "extra" and pocket the profit. While you may not make a profit from these little puffs, you will gain a sweet something extra.

½ cup water
4 tablespoons butter
½ cup flour
3 eggs
¼ cup sliced almonds

Preheat oven to 375°. Combine water and butter in a saucepan and bring to a boil, making sure butter dissolves. Lower heat. Add flour and stir until mixture pulls away from the sides of pan. Transfer mixture to a bowl. Beat in eggs, one at a time, until mixture is shiny. Chill dough for about 30 minutes.

Butter a nonstick baking sheet. Shape dough into 1½-inch balls. (This can be done in one of two ways: either fill a pastry bag fitted with a round tip and pipe little mounds onto the baking sheet or drop teaspoons of dough onto the baking sheet.) Place dough 2 inches apart on baking sheet. Top each mound with a sliver of almond and bake until golden brown, about 12 to 15 minutes. Remove and cool.

Yields approximately 20 profiteroles

Profiteroles are basically miniature cream puffs that can be stuffed with a sweet or savory filling. Profiteroles can be frozen after they have been piped out. When ready to bake, they can be transferred directly from the freezer to the oven with no thawing necessary.

Hazelnut Biscotti

4 cups flour

2 cups sugar

2 teaspoons baking powder

2 cups chopped toasted hazelnuts

6 eggs

4 tablespoons hazelnut liqueur

2 teaspoons almond extract

2 teaspoons vanilla extract

Preheat oven to 350°. Place dry ingredients in a food processor. In a separate bowl, combine wet ingredients. Add wet ingredients to the processor and process until a dough ball is formed. Place dough on a greased baking sheet and roll into a 3-inch wide log. Bake for 20 minutes. Remove and cool.

Slice log on a diagonal into ½-inch wide slices. Lay slices on a greased baking sheet and bake for 15 minutes until golden. Remove and cool. Serve with coffee.

Yields 2 dozen

from the cooking school at la
campagne ~ from the cooking
school at la campagne ~ from the
cooking school at la campagne ~
**from the cooking school at la
campagne** ~ from the cooking
school at la campagne ~ from the
cooking school at la campagne ~
from the cooking school at la
campagne ~ from the cooking
school at la campagne ~ from the
cooking school at la campagne ~
from the cooking school at la
campagne ~ from the cooking
school at la campagne ~ from the
cooking school at la campagne ~
from the cooking school at la
campagne ~ from the cooking
school at la campagne ~ from the

La Campagne

dramatic desserts

Tulipe Cookies

Tuile cookies are made from a basic stencil paste that is molded into a variety of shapes. We like to shape them into little baskets — tulipes — to hold chocolate mousse and raspberries. The possibilities are endless!

2 egg whites
¾ cup flour
½ cup confectioners' sugar
2½ tablespoons unsalted butter, melted and cooled
1 tablespoon heavy cream
Mocha Hazelnut Mousse (Recipe appears on page 241.)
1 cup raspberries, hulled
Sweet Whipped Cream (Recipe appears on page 227.)

Preheat oven to 450°. Whisk egg whites in a bowl until frothy. Sift in flour and sugar and whisk until just combined. Stir in butter and heavy cream until smooth.

Place 6 mounds of batter (1 tablespoon each) well apart on a greased baking sheet. Spread batter as thinly as possible with the back of a spoon to form 4-inch circles. Bake for 5 to 7 minutes, until cookies are just brown around the edges. While still hot, carefully lift cookies off sheet and mold them over the ends of upturned rock glasses or ramekins to form cupped shapes. Repeat until all batter is used.

When cookies are completely cooled, remove from glasses, and fill with mousse. Garnish with raspberries and as much whipped cream as you like.

Yields 16 desserts

Tulipes are perfect for summer entertaining. Fill them with low-fat frozen yogurt or ice cream and top with fresh fruit such as mango, papaya, and berries. Be prepared for lots of "oohs" and "aahs."

Strawberry Napoleon

Looking for an impressive dessert? You've found it. Made with precariously stacked layers of crispy pastry and sweet cream, this dessert will be the triumphant end to any elegant evening.

1 sheet frozen puff pastry, thawed
Pastry Cream (Recipe appears on page 298.)
2 pints strawberries, hulled and sliced
1 cup Sweet Whipped Cream (see recipe)

A French dessert, napoleons are named not for the infamous, short dictator but for the neapolitan style of layering pastry. Filled with pastry cream and then dusted with confectioners' sugar or thinly glazed, napoleons have been known to ruin a diet or two.

Preheat oven to 425°. Roll out pastry on a lightly floured work surface. Cut pastry to measure 12 x 12-inches. Transfer to a baking sheet and weigh down with a weight or heavy pan. Bake for 20 minutes.

Cut baked puff pastry into 12 squares. Spread half the pastry cream onto 4 squares. Place half the strawberries on pastry cream; then top with half the cream. Add another pastry square to each stack and repeat procedure, using remaining pastry cream, strawberries, and whipped cream. Cover with remaining pastry squares. Dust with confectioners' sugar.

Serve as is or with Chocolate Sauce (Recipe appears on page 295.).

Serves 4

Sweet Whipped Cream

1 cup heavy cream
1 to 2 tablespoons confectioners' sugar (depending on your sweet tooth)
½ teaspoon pure vanilla extract

Beat cream with an electric mixer at medium speed until thickened and frothy. Add sugar and vanilla and continue beating until cream holds soft peaks. Store covered in refrigerator for up to 1 hour.

Crispy Pear Packages with Chocolate Sauce

An air of mystery surrounds these pretty packages. Crack into the crispy crust and . . . well, we don't want to spoil the surprise. You'll just have to make them and see for yourself.

4 Anjou pears, peeled and cored
1 small cinnamon stick
1 vanilla bean, split
4 cups water
1 cup sugar
4 sheets phyllo dough, thawed
1 egg, beaten
Chocolate Sauce (Recipe appears on page 295.)

Cut pears into quarters. Combine cinnamon stick, vanilla bean, water, and sugar in a saucepan over medium-high heat. Bring to a simmer and add pear pieces. Cook until pears are tender, about 8 to 10 minutes. Remove pears from pan with a slotted spoon.

Preheat oven to 375°. Grease a baking sheet. Lay 1 phyllo sheet out on a work surface. Spoon one-quarter pears onto center of sheet. Wrap pears in dough and place, seam side down, on baking sheet. Brush with egg wash. Repeat with remaining phyllo sheets and pears. Bake until brown, about 5 to 8 minutes. Serve warm with chocolate sauce.

Serves 4

Types of pears

Anjou – large, egg-shaped, yellowish-green with red flecks, sweet flavor

Asian – over 100 varieties from huge golden brown to tiny yellow green, sweet flavor

Bartlett – large, bell-shaped, red or yellowish-green, musky sweet flavor

Bosc – long, thin-necked, russet color, tart flavor

Comice – round, green color, very juicy, sweet flavor

Neils – large, round, dark green color, spicy flavor

Seckel – tiny, russet color, spicy and sweet flavor

Poached Peaches with Caramel Ginger Sauce and Ice Cream

What's the scoop on this dessert? We replace the pit with a ball of ice cream and turn plain peaches into the perfect luncheon dessert.

2 cups plus 7 tablespoons sugar

4 cups water

1 vanilla bean

4 peaches, washed

½ cup heavy cream

3 ounces crystallized or candied ginger

1 cup vanilla ice cream

4 ounces pistachios, toasted

Crystallized ginger is fresh ginger that has been cooked in a sugar syrup and coated with coarse sugar. Minced crystallized ginger gives a peppery kick to cakes or pies. Sprinkle it over fresh fruit, custard, or ice cream. Look for crystallized ginger in the spice section of most food stores.

Heat 2 cups sugar, water, and vanilla bean in a saucepan over high heat. Boil for 10 minutes. Add peaches and simmer for 10 minutes. Cover and turn off heat.

In a separate pan, heat remaining 7 tablespoons sugar over medium-high heat until very dark but not burned. In a separate pan, bring cream and ginger to a boil. Remove sugar from heat. Slowly pour cream into sugar, stirring to combine.

When peaches are tender and slightly cooled, peel, halve, and remove pits. Place a ball of ice cream in place of each pit. Ladle sauce over peaches and sprinkle with pistachios.

Serves 8

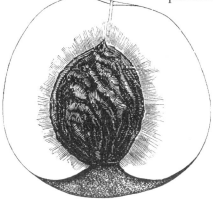

Applejack Apple Puff

Normandy is one of the only regions in France that has no vineyards. What the area does have is apples . . . lots and lots of apples. There may not be much wine in Normandy, but who needs wine when you have Calvados, an apple brandy that is the secret ingredient of this favorite dessert.

1 sheet frozen puff pastry, thawed

1 egg white

11 tablespoons confectioners' sugar

4 tablespoons sliced toasted almonds

4 tablespoons butter

1 pound Granny Smith apples, peeled, cored, and sliced

10 tablespoons granulated sugar

2 ounces Calvados

Preheat oven to 400°. Roll out pastry on a lightly floured work surface and cut in half. Place pastry on a baking sheet and prick with a fork.

Combine egg white and confectioners' sugar in a mixing bowl and mix for 2 minutes. Spread sugar mixture on one pastry half. Sprinkle with 2 tablespoons almonds. Bake both sheets for 15 to 20 minutes.

Melt butter in a sauté pan over medium heat. Add apples and granulated sugar and sauté for 15 minutes. Add Calvados and remaining almonds and stir to combine.

Place plain pastry square on a serving platter. Top with apples and cover with glazed pastry square (glazed side up). Serve warm. We like it with a spoonful of cold Crème Fraîche (Recipe appears on page 289.).

Serves 4 to 6

Calvados (also known as applejack) is a dry, fiery apple brandy made in Calvados, which is in the Normandy region of northern France. It is used for flavoring desserts, chicken, pork, and veal.

Paris-Brest

In 1891, a French pastry chef created this pastry which resembles a bicycle wheel in honor of the famous bicycle race from Paris to Brest. Traditionally filled with a praline-flavored mixture of pastry cream, buttercream, and Italian meringue, we fill ours with praline powder and pastry cream.

Choux Paste (Recipe appears on page 299.)
1 egg, beaten
¾ cup sliced almonds
½ cup sugar
Pastry Cream (Recipe appears on page 298.)
Confectioners' sugar

Called "pâte feuilletée" in French, puff pastry requires patience and care in its preparation. The process of rolling and folding dough results in up to 500 to 600 layers of this buttery treat. Baking the dough produces a flaky pastry that can be used in making croissants, napoleons, and other French delights.

Preheat oven to 350°. Butter a large baking sheet. Put choux paste into a pastry bag fitted with a large plain tip. Pipe a 9-inch circle onto prepared baking sheet. Fill in circle with choux paste. Pipe two more circles on top of original circle. Brush with egg and sprinkle ¼ cup sliced almonds on top. Pipe remaining paste to form 8 small eclairs (about the size and shape of a thumb) on the same baking sheet. Brush with egg. Bake for 10 to 15 minutes until golden brown. Remove from oven and cool.

Melt sugar in a saucepan over medium heat. Add remaining ½ cup almonds and cook until mixture is a light caramel color. Pour mixture onto oiled sheet pan and cool until set. When cool, break praline into pieces. Place pieces in a food processor and grind into a powder. Fold praline powder into pastry cream. Reserve.

Carefully cut the circle in half horizontally. Place pastry cream in a pastry bag fitted with a star tip. Pipe about half the cream into the bottom half of circle. Cover with top half of circle. Pipe some cream into eclairs and arrange eclairs in the center of circle to form spokes. Pipe remaining cream between eclairs. Dust with confectioners' sugar and serve.

Serves 8

Caramel-Orange Bûche de Noël

1½ cups sliced toasted almonds

2 teaspoons flour

6 large eggs, separated

5 tablespoons firmly packed brown sugar

1 teaspoon grated orange zest

½ teaspoon vanilla

½ teaspoon cream of tartar

⅛ teaspoon salt

Orange Buttercream (Recipe appears on page 233.)

Confectioners' sugar

Preheat oven to 300°. Butter a 11 x 17-inch baking sheet. Line with parchment paper. Butter and flour paper. Combine almonds and flour in a food processor and process until almonds are coarsely ground.

Combine egg yolks and brown sugar in a mixing bowl and beat for 5 minutes. Stir in zest and vanilla. In a separate bowl, beat egg whites, cream of tartar, and salt until stiff. Fold egg whites into yolk mixture. Fold in almond mixture.

Spread batter in prepared sheet. Bake for 30 minutes. Slide cake and parchment paper onto a rack and cool. Loosen parchment from cake and invert cake onto another parchment-lined baking sheet. Spread half of orange buttercream over cake, leaving a ½-inch border all around. Roll up cake, jelly roll style, starting at the top long end and rolling forward. Arrange rolled cake, seam side down, on a serving platter. Cut 2 inches off each end on a bias. Attach ends to top of cake with buttercream to form branches. Spread remaining buttercream over cake, including trimmed ends. Chill for 1 hour. Dust with confectioners' sugar. Garnish with holly branches and cranberries and slice to serve.

Serves 8 to 10

Bûche de Noël resembles a yule log and is the traditional centerpiece of the holiday table. There is no "right" way to do this festive dessert: you can decorate it any way you like. Children in particular come up with lots of creative ideas.

Orange Buttercream

Buttercream can be used as both a filling and a frosting for cakes and desserts. Always use high-quality sweet butter.

6 large egg yolks

⅓ cup firmly packed brown sugar

2 tablespoons flour

1½ cups half-and-half

8 ounces white chocolate, chopped

1½ teaspoons grated orange zest

1 cup butter

1 tablespoon orange liqueur

Whisk together yolks, sugar, and flour in a mixing bowl. Bring half-and-half to a boil in a heavy saucepan. Slowly whisk hot liquid into egg yolk mixture. Return mixture to saucepan. Add white chocolate and zest and simmer until smooth. Remove from heat, cover, and allow to cool completely.

Beat butter and liqueur in a mixing bowl until fluffy. Stir in cooled cream. Store in refrigerator for up to 2 weeks but bring to room temperature before using.

Croquembouche

Literally "crunch in the mouth," croquembouche is a French dessert specialty. It consists of small custard-filled cream puffs that are shaped into a cone and glazed with caramelized sugar. It is often used as the centerpiece at French weddings, First Communion celebrations, and Christmas parties. We suggest you make it anytime you feel festive.

Choux Paste (Recipe appears on page 299.)
1 egg, beaten
Pastry Cream (Recipe appears on page 298.)
1 cup granulated sugar
⅓ cup water

Preheat oven to 400°. Line a baking sheet with parchment paper. Place choux paste in a pastry bag fitted with a ½-inch plain tube. Pipe 1-inch mounds onto the baking sheet, 1 inch apart. Brush with egg wash. Bake for 20 to 25 minutes or until puffs are firm and brown. Pierce bottoms of each puff with the tip of a small knife.

Place pastry cream in a pastry bag fitted with a small tip. Pipe cream into choux puffs.

Combine sugar and water in a saucepan over high heat. Bring to a boil and cook until mixture is light golden brown.

Dip choux puffs in caramel and arrange in a 10-inch ring on a large serving platter. Fill the ring with more dipped puffs. Build a second, slightly smaller layer in the same manner. Continue the process, layer by layer, until a conical shape is formed. Drizzle remaining caramel over entire croquembouche. Garnish with spun sugar, candies, flowers, etc., using the caramel as an adhesive. Pull apart to eat, taking one cream puff at a time.

Serves up to 20

Cappuccino Cheesecake

Although the French consider cheesecake to be a plain, country-style dessert, there's nothing plain about this creamy coffee-flavored confection.

½ cup butter

2 cups graham cracker crumbs

½ teaspoon cinnamon

1½ cups sugar

2½ pounds cream cheese, softened

4 large eggs, room temperature

½ cup sour cream

1 teaspoon vanilla extract

½ cup espresso, cooled

Try to avoid lumps in your cheesecake. Lumps are caused by adding the eggs to the cream cheese too fast or by not scraping down the sides of the mixing bowl.

Preheat oven to 325°. Melt butter in a saucepan over medium heat. Stir in graham cracker crumbs, cinnamon, and ½ cup sugar. Press mixture into the bottom of a 10-inch springform pan. Reserve.

In a large mixing bowl, beat cream cheese and remaining sugar for 1 minute on high speed. Scrape down sides with a rubber spatula. Lower speed and add eggs, one at a time. Scrape down sides. Stir in remaining ingredients. (Do not overbeat: the less air incorporated, the better.)

Pour mixture into prepared pan and place in a water bath. Bake for 80 minutes. Set on rack to cool before removing from pan.

Serves 10

from the cooking school at la campagne ~ from the cooking school at la campagne ~ from the cooking school at la campagne ~ from the cooking school at la campagne ~ from the cooking school at la campagne ~ from the cooking school at la campagne ~ from the cooking school at la campagne ~ from the cooking school at la campagne ~ from the cooking school at la campagne ~ from the cooking school at la campagne ~ from the cooking school at la campagne ~ from the cooking school at la campagne ~ from the cooking school at la campagne ~ from the cooking school at la campagne ~ from the cooking school at la campagne ~ from the

comforting
conclusions

Clafouti

Clafouti is a type of puffy French fruit pancake. Although cherries are usually used, other fruits such as apples, apricots, berries, or plums may be substituted. Clafouti is not only a refreshing summer dessert (or brunch entree), it is also a great way to use bruised or overabundant seasonal fruit.

3 eggs

1¼ cups milk

½ cup sugar

Pinch of salt

1 teaspoon rum

1 teaspoon vanilla extract

½ cup flour

3 cups pitted fresh cherries

Confectioners' sugar

Preheat oven to 350°. Place eggs, milk, sugar, salt, rum, vanilla, and flour in a blender and process for 1 minute. Pour batter to ¼ inch in an 8- or 9-inch Pyrex pie plate. Warm a burner on medium heat. Set pie plate over burner for 1 to 2 minutes or until a film has set. Remove from heat. Pour in cherries and spread to cover bottom of plate. Cover with remaining batter. Bake for 40 to 50 minutes or until an inserted skewer comes out clean. (The clafouti will be puffy and brown.) Sprinkle with confectioners' sugar and serve warm.

Serves 6 to 8

clafouti
[kla-foo-TEE]

This country dessert, originally from the Limousin region in France, is made by topping a layer of fresh fruit with custard.

Oeufs à la Neige

Also called Floating Island, this longtime favorite French dessert is still served in Michelin three-star restaurants.

3 cups milk
1 vanilla bean, split and scraped
8 egg whites
⅔ cup plus ½ cup sugar
8 egg yolks
Caramel (Recipe appears on page 295.)

Combine milk and vanilla bean in a heavy saucepan over medium-high heat and bring to a simmer. Reduce heat and cook until steam just rises off the top.

Meanwhile, beat egg whites to soft peaks. Gradually add ⅔ cup sugar, whipping continuously until stiff, shiny peaks are formed. (Do not over whip egg whites). Drop 1 tablespoon whipped egg whites into hot milk and cook until firm, about 3 to 4 minutes, turning once. Remove and place on a paper towel-lined baking sheet. Repeat with remaining meringue. Cool and reserve.

After all meringue portions are poached, bring milk back to a simmer. Whisk together yolks and ½ cup sugar in a bowl. Slowly add milk to yolks until well incorporated. Return contents to saucepan. Cook on low heat, stirring often, until mixture is thick enough to coat the back of a spoon. Transfer to a bowl, cool, and reserve.

Place custard on a serving plate, top with meringues, and drizzle with caramel.

Serves 6

The meringues and custard should be prepared in advance, and the caramel should be prepared at service time.

Raspberry Lemon Mousse with Lavender Orange Sauce

¾ ounce gelatin powder
¾ cup fresh lemon juice
10 tablespoons heavy cream
6 eggs, separated
1¾ cups sugar
3 tablespoons flour
½ pound raspberries, hulled
Lavender Orange Sauce (Recipe appears on page 299.)

Soften gelatin in cold water according to package directions. Bring lemon juice and heavy cream to a boil in a heavy-bottomed saucepan. Whisk egg yolks with ½ cup sugar. Add flour and whisk until thickened. Whisk one-third heavy cream into egg mixture and then pour combined mixture back into saucepan. Stir in softened gelatin.

Combine 1 cup sugar and egg whites in a stainless steel mixing bowl. Heat over a double boiler, whipping periodically to prevent egg whites from cooking, until a candy thermometer reads 140°. Remove from heat. Whip with electric mixer until mixture is cool and whites are stiff and glossy. Gently fold egg white mixture into lemon mixture.

Place a piece of buttered parchment paper on a sheet tray. Set a 10- or 12-inch ring mold on top of parchment paper. Pour half of lemon mousse into the mold. Cover with raspberries and then top with remaining mousse. Smooth with a spatula. Refrigerate.

When ready to serve, remove ring mold. Sprinkle mousse with remaining ¼ cup sugar and place under a preheated broiler until sugar caramelizes. Transfer mousse from parchment paper to a serving plate. Top with lavender orange sauce.

Serve 4 to 6

It is rumored that lavender can . . .

make cows produce sweet milk

invoke gods

heal wounds

give strength to women during childbirth

stop insomnia

protect children from the evil eye

drive evil demons from people

act as a tranquilizer

remind you to make a reservation at La Campagne for lunch, brunch, or dinner!

Mocha Hazelnut Mousse

At La Campagne we serve mousse in wide-mouthed stemmed glasses with biscotti and a sprig of mint. This subtle coffee-chocolate-flavored mousse is also a lovely filling for profiteroles.

3 ounces semi-sweet chocolate

1½ tablespoons espresso

2 eggs, separated

1½ teaspoons butter, softened

1 teaspoon hazelnut liqueur

1½ tablespoons sugar

Heat chocolate and coffee in a saucepan over low-medium heat. Stir to melt chocolate. Simmer until mixture is slightly thickened. Remove from heat. Add yolks, one at a time, beating thoroughly after each addition. Beat in butter and liqueur until well combined. Cool to room temperature.

In a separate bowl, beat egg whites with an electric mixer until foamy. Add sugar and beat until stiff peaks form, about 30 seconds. Fold whites gently into chocolate mixture. Transfer mousse to a serving dish or individual dessert cups. Refrigerate until set, about 2 hours.

Yields 2½ cups

Crème Brûlée

In 17th century England, this rich dessert was extremely popular. Later, the French named it crème brûlée — "burnt cream" — and the dish became a staple on restaurant menus. It is our number one selling dessert.

4 cups heavy cream
1 vanilla bean, split
1 strip orange peel
5 large egg yolks
½ cup granulated sugar
4 tablespoons coarse raw sugar

Preheat oven to 350°. Place four 4½-inch round, ¾-inch deep ramekins in a roasting pan.

Combine cream, vanilla bean, and orange peel in a heavy-bottomed saucepan over medium heat and scald. Cover and allow to infuse for 10 minutes. Meanwhile, whisk together yolks and granulated sugar in a mixing bowl. Whisk hot cream into yolks. Strain and pour into ramekins. Pour boiling water into roasting pan to reach about half way up the sides of ramekins. Cover pan with aluminum foil. Bake for 35 to 40 minutes.

Remove ramekins and chill overnight. Sprinkle raw sugar over cooked custard. Place ramekins under broiler and allow sugar to caramelize. Serve immediately.

Serves 4

Always very good, crème brûlée turns glorious when topped with bite-sized fresh fruit. Try these combinations:

apricots and strawberries

pears and currants

blood oranges and raspberries

mangoes and blackberries

peaches and blueberries

sour cherries and plums

Chocolate Crème Brûlée

4 cups heavy cream
Pinch of fresh coffee grinds
5 egg yolks
½ cup granulated sugar
3 tablespoons cocoa powder
4 tablespoons coarse raw sugar

Preheat oven to 350°. Place four 4½-inch round, ¾-inch deep ramekins in a roasting pan.

Combine cream and coffee grinds in a heavy-bottomed saucepan over medium heat and bring to a boil. Cover and allow to infuse for 10 minutes. Meanwhile, whisk together yolks and granulated sugar in a mixing bowl. Sift in cocoa powder. Whisk hot cream into yolk mixture. Strain and pour into ramekins. Pour boiling water into roasting pan to reach about halfway up the sides of ramekins. Cover pan with aluminum foil. Bake for 35 to 40 minutes. Remove and chill overnight.

Sprinkle raw sugar over cooked custard. Place ramekins under broiler and sugar caramelizes. Serve immediately.

Serves 4

Ginger Vanilla Crème Brûlée

Ginger spices up this smooth sweet dessert.

2 cups heavy cream
1 vanilla bean, split lengthwise, or 1 teaspoon vanilla extract
1 tablespoon grated ginger
6 egg yolks
½ cup plus 4 tablespoons sugar

Preheat oven to 325°. Combine cream, vanilla bean, and ginger in a 2-quart saucepan and bring to a simmer. In a separate bowl, combine yolks and ½ cup sugar and whisk until smooth. Slowly whisk cream mixture into egg yolk mixture. When thoroughly combined, strain mixture into another bowl. Divide mixture among four 8-ounce ramekins. Place ramekins in a water bath and bake for 40 to 50 minutes until custard is set. Remove from oven and cool.

Sprinkle 1 tablespoon sugar on top of each crème brûlée. Place ramekins under a broiler until sugar has caramelized or use a torch to caramelize sugar. Serve immediately.

Serves 4

Crème Caramel

In France, this custard presentation is called Crème Renversèe — "cream turned upside down." We love how this "cream" looks when plated — quivering and cool with its delicious caramel glaze dripping over the top and around the base.

¼ cup water

1 cup sugar

2 cups milk

1 vanilla bean, split

2 large eggs

2 egg yolks

Mix water and ½ cup sugar in a saucepan. Place over high heat and cook until mahogany in color. Pour into four 4-inch round, ¾-inch deep ramekins. Place ramekins in a roasting pan.

Preheat oven to 350°. Combine milk, vanilla bean, and remaining sugar in a heavy-bottomed saucepan over medium heat and bring to a boil. Cover and allow to infuse for 10 minutes. Meanwhile, whisk together eggs and egg yolks in a mixing bowl. Whisk hot milk into eggs. Strain and pour into caramel-lined ramekins. Pour boiling water into roasting pan to reach about halfway up the sides of ramekins. Cover pan with aluminum foil. Bake for 40 to 50 minutes until custard is firm. Remove ramekins and chill overnight. (Chilling at least 12 hours and as much as 48 hours allows the caramelized sugar to liquify.)

Run a paring knife around the edge of the custard and unmold onto serving plates. Some caramel will run off custard and pool on plate.

Serves 4

Crème caramel and crème brûlée are almost opposites. Crème caramel uses milk and eggs; crème brûlée uses cream and yolks. While the sugar in crème caramel is first caramelized and then poured into the bottom of the ramekins, crème brûlée is topped with sugar that is later caramelized. Finally, crème caramel is inverted and served on a plate, and crème brûlée is served in the ramekin.

The similarities? Both are out of this world.

Chocolate Soufflé

*Chocolate soufflé . . . sounds decadent, delicious, and difficult.
It is, it is, and it isn't. Make one and see for yourself.*

3 egg yolks
½ cup sugar
⅓ cup flour
Pinch of salt
1½ cups milk
6 ounces semi-sweet chocolate, cut into small pieces
1¼ cups egg whites
½ teaspoon cream of tartar
Confectioners' sugar

Preheat oven to 375°. Grease six 6-ounce soufflé dishes with butter. Dust dishes with cocoa powder. Make paper collars (see sidebar) and reserve.

Whisk together egg yolks, ¼ cup sugar, flour, and salt in a mixing bowl.

Scald milk in a small saucepan over medium-high heat. Gradually add scalded milk to egg mixture, one ladleful at a time, whipping constantly. When all hot milk has been added, immediately add chocolate pieces. Stir until chocolate is melted and smooth. Cover with plastic wrap and reserve.

In a separate bowl, whip egg whites with an electric mixer until soft peaks form. Add remaining sugar and cream of tartar and whip until peaks are stiff and shiny. Fold half of egg whites into chocolate base. Repeat with remaining whites.

Divide soufflé mixture among prepared dishes. Attach paper collars. Bake on lowest rack of oven for 30 to 35 minutes. An inserted skewer should come out barely moist. Remove collars, dust with confectioners' sugar, and serve immediately.

Serves 6

To make a paper collar

Measure pieces of wax paper 1½ times as long as the diameter of the soufflé dish and twice as high. Wrap the paper around the dish so that the lower edge of the paper rests on the countertop. Secure the paper with tape or a paper clip.

Grand Marnier Soufflé

A soufflé rises because air which is trapped in the egg whites becomes lighter and expands as it is heated. You'll be happy to know that liqueur soufflés such as the popular Grand Marnier soufflé always rise higher than fruit soufflés because the evaporated alcohol fumes help push the air and the soufflé up.

8 eggs, separated
⅔ cup plus 2 tablespoons sugar
⅓ cup orange liqueur such as Grand Marnier
2 tablespoons butter
Confectioners' sugar

Preheat oven to 450°. Butter six 1¼-cup ramekins. Use 2 tablespoons sugar to coat ramekins, tapping off excess. Refrigerate.

Beat yolks and ⅓ cup sugar in a stainless steel bowl set over simmering water, whisking until mixture is the consistency of heavy cream. Add liqueur. Transfer to a mixing bowl set over ice. Beat until cool.

Beat egg whites until frothy. Add remaining ⅓ cup sugar and beat until stiff peaks form. Fold whites into yolk mixture.

Spoon mixture into prepared ramekins. Place ramekins on a baking sheet and bake for 12 to 15 minutes. Sprinkle with confectioners' sugar.

Serves 6

Grand Marnier is a golden French liqueur with an aged cognac base that is flavored with the peel of an orange.

Individual Raspberry Soufflés

2⅓ pounds fresh or frozen raspberries
2½ tablespoons framboise or other raspberry liqueur
1¾ cups plus ⅓ cup sugar
4 cups water
Juice of 1 lemon
2 cups milk
6 large egg yolks
½ cup flour, sifted
Butter
10 large egg whites
Pinch of salt
Confectioners' sugar

Preheat oven to 425°. Butter six 4-inch round, 2½-inch deep ramekins. Coat inside of each with sugar. Refrigerate.

Select 18 well-formed raspberries and place in a shallow bowl. Sprinkle with 1¼ tablespoons framboise. Reserve.

Place remaining raspberries, 1½ cups sugar, and water in a saucepan over high heat. Bring to a boil and cook for 5 minutes. Remove from heat and transfer to a food processor or blender and puree. Push through a fine sieve to remove seeds.

Place one-third puree in a bowl with remaining framboise and lemon juice. Stir to combine and keep warm. Return remaining two-thirds puree to pan. Cook over low heat until mixture is the consistency of jam.

Combine milk and ⅓ cup sugar in a saucepan over high heat. Bring to a boil and remove from heat. Whisk together egg yolks and ¼ cup sugar in a bowl. Stir in flour. Whisk in hot milk. Return mixture to pan and simmer for 3 minutes, stirring constantly. Transfer pastry cream to a large mixing bowl and dot surface with butter.

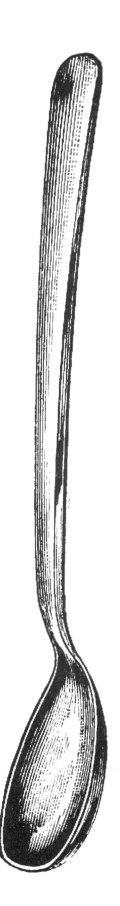

Fold raspberry "jam" into pastry cream. In a mixing bowl, whip egg whites until frothy. Add pinch of salt and whip until soft peaks form. Fold one-third whites into pastry cream. When incorporated, fold in remaining whites.

Pour pastry cream mixture into prepared ramekins halfway to the top. Put 3 reserved raspberries into each ramekin. Fill with remaining pastry cream mixture. Level tops with a knife. Bake for 10 minutes. Dust with confectioners' sugar and serve with warm raspberry puree.

Serves 6

Warm Chocolate Velvet

What is more universal then the pleasure derived from the melting of chocolate on one's tongue? A few things perhaps, but it is no wonder that the cocoa tree's genus, Theobroma, *translates into "food of the gods."*

16 ounces semi-sweet chocolate

14 ounces butter

8 eggs

2 cups sugar

2 cups all-purpose flour

½ cup cocoa powder

1½ teaspoons baking powder

Preheat oven to 375°. Butter and flour twelve 4-ounce ramekins. Melt chocolate and butter in a bowl over a simmering double boiler. Whisk in eggs and sugar over a boiling double boiler until very hot (140°), about 5 minutes.

Sift together flour, cocoa powder, and baking powder. Fold dry ingredients into chocolate mixture. Fill prepared ramekins with mixture and bake for 15 to 20 minutes. Serve warm.

Serves 12

The world's finest cocoa beans traditionally come from Venezuela and Costa Rico. Unsweetened cocoa powder is the finely ground product that remains after the cocoa butter has been extracted from the cocoa mass. There are 2 types of cocoa power: Dutch process and natural unsweetened. We prefer Dutch process because it has a smoother flavor and a darker color. It also dissolves easier in liquid.

Vanilla Ice Cream

This extra thick and rich ice cream should be cooked over very low heat or in a double boiler so the egg yolks do not scramble.

6 large egg yolks
1 cup sugar
1½ cups half-and-half
2 vanilla beans, split
1 cup heavy cream

Beat yolks and sugar until thickened. Reserve.

Bring half-and-half and vanilla beans to a simmer in a heavy saucepan. Lower heat to low. Slowly beat hot half-and-half mixture into egg yolk mixture; then pour combined mixture back into saucepan. Cook, stirring constantly, until mixture is thick enough to coat the back of a spoon. (Be careful to not let mixture boil.) Remove from heat and pour mixture through a strainer into a large, clean bowl. Cool slightly, then stir in cream.

Cover and refrigerate until cold. Freeze in ice cream machine according to manufacturer's instructions.

Yields about 1 quart

Chocolate Truffle Rum Ice Cream

Ganache is used to make truffles. This recipe uses the same ingredients that comprise ganache — scalded cream and bittersweet chocolate — and adds a smooth shot of rum. As with ganache, use the best quality chocolate available.

2 large egg yolks
½ cup sugar
1 cup milk
½ cup premium rum
¾ cup cocoa powder
6 ounces bittersweet chocolate, chopped
1½ cups heavy cream
1 teaspoon vanilla extract

Beat yolks and sugar until fluffy. Reserve.

Bring milk and rum to a simmer in a heavy saucepan. Whisk in cocoa and bring mixture back to a simmer. Stir for 3 minutes. Slowly beat hot milk mixture into egg yolk mixture; then pour combined mixture back into saucepan. Cook, stirring constantly, until mixture is thick enough to coat the back of a spoon. (Be careful to not let mixture boil.) Remove from heat and pour mixture through a strainer into a large, clean bowl.

Place chopped chocolate in a bowl. Bring cream to a simmer in a saucepan and pour over chocolate. Stir until chocolate is melted and smooth. Pour chocolate mixture into custard and combine well. Stir in vanilla.

Cover and refrigerate until cold. Freeze in ice cream machine according to manufacturer's instructions.

Yields about 1 quart

ganache

[gahn-AHSH]

Ganache is a very versatile rich chocolate icing made of chocolate and cream. It is usually poured over cakes or tortes but can also be used as a filling, an ingredient in complex desserts, or the basis for truffles.

Burnt Sugar Ice Cream

Intense caramel color and flavor make this ice cream a natural complement to hot-from-the-oven apple pie.

1½ cups sugar
½ cup water
2 cups heavy cream
8 egg yolks, whisked
2 cups milk

Place sugar and water in a heavy saucepan and dissolve sugar. Cook liquid on high heat until sugar is a dark caramel color. Slowly and carefully add heavy cream in intervals, whisking between each addition. (The cream will bubble violently and emit a lot of steam, so be careful to not get burned.) When cream is incorporated, slowly whisk mixture into egg yolks. Whisk in milk.

Freeze in an ice cream maker according to manufacturer's instructions.

Yields 1½ quarts

Lavender Ice Cream

What is the taste of lavender? Woodsy, sweet, pungent, citrus, even a bit minty. What's the taste of lavender ice cream? Wild.

6 large egg yolks

2 teaspoons vanilla extract

¾ cup honey

2 cups milk

1 cup heavy cream

1 tablespoon dried lavender blossoms

Beat yolks with vanilla and honey until mixture triples in volume. Bring milk, heavy cream, and lavender to a simmer in a heavy saucepan over medium heat. Whisk one-third milk mixture into yolk mixture; then pour combined mixture back into saucepan. Cook, stirring constantly, until mixture coats the back of a spoon.

Remove from heat and pour mixture through a strainer into a large, clean bowl. Cool over a bowl of ice water. Cover and refrigerate until cold. Freeze in an ice cream maker according to manufacturer's instructions.

Yields approximately 1 quart

Summer is an appropriate time to enjoy lavender (especially lavender ice cream). In ancient times, people believed that lavender was a remedy for colds, wounds, aches, and even sadness, so they burned it as a divine offering on midsummer's nights.

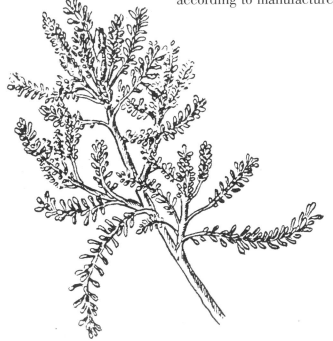

from the cooking school at la campagne ~ from the cooking school at la campagne ~ from the cooking school at la campagne ~ from the cooking school at la campagne ~ from the cooking school at la campagne ~ **from the cooking school at la campagne** ~ from the cooking school at la campagne ~ from the cooking school at la campagne ~ from the cooking school at la campagne ~ from the cooking school at la campagne ~ from the cooking school at la campagne ~ from the cooking school at la campagne ~ from the cooking school at la campagne ~ from the cooking school at la campagne ~ from the cooking school at la campagne ~ from the

La Campagne

brunch

Buttermilk Scones

Better than your mom used to make, these scones can be topped with butter or jam, but I like them plain and hot out of the oven.

3 cups all-purpose flour

⅓ cup sugar

2½ teaspoons baking powder

½ teaspoon baking soda

¾ teaspoon salt

¾ cup cold unsalted butter, cut into small pieces

1 cup buttermilk

1 tablespoon grated orange or lemon zest

¼ cup unsalted butter, melted

¼ cup sugar

4 tablespoons diced dried fruits, optional

Preheat oven to 425°. In a medium bowl, combine flour, sugar, baking powder, baking soda, and salt and stir with a fork. Add cold butter pieces. Use a pastry blender or two knives to work butter into flour mixture until mixture resembles coarse cornmeal. (Don't worry if a few large butter pieces remain; they'll add to the scones' flakiness.) Pour in buttermilk and zest and mix with a fork until ingredients are just moistened and dough pulls away from the side of bowl. (Add another tablespoon of buttermilk if dough looks dry.)

Turn dough onto lightly floured surface. Knead briefly, about 10 to 12 turns. Roll or pat dough to ½-inch thick. Cut with a floured 2-inch round cutter or cut into triangles with a sharp knife. Place scones onto an ungreased baking sheet. Brush each with melted butter and sprinkle with sugar. Bake for 10 to 12 minutes. Immediately remove from baking sheet to cool.

Yields about 1 dozen

True buttermilk is simply the liquid left after butter is churned. Commercially produced, cultured buttermilk is made by adding bacteria to skim milk to give it a tart flavor.

Cranberry Ginger Muffins

Although our muffin selection changes weekly, this is our all time favorite. Be sure to use grated ginger, not dried, for maximum flavor.

Cultivated in the more northern areas of this continent, the cranberry can be found freshest in the local market from midfall to early winter. Don't limit the use of this tart berry to Thanksgiving sauce. It's delicious in pies, jams, and baked goods. Sprinkle a few on salads too.

⅔ cup apple juice

1 cup oil

1 egg

1 teaspoon vanilla

¼ cup sugar

¼ cup packed brown sugar

½ cup jellied cranberry sauce

2 cups flour

1 teaspoon baking powder

2 teaspoons grated ginger

Preheat oven to 375°. Grease bottoms only of 12 medium muffin cups or line with paper baking cups. Combine apple juice, oil, egg, vanilla, sugars, and cranberry sauce. In a separate bowl, combine flour, baking powder, and ginger. Add dry ingredients to wet mixture and blend until ingredients are moistened. (Batter should be lumpy; do not overmix.) Spoon batter into prepared muffin cups, filling each three-quarters full. Bake for 15 to 18 minutes until nicely colored and an inserted toothpick comes out clean.

Yields 12 muffins

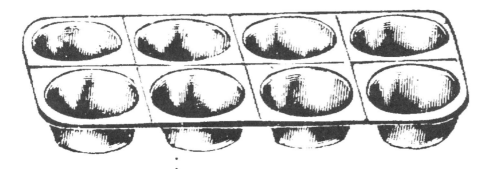

Apple Walnut Breakfast Squares

A childhood favorite of one of our chefs, these breakfast squares will get you going in the morning, but they're also a great addition to any lunch box or picnic basket. In a pinch they even make for a great dessert when topped with some sweet whipped cream.

5 tablespoons butter

1 cup sugar

1 egg

1 teaspoon vanilla extract

3 apples, peeled, cored and shredded

¾ cup chopped toasted walnuts

1½ cups all-purpose flour

1 teaspoon cinnamon

¾ teaspoon baking soda

½ teaspoon salt

½ teaspoon allspice

½ teaspoon nutmeg

Preheat oven to 325°. Grease and lightly flour a 9-inch square bread pan. Cream butter, sugar, and egg together with an electric mixer until light and fluffy. Stir in vanilla, apples, and walnuts.

In a separate bowl, combine dry ingredients. Stir dry ingredients into apple mixture. Pour batter into prepared pan and bake until an inserted toothpick comes out clean, about 1 hour.

Cut into squares and serve warm or at room temperature.

Serves 6 to 8

Potato-Chive Blini

Chopped chives add a fleck of color and dash of freshness to these sturdy, handheld mini pancakes. You can also add grated carrot or zucchini to the batter for even more flavor, color, and texture.

1 pound russet potatoes, peeled and quartered
¼ cup milk
4 tablespoons flour
3 large eggs
3 large egg whites
½ teaspoon chopped chives
Salt and pepper
Oil

Cook potatoes in boiling salted water until tender, about 30 minutes. Push potatoes through a ricer or puree in a food processor. Transfer potatoes to a large mixing bowl. Stir in milk and flour. Beat in eggs, one at a time.

In a separate bowl, beat egg whites until stiff peaks form. Fold whites and chives into potato mixture. Season to taste with salt and pepper.

Heat a small skillet over medium heat. Coat with a thin layer of oil. Pour 1 tablespoon batter into skillet and cook until bubbles start breaking on the uncooked side, about 2 minutes. Turn blini over with a spatula and finish cooking, about 1 minute. Repeat with remaining batter. Keep blini warm until ready to serve. Serve with caviar, gravlax, or Sunday Scrambled Eggs (Recipe appears on page 260.).

Serves 8

Although blini are most often used to serve caviar, they can be a base for hors d'oeuvres. Some nice toppings would include:

swirls of smoked salmon with crème fraîche

rillettes, tapenade, aïoli, or pesto

goat cheese and fresh rosemary

chopped roasted vegetables

Sunday Scrambled Eggs

Scrambled eggs were the first thing I ever learned to cook. With this version — the culmination of over 35 years of tinkering with the basic egg and milk "recipe" — I believe I have reached egg nirvana.

3 eggs, beaten
Salt and pepper
1 teaspoon fresh butter
3 teaspoons sour cream
1 teaspoon minced onion
1 teaspoon chopped chives or parsley

Season beaten eggs with salt and pepper to taste. Melt butter in a skillet over medium heat. Pour eggs into hot pan and gently whisk until eggs are cooked but very moist. Remove pan from heat and stir in sour cream, onion, and chives or parsley. Serve as is, with caviar, or atop Potato-Chive Blini (Recipe appears on page 259.).

Serves 2

Chives are easy to grow and give a delicate onion-like flavor to food, especially salads, sauces, vegetables, meat, poultry, fish, and egg and cheese dishes. We also add them to herb butters and cheeses, salad dressings, dips, and breads. The flavor and nutrients are diminished during cooking, so add chives in the final minutes of cooking or sprinkle over foods after they are plated.

Truffled Scrambled Eggs

With so many people watching their cholesterol, eating eggs has become something of a luxury. So we've made them luxurious with the addition of truffles, cream, and butter. Serve this dish for a celebration breakfast with a bottle of champagne and count your blessings instead of your cholesterol.

2 canned black truffles

10 large eggs

8 tablespoons unsalted butter

½ teaspoon salt

White pepper to taste

2 tablespoons heavy cream

Dice 1½ truffles and reserve. Slice remaining truffle half and reserve. Set a fine strainer over a bowl. Break eggs into strainer, pierce yolks, and allow eggs to drip into bowl.

Melt 2 tablespoons butter in a double boiler or a stainless steel mixing bowl set over boiling water. Add eggs and stir constantly with a spatula for 1 to 2 minutes. Season with salt and pepper and cook 7 to 8 minutes. Add remaining butter, a little at a time. When eggs have bound together and there are very few curds, whisk in cream and diced truffles. Cook for 1 minute.

Spoon eggs into warmed glass bowls or puff pastry cups and garnish with truffle slices.

Serves 4 to 6

Prepare truffles by lightly brushing, peeling (not necessary with white truffle), and slicing or shaving as thin as possible. A truffle slicer is a convenient tool that has an adjustable blade held at a 45 degree angle. Simply press the truffle down and across the blade for thin slices of this most delicious fungus.

Nest of Egg Niçoise

Baked tomatoes form a jaunty container for robust vegetable-laden scrambled eggs. Easily assembled ahead of time, be sure to serve them hot from the oven.

4 large tomatoes

Salt and pepper

3 tablespoons olive oil

1 small onion, minced

2 cloves garlic, chopped

3 tablespoons chopped black olives

4 juniper berries

1 teaspoon thyme leaves

4 eggs

Preheat oven to 400°. Cut tops off tomatoes. Carefully scoop out the fruit and reserve. Place tomatoes in an ovenproof dish. Season with salt and pepper and drizzle with 1 tablespoon olive oil. Bake for 7 minutes.

Meanwhile, heat remaining olive oil in a saucepan over medium heat. Add onion and garlic and cook until soft, about 5 minutes. Roughly chop reserved tomato fruit and add to pan. Add olives, juniper berries, thyme, and salt and pepper to taste. Cook for 5 minutes.

Pour sauce into each baked tomato, reserving 4 teaspoons. Crack 1 egg into each tomato. Cover each egg with 1 teaspoon reserved sauce. Return to oven and bake for 10 minutes. Serve immediately.

Serves 4

Rarely eaten raw, bitter juniper berries are mostly used to flavor meats, poultry, egg dishes, and sauces. Some might argue that the greatest culinary contribution of these blue-black berries is their use in the flavoring of gin.

Phyllo Baked Eggs with Tomato and Prosciutto

A favorite brunch entree on Mother's Day, these puffed packets look terrific when cut open with a grand flourish at the table.

12 sheets phyllo dough

8 tablespoons tomato sauce

4 eggs

2 tablespoons melted butter

8 slices proscuitto, cut into strips

Preheat oven to 375°. Brush 3 sheets phyllo with butter and stack together. Repeat with remaining dough to form 4 stacks. Place stacks on a nonstick baking sheet.

Place 2 tablespoons tomato sauce in the center of each stack. Break egg over sauce. Fold phyllo in half to cover egg. Brush with butter and bake for 10 minutes. Transfer to a serving platter, cut each packet in half, and sprinkle with proscuitto.

Serves 4

Working with phyllo

Thaw frozen phyllo in the refrigerator overnight. Phyllo will become very brittle so do not open the package until you are ready to use the sheets. Then keep the sheets you are using covered with a damp cloth to keep them from drying out.

Smoked Salmon Scrambled Eggs in Puff Pastry

Don't just reserve this unabashedly elegant entree for special occasion brunches: it's so good you'll want it morning, noon, and night. Do not oversalt as the salmon is salty enough.

2 sheets frozen puff pastry, thawed

4 tablespoons unsalted butter

8 eggs

Salt and pepper

¼ cup Crème Fraîche (Recipe appears on page 289.) or
   heavy cream, chilled

1 small onion, minced

1 bunch chives, finely cut

8 slices smoked salmon

Preheat oven to 425°. Roll out pastry onto a lightly floured work surface. Cut pastry into four 4 x 4-inch squares. Place pastry on a nonstick baking sheet and bake for 15 minutes.

Melt butter in a saucepan over medium heat. Beat eggs, season with salt and pepper, and pour into pan. Stir gently with a wooden spoon, scraping eggs from sides and bottom of pan until cooked to desired doneness. Remove from heat and stir in cold crème fraîche. Stir in onions and chives. Season to taste with salt and pepper.

Place puff pastry on 4 serving plates. Top with eggs and cover with smoked salmon.

Serves 4

You can make a whole meal out of smoked salmon and we often do. Slice the cold salmon as thinly as possible on the diagonal just prior to serving. Splash with a touch of lemon juice and serve the delicate slivers with pumpernickel, caviar, sour cream, or dill. Salmon is also fantastic with cream cheese and tomato and onion slices on lightly toasted onion bagels.

Potato Pesto Pancakes

We've updated Grandmom's "egg in the hole" recipe by replacing ho-hum toast with peppy potato pancakes and topping each off with a heady dollop of pesto.

1 red pepper, cut into small strips

1 green pepper, cut into small strips

1 onion, cut into small strips

1 teaspoon chopped garlic

3 medium russet potatoes, shredded

Salt and pepper

1 teaspoon olive oil

1 teaspoon dry oregano

4 eggs

2 teaspoons Pesto (Recipe appears on page 288.)

Preheat oven to 400°. Combine peppers, onion, and garlic in a bowl. Stir in potatoes. Season with salt and pepper.

Heat oil in a nonstick skillet over medium-high heat. Divide mixture into four portions. Place a portion of potato mixture into skillet and press with a spoon to form a round cake. When browned, flip cake and make a hole in the center with a spoon. Place cake on a nonstick baking sheet. Repeat process with the three remaining potato portions.

Break 1 egg into each hole. Bake for 3 to 4 minutes until eggs are cooked. Sprinkle with pesto and serve.

Serves 4

Cheese Soufflé

The perfect soufflé comes out of the oven crisp on the outside, creamy on the inside, and trembling high above its mold. Our perfect cheese soufflé is rich enough to be served sans sauce for brunch, lunch, or even a light dinner — just make sure to serve it as soon as it comes out of the oven.

2 tablespoons melted butter

1 cup freshly grated Parmesan cheese

6 tablespoons unsalted butter, softened

¾ cup flour

2 cups milk

7 eggs, separated

⅓ cup grated Gruyère cheese

¼ teaspoon cayenne pepper

¼ teaspoon ground nutmeg

2 teaspoons salt

Preheat oven to 400°. Coat the inside of eight 5-ounce soufflé cups with melted butter. Dust with 2 tablespoons Parmesan cheese. Reserve.

Cut butter into flour. Scald milk in a small saucepan over medium-high heat. Whisk flour mixture into milk and cook to a thick paste, stirring constantly. Remove from heat. Add egg yolks, one at a time, stirring constantly. Stir in remaining Parmesan cheese, Gruyère cheese, cayenne, nutmeg, and salt.

In a separate bowl, whip egg whites until stiff peaks form. Fold whites into batter one-third at a time.

Fill soufflé cups three-quarters full. Bake for 15 minutes. Serve immediately.

Serves 8

Nothing strikes fear in the heart of the amateur chef quite like the word soufflé. Although baked soufflés require unmistakable timing and must be served immediately, they are not difficult to assemble and the result is worth the worry.

Mint Frittata with Tomato

Frittata is an Italian-style omelette whose ingredients are cooked together in a skillet, finished in the oven, and cut into wedges. A refreshing burst of mint makes this frittata unique.

2 large plum tomatoes, diced

3 tablespoons olive oil

1 tablespoon balsamic vinegar

Salt and pepper

8 large eggs, lightly beaten

2 tablespoons grated Pecorino Romano cheese

1 tablespoon fresh breadcrumbs

3 tablespoons chiffonade mint leaves

An ancient symbol of hospitality, mint is grown all over the world, most notably native to Europe and Asia.

Combine tomatoes, 1 tablespoon oil, and vinegar. Season to taste with salt and pepper. Reserve.

In a separate bowl, beat together eggs, cheese, breadcrumbs, mint, and salt and pepper to taste.

Preheat oven to 400°. Heat remaining oil in a nonstick skillet over medium-high heat. Pour in egg mixture and stir until the bottom is set but the top is still runny, about 6 minutes. Place in oven until lightly browned, about 3 to 4 minutes. Remove from oven and cool for 2 minutes. Loosen bottom with a spatula and invert on a large serving plate. Top with tomatoes, cut into wedges, and serve immediately.

Serves 4

Poached Figs with French Toast

*The enticing flavors of cinnamon, ginger, and port give a
sophisticated accent to the sweet stickiness of fresh figs.
Although extremely perishable, use fresh figs whenever possible.
They are available in stores from June through October.*

2 cups port wine

Peels of 1 lemon

Peels of 1 orange

1 cinnamon stick

1 vanilla bean

3 black peppercorns or 1 chunk ginger

16 figs

1 egg, beaten

½ cup milk

2 tablespoons sugar

4 thick slices stale bread

2 tablespoons butter

Combine port wine, lemon and orange peels, cinnamon
stick, vanilla bean, and peppercorns in a saucepan and
bring to a simmer. Add figs and poach for 10 minutes.
Remove from heat, cover, and allow to sit for 30 minutes.

Remove figs and reserve. Strain poaching liquid into
another pan and cook over medium heat until syrupy.

Whisk together egg, milk, and sugar in a mixing bowl.
Soak bread in mixture for about 5 minutes. Melt butter in a
nonstick skillet over medium heat. Sauté bread in butter
until golden brown on both sides.

Spoon 2 or 3 tablespoons warm syrup into the center of 4
warm plates. Top with French toast and arrange figs around
toast. Drizzle with remaining syrup.

Serves 4

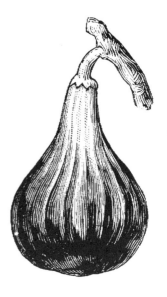

Banana Stuffed Brioche French Toast with Mango Syrup

Bananas, raspberries, and macadamia nuts give a fresh twist to an old French favorite. Make some extra mango syrup: it tastes great drizzled over vanilla ice cream or pound cake.

3 bananas, peeled and sliced into disks

2 tablespoons lemon juice

Zest of 2 lemons

12 slices brioche (each 1½ inches thick)

6 eggs, beaten

1 cup heavy cream

1 teaspoon vanilla extract

1 tablespoon sugar

Pinch of salt

½ teaspoon cinnamon

¼ teaspoon nutmeg

6 tablespoons unsalted butter

½ pint raspberries

4 tablespoons chopped macadamia nuts

Mango Syrup (Recipe appears on page 271.)

Toss bananas with lemon juice and zest. Cut a pocket into each bread slice and stuff with bananas. Reserve.

Preheat oven to 375°. Whisk together eggs, cream, vanilla, sugar, salt, cinnamon, and nutmeg. Soak bread in mixture until very soft. Melt butter in a skillet over medium heat. Sauté soaked bread until golden brown on both sides. Transfer to a baking sheet and bake until bread puffs, about 3 to 4 minutes.

Divide bread among 4 warm plates. Top with raspberries and macadamia nuts. Serve with mango syrup.

Serves 4

Originating and sacred in India, mangoes change from yellow to orange as they ripen at room temperature. This exotic fruit is wonderful eaten raw by itself, in salad, or atop ice cream and provides an excellent base for syrups and salad dressings. Look for mangos throughout the summer in your local produce section.

Tonga Toast

When we list this on our brunch menu, kids invariably order it, but it's the adults who truly fall for the unique coffee-flavored syrup.

1 loaf French bread
3 to 4 bananas, peeled
4 eggs
1 cup milk
1 tablespoon sugar
1 teaspoon cinnamon
4 tablespoons butter
Espresso Syrup (see recipe)

Slice bread lengthwise without cutting all the way through. Open loaf and scoop out a ½-inch-deep pocket. Place bananas in the channel and close bread, pressing down firmly. Slice loaf on a bias into 1-inch slices. Reserve.

Whip together eggs, milk, sugar, and cinnamon in a mixing bowl. Dip bread slices into mixture and drain.

Melt butter in a nonstick skillet over medium heat. Sauté soaked bread until golden brown on both sides. Serve with espresso syrup.

Serves 4 to 6

Espresso Syrup

1 cup strongly brewed espresso
1½ cups maple syrup

Heat espresso in a saucepan until liquid is reduced by half. Add syrup. Simmer until combined. Serve warm.

Mango Syrup

4 ripe mangoes, peeled and pitted
1 tablespoon lemon juice
½ cup water
¼ cup sugar
1 tablespoon orange liqueur

Combine mangoes and lemon juice in a blender and puree.
Combine water and sugar in a saucepan and bring to a boil. Remove from heat and allow to cool completely. Combine mango puree, sugar syrup, and liqueur. Refrigerate overnight.

Curd is a creamy mixture made by combining and cooking citrus juice, sugar, butter, and egg yolks. When cooled, the mixture becomes thick enough to spread and can be used as a topping for breads, muffins, scones, and other baked goods. Jarred curd is also available in specialty stores.

Lemon Curd

¾ cup plus 2 tablespoons sugar
12 tablespoons unsalted butter
½ cup freshly squeezed lemon juice
4 egg yolks
1 egg

Combine sugar, butter, and lemon juice in a heavy-bottomed saucepan over medium-high heat. Bring to a boil and remove from heat.
In a separate bowl, whisk egg yolks and egg. Whisk one-third hot lemon mixture into eggs, stirring constantly. Pour mixture back into pan. Cook over low heat, whisking until mixture thickens, for about 5 minutes. Remove from heat, cover, and refrigerate at least 1 hour.

Pancakes with Lemon Curd

What better way to celebrate New Year's Day or just sleeping late than with light pancakes wrapped around tangy lemon curd.

2 cups flour
3 eggs
1¼ cups milk
1 teaspoon salt
1 teaspoon butter, melted and cooled
Lemon Curd (Recipe appears on page 271.)

Place flour in a shallow mixing bowl. Make a well in the center of flour. In a separate bowl, beat eggs and salt and pour into center of the well. Slowly whisk in milk until mixture becomes a smooth liquid paste. Stir in butter.

Coat a skillet with nonstick spray or vegetable oil. Heat skillet over medium heat. Pour about ¼ cup batter into pan. Flip pancake when edges turn brown. Transfer pancake to a heated plate and keep warm. Continue process with remaining batter.

Spread 1 tablespoon lemon curd on each pancake, fold in half, and serve.

Yields 16 pancakes

In Provence, pancakes aren't thick like American flapjacks. Instead, you'll find big, thin, irregularly shaped pancakes served hot off a black grill with a dash of sugar or salt. They are then rolled into tubes or folded into triangular or rectangular packets and filled with butter, cheese, honey, or preserves.

Apple Walnut Crêpes

4 apples, peeled, cored, and diced
1 cup chopped walnuts
4 tablespoons butter
½ cup packed brown sugar
½ teaspoon cinnamon
6 Basic Crêpes (see recipe)
Confectioners' sugar

Sauté diced apples and walnuts in butter for 2 minutes over medium heat. Add brown sugar and cinnamon and continue to cook until liquid is thick, about the consistency of syrup. Remove from heat and cool.

Preheat oven to 350°. Place 2 tablespoons filling in the center of each crêpe and roll into a cigar shape. Bake for 5 to 7 minutes. Sprinkle with confectioners' sugar and serve.

Serves 4 to 6

Basic Crêpes

4 eggs
3 cups milk
1 cup water
2 cups all-purpose flour
3 tablespoons vegetable oil

Whisk together eggs, milk, and water. Sift in flour. Whisk in oil. Strain to remove lumps. Allow batter to rest for 30 minutes.

Heat a nonstick 8-inch pan over medium-high heat. Brush lightly with melted butter. Ladle ¼ cup batter into center of pan. Twirl pan to allow batter to spread evenly over pan. Cook for about 30 seconds or until edges are brown and underside is golden. Flip and cook for 1 minute more. Slide crêpe onto plate. Repeat until all batter is used, stacking finished crêpes between wax paper or off center for easy separation. Allow crêpes to cool.

Other crêpe fillings

scrambled eggs and truffles

salmon mousse

caramelized onions and Asiago cheese

sun-dried tomatoes and goat cheese

creamed spinach

fresh fruit and whipped cream

sautéed apples with raisins, brown sugar, and crème fraîche

bananas, shaved chocolate, and Nutella

ice cream and caramel sauce

Gratin of Fresh Berries

Berry season is all too short, so as soon as they appear in the markets we incorporate them into every part of the menu. We even teach a whole class on berries! Brightened by a splash of Grand Mariner, this simple combination of fresh berries and cream can be served as a brunch entree or dessert.

2 pints mixed berries, washed and hulled

¾ cup sugar

Juice of 1 lemon

½ cup heavy cream

4 large egg yolks

1 tablespoon Grand Marnier

Puree 1 cup berries, ½ cup sugar, and lemon juice in a blender or food processor. Transfer to a saucepan and bring to a boil. Add remaining berries. Remove from heat and reserve.

Whip heavy cream until stiff peaks form. Reserve.

Preheat broiler. Whisk remaining sugar, yolks, and liqueur in a bowl set over a double boiler until mixture is consistency of lightly beaten cream. Remove from heat. Fold whipped cream into egg mixture. Pour berry mixture into an ovenproof gratin dish. Top with cream mixture and spread smooth. Place under broiler and brown.

Serves 4

The blackberry, a black or dark purple fruit, is found throughout the United States. The largest but most scarce of all the American berries, blackberries are prized for their sweet-tartness and size. Eat these beauties by the handful or use them to make pies and jams.

Fresh Fruit Glazed with Sabayon

Sabayon can be served hot or cold. Be patient with the whisking — you'll be more than pleased with the results. Although more often considered a dessert, we like to serve this with warm scones and the Sunday paper.

2 oranges, peeled and sectioned

2 cups fresh berries (or seasonal fruit), hulled

3 egg yolks

4 tablespoons sugar

¼ cup Marsala wine

¼ cup dry white wine

1 teaspoon lemon zest

1 teaspoon orange zest

Mint leaves

Combine oranges and berries in a serving bowl and reserve. (Large berries such as strawberries should be halved.)

Combine egg yolks, sugar, Marsala wine, white wine, and zests in a stainless steel bowl. Whisk over a double boiler until mixture is thick and creamy, about 10 to 20 minutes.

Pour sabayon over fruit and garnish with mint leaves.

Serves 4

from the cooking school at la campagne ~ from the cooking school at la campagne ~ from the cooking school at la campagne ~ from the cooking school at la campagne ~ from the cooking school at la campagne ~ from the cooking school at la campagne ~ from the cooking school at la campagne ~ from the cooking school at la campagne ~ from the cooking school at la campagne ~ from the cooking school at la campagne ~ from the cooking school at la campagne ~ from the cooking school at la campagne ~ from the cooking school at la campagne ~ from the cooking school at la campagne ~ from the

basics

Chicken Stock

You don't have to buy chicken backs every time you want to make stock. Whenever you roast a chicken, simply use the carcass to make your stock.

4 pounds chicken backs, chopped

8 quarts water

2 tablespoons salt

2 carrots, roughly chopped

2 stalks celery, roughly chopped

2 onions, chopped

2 leeks, white part only, washed and chopped

6 parsley stems

Bouquet garni

2 tablespoons peppercorns, cracked

Combine all ingredients in a large stockpot. Bring to a boil. Skim foam and lower to a simmer. Simmer, skimming often, for 2 hours. Strain, allow to cool, and refrigerate. Do this a day ahead for easier removal of fat. Fat will solidify and can be carefully skimmed off.

Yields 4 quarts

Beef Stock

Roasting the vegetables with the bones results in a deeper, more satisfying flavor.

10 pounds beef bones
2 carrots, peeled and chopped
3 stalks celery, chopped
3 tomatoes, chopped
2 onions, chopped
1 head garlic, split in half
1 tablespoon dry thyme
4 bay leaves
2 tablespoons black peppercorns
1 teaspoon salt

Preheat oven to 450°. Place bones and vegetables in a roasting pan. Roast until vegetables are dark golden brown, about 30 to 40 minutes. Use a slotted spoon to transfer bones and vegetables to a stockpot. Add remaining ingredients, except salt, and enough water to cover bones and bring to a boil. Reduce heat and simmer for 10 hours, occasionally skimming the scum that forms on top.

Pour contents through a fine mesh strainer into another container and season with salt. Discard solids. Allow stock to cool to room temperature. Skim off the fat. Store up to 1 week in refrigerator or freeze.

Yields 2 quarts

This stock is a good base for soups and sauces, but it can also be enjoyed as is. Consider these garnishes:

diced cooked vegetables with cooked barley

blanched diced celery and leeks

cooked egg noodles and carrots

roasted cubed lean beef

sliced sautéed wild mushrooms

Fish Bouillon

Fish carcasses can usually be obtained for free (or almost free) from your fishmonger.

4 pounds fish carcasses (Flounder or snapper are best.)
1 stalk celery, chopped
1 onion, chopped
1 carrot, chopped
1 sprig thyme
2 bay leaves
½ lemon
¼ cup white wine
2 tablespoons kosher salt
1 teaspoon black peppercorns
1 gallon cold water

Place ingredients in an 8-quart stockpot and bring to a boil. Lower heat and simmer for 30 minutes, skimming any scum that rises to the top. Strain through a fine mesh sieve, pressing the solids to extract juices. Use immediately as a basis for soups or cool to room temperature and then refrigerate for up to 3 days or freeze for up to 2 months.

Yields 3 quarts

bouillon
[BOOL-yahn]

Any broth made by cooking vegetables, poultry, meat, or fish in water. The liquid that is strained off after cooking is the bouillon, which can form the base for soups and sauces.

Demi-glace

This is a rich, brown glossy sauce that is often used as a base for other sauces and soups.

10 pounds veal marrow bones, cut into 2-inch pieces
2 carrots, peeled and chopped
2 stalks celery, chopped
2 ripe tomatoes, chopped
4 tablespoons tomato paste
1 head garlic, cut in half
1 tablespoon black peppercorns
1 large onion, peeled and chopped
2 sprigs fresh thyme or 1 tablespoon dry
1 bay leaf

Preheat oven to 450°. Place bones in a roasting pan and roast until light brown, about 30 to 40 minutes. Add vegetables and garlic and roast until bones are deep brown but not burned. Use a slotted spoon to transfer bones and vegetables to a stockpot. Add remaining ingredients and enough cold water to cover bones. Bring to a boil. Reduce heat to low and simmer for 12 hours, occasionally skimming the scum that forms on top. Pour contents through a fine mesh strainer into another container. Discard solids. Allow stock to cool to room temperature. Skim off the fat. Store for up to 2 weeks in refrigerator or freeze.

Yields 1 quart

Beginning in the last half of the 19th century, chefs would prepare basic sauces on a daily basis. These "mother sauces" included 2 whites — velouté and béchamel — and 2 browns — espagnole and demi-glace.

Chicken Velouté

Velouté, French for "possessing the texture of velvet," is a sauce made be combining classic white stock and white roux.

1 quart Chicken Stock (Recipe appears on page 278.)
½ cup flour
5 tablespoons butter
Salt and pepper

Melt butter in a small sauté pan over medium heat. Slowly whisk in flour to make a smooth roux. Cook for 5 minutes, stirring constantly. Remove from heat and cool.

Bring stock to a boil in a 2-quart saucepan. Whisk in roux a little at a time. Lower heat and simmer for 10 minutes. Season with salt and pepper and strain. Refrigerate for up to 7 days or freeze.

Yields 1 quart

Sage Butter Sauce

Serve with Chicken and Spinach Tortellini (page 182) or over pasta, chicken, or asparagus.

1 tablespoon olive oil
12 leaves sage, julienned
1 teaspoon chopped garlic
1 shallot, minced
¼ cup white wine
6 tablespoons butter
Salt and pepper

Heat olive oil in a saucepan over medium heat. Add sage, garlic, and shallot and sauté until translucent. Deglaze with wine and cook until liquid is reduced by half. Slowly swirl in butter, a little at a time, until sauce is smooth. Season to taste with salt and pepper.

Serves 4 to 6

Béchamel Sauce

Béchamel is a white sauce often used as a base for other sauces. It was named after its inventor, the Marquis Louis de Béchameil, a steward to Louis XIV.

½ cup unsalted butter
1 small yellow onion, chopped
1 small carrot, chopped
½ stalk celery, chopped
¼ cup all-purpose flour
4½ cups milk, scalded
Salt and pepper
Pinch of nutmeg
Bouquet garni (See sidebar on page 78.)

Melt butter in a large saucepan over medium heat. Add vegetables and sauté until onions are translucent. Remove from heat; stir in flour. Return to heat and cook for 5 to 7 minutes, stirring occasionally. Remove from heat and slowly stir in scalded milk. Return to heat; bring to a boil. Season with salt and pepper and nutmeg. Add bouquet garni. Simmer for 35 minutes. Strain and cool completely.

Yields 1 quart

Béarnaise Sauce

Béarnaise is a classic French sauce made with a reduction of vinegar, tarragon, and shallots. It is often served with meat (such as Heart-Shaped Beef Wellington on page 106), fish, and vegetables. We especially like it with scrambled or poached eggs.

¼ cup white wine vinegar

1 shallot, chopped

1 teaspoon cracked black pepper

1 tablespoon dry tarragon

4 egg yolks

1 tablespoon water

½ cup Clarified Butter (Recipe appears on page 287.)

Salt and pepper

Combine vinegar, shallot, pepper, and tarragon in a saucepan over medium heat. Cook until all liquid evaporates. Reduce heat to low.

In a small bowl, whisk yolks with water. Add yolks to the reduction and whisk until fluffy and cooked. (You should see the bottom of the pan.) Slowly pour in butter, whisking constantly. Season to taste with salt and pepper.

Yields 1 cup

Mousseline Sauce

Also known as chantilly sauce, mousseline sauce is a variation of hollandaise sauce. It is often served with poached fish or vegetables (such as White Asparagus on page 188).

4 egg yolks
1 teaspoon white wine
4 tablespoons butter, cut into small pieces
Salt and pepper
2 ounces heavy cream

Whisk together yolks and wine in the top pan of a double boiler. Cook yolk mixture over medium heat, whisking continuously until mixture begins to thicken. Remove pan from heat and add butter, a few pieces at a time, whisking until fully incorporated. Season to taste with salt and pepper. Whip heavy cream and fold into sauce.

sauce verte
[VEHRT]

Although the name means "green sauce" in French, sauce verte is actually just a green-colored mayonnaise. It is often served with cold fish dishes (such as Lobster and Salmon Terrine on page 29).

Sauce Verte

1 cup fresh spinach leaves, finely chopped
3 egg yolks
1 tablespoon Dijon mustard
½ teaspoon salt
½ teaspoon pepper
¼ cup lemon juice
2 cups vegetable or olive oil

Squeeze spinach to extract juice. Discard spinach and reserve juice. Combine yolks, mustard, salt, pepper, and lemon juice in a food processor. Puree until smooth. With motor running, add oil in a slow, steady stream until mixture reaches the consistency of thick mayonnaise. Add more salt, pepper, and lemon juice if needed. Stir in spinach juice. Transfer to a clean container and refrigerate.

Yields 2½ cups

Orange Beurre Blanc

Although a traditional beurre blanc does not contain heavy cream, this one does. It acts as a stabilizer so the sauce will last longer during service.

Zest and juice of 2 oranges
1 cup white wine
½ cup heavy cream
2 tablespoons Triple Sec
1 stick butter
Salt and pepper

Heat orange zest and juice in a saucepan over medium heat until juice thickens to a syrup. Add wine and cook until liquid is reduced by half. Add cream and cook until sauce thickens slightly. Add Triple Sec and bring to a simmer. Slowly add butter, a few pieces at a time, swirling until well incorporated. Season with salt and pepper.

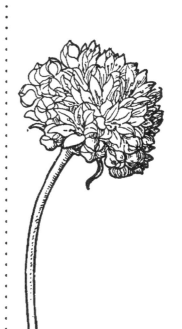

Chive Beurre Blanc

½ cup white wine vinegar
½ cup dry white wine
3 tablespoons chopped shallots
1 bay leaf
4 tablespoons heavy cream
½ pound unsalted butter, cubed
Salt and pepper
1 tablespoon chopped chives

Combine vinegar, wine, shallots, and bay leaf in a saucepan. Simmer over medium heat until liquid reduces to 2 tablespoons. Add cream and simmer for 2 minutes. Reduce heat to medium-low. Stir in butter, one piece at a time, allowing each piece to incorporate before adding another. Strain. Season with salt and pepper. Stir in chives.

Clarified Butter

Because there are no milk solids, clarified butter has a higher burning point than whole butter.

1 cup butter

Melt butter in a heavy saucepan over medium heat until butter bubbles. Remove from heat and let stand for 10 minutes. Skim off all foamy solids from the top. Spoon or pour the clear butterfat into a container. Discard residue that remains in the bottom of pan.

Fennel Butter

Melt fennel butter over fish, spread on toast, or toss with vegetables.

½ pound plus 2 tablespoons butter, softened
1 bulb fennel, diced
1 tablespoon minced garlic
¼ cup Pernod or other anise-flavored liquor
1 teaspoon chopped fresh thyme
Salt and pepper

Heat 2 tablespoons butter in a sauté pan over medium-high heat. Add fennel and cook until well browned and caramelized. Add garlic and Pernod and cook for 1 minute. Remove from heat and cool. Place fennel mixture, remaining butter, thyme, and salt and pepper in a food processor and process until smooth. Refrigerate until ready to serve.

beurre manié
[burr-mahn-YAY]

Literally "kneaded butter" in French, beurre manié is a paste made of softened butter and flour. It is used to thicken sauces.

Beurre Manié

2 tablespoons butter, room temperature
3 tablespoons flour

Blend butter and flour in a bowl until smooth. Refrigerate.

Pesto

We suggest you make a double batch of pesto. Freeze the extra in small ice cube trays. When frozen, transfer to a resealable freezer bag so you always have some available.

1 cup fresh basil leaves, washed and drained
2 tablespoons pine nuts
1 tablespoon chopped garlic
¼ cup extra virgin olive oil
1 tablespoon grated locatelli cheese
Salt and pepper

Place basil, pine nuts, and garlic in a food processor and process into a coarse paste. With the motor running, add oil in a slow, steady stream. Add cheese. Season with salt and pepper to taste. Store covered in refrigerator but bring to room temperature before serving.

Yields 1 cup

Pistou

3 cloves garlic
3 cups packed fresh basil leaves
½ teaspoon salt
6 tablespoons olive oil
¾ cup grated Parmesan cheese
Black pepper

Place garlic in a food processor and finely chop. Add basil and salt and process until basil is finely chopped, scraping down sides of bowl occasionally. With motor running, add oil in a slow, steady stream. Add cheese and process. Transfer to a serving bowl and season with pepper to taste.

Yields ½ to ¾ cups

What to do with pesto . . .

serve over hot pasta

garnish soup

spread on bruschetta

mix with breadcrumbs to form a coating for fish or chicken

make a salad dressing

toss with Jersey tomatoes

combine with goat cheese and spread on bread or stuff in profiteroles

Crème Fraîche

Crème fraîche is a matured, thickened heavy cream with a slightly tangy, almost nutty flavor. Sold for big bucks in specialty stores, crème fraîche is easy and inexpensive to make at home and can be stored for up to 10 days in the refrigerator.

1 cup heavy cream
1 tablespoon buttermilk

Combine heavy cream and buttermilk in a nonreactive bowl. Cover with plastic wrap and set out overnight (8 to 24 hours) in a warm place. (Don't worry, it won't spoil.) When thickened to the consistency of sour cream, stir well, transfer to a lidded jar, and refrigerate.

Yields 1 cup

What to do with crème fraîche . . .

serve atop fruit and desserts

add to soups and sauces

spoon over buttered warm veggies

whisk into salad dressings

spread on muffins, scones, and bagels

eat by spoonfuls

Rouille

To make Yellow Pepper Rouille, substitute roasted yellow bell pepper for red. Serve Rouille as a garnish for fish or fish stews (such as Bouillabaisse on page 84).

4 cloves garlic
2 egg yolks
½ teaspoon crushed red pepper
½ red bell pepper, roasted and skinned
1 cup olive oil
Salt

Place garlic, egg yolks, crushed red pepper, and roasted pepper in a food processor. Puree until smooth. With motor running, add oil in a slow, steady stream until mixture reaches the consistency of thick mayonnaise. Season with salt and serve.

Yields 1½ cups

Tomato Basil Coulis

For additional kick, add roasted garlic or roasted red peppers.

½ cup plus 1 teaspoon olive oil
3 whole tomatoes, chopped
1 small onion, chopped
½ cup water
Salt and cayenne pepper
1 bunch basil, chopped

Heat ½ cup oil in a saucepan over medium heat. Add tomatoes, onion, and water. Season with salt and cayenne. When tomatoes are very well cooked, add basil. Transfer to a blender and puree. Add remaining olive oil and season with salt and pepper.

Roasted Red Pepper Coulis

3 red bell peppers, roasted, seeded and pureed
1 clove garlic
½ cup olive oil
Salt and pepper

Combine pureed peppers, garlic, and olive oil in a blender. Puree and season to taste with salt and pepper.

Horseradish Cream

¼ cup horseradish
¼ cup mayonnaise
¼ cup heavy cream
Salt and pepper

Mix horseradish with mayonnaise. Whip heavy cream and add to mixture. Season with salt and pepper.

coulis
[koo-LEE]

Coulis is a thick vegetable or fruit puree. Butter, cream, or crème fraîche may be added to a coulis. Coulis can be used to add color and flavor to most any dish. Try it as a garnish for meat, fish, poultry, or soups.

Shallot Confit

10 shallots, sliced
1 cup Burgundy wine
1 cup red wine vinegar
¼ cup sugar
½ teaspoon crushed juniper berries
1 sprig fresh thyme, stemmed and chopped
¼ teaspoon cracked black pepper

Place all ingredients in a heavy sauté pan over medium heat. Simmer, stirring occasionally, until all liquid is absorbed. Serve hot or at room temperature.

Serve these vegetable confits as a side dish or garnish for meats, poultry, seafood, and omelets. They also make a snazzy spread for sandwiches, breads, and hors d'oeuvres.

Red Onion Confit

3 tablespoons olive oil
2 large red onions, thinly sliced
3 tablespoons dried currants
3 tablespoons red wine vinegar
1 tablespoon Chicken Stock (Recipe appears on page 278.)
2 teaspoons chopped fresh thyme
½ teaspoon sugar
Salt and pepper

Heat oil in a large skillet over medium heat. Add onions and sauté for 5 minutes. Stir in remaining ingredients and cook for 30 to 45 minutes or until onions are deep brown. Add water if pan becomes too dry. Season with salt and pepper. Serve hot or at room temperature.

Gremolada

Use gremolada as a garnish with meats and fish or incorporate into tomato-based sauces.

1 tablespoon finely grated lemon zest
1 tablespoon chopped rosemary
3 tablespoons chopped Italian parsley
3 anchovy fillets, chopped

Thoroughly combine ingredients in a small bowl.

Herbes de Provence

½ teaspoon dry thyme
½ teaspoon dry basil
¼ teaspoon dry lavender
¼ teaspoon dry rosemary
¼ teaspoon fennel seed
1 crumbled bay leaf

Combine herbs and mix thoroughly.

Croutons

For Garlic Croutons, rub bread with garlic cloves before spreading on oil or butter.

Olive oil or butter
6 slices crusty French bread

Preheat oven to 275°. Spread olive oil or butter on both sides of bread. Baked on an ungreased baking sheet, turning once during baking, until golden and crisp, about 25 to 35 minutes. Cool slightly and cut into cubes.

Rosemary, lavender, thyme, and fennel grow wild and abundant in Provence. These herbs along with basil and bay leaf make up herbes de Provence, an herbal blend widely used in Provençal cooking. Don't worry if you see a different combination of herbs labled "herbes de Provence." There is no hard and fast rule, and the blend can change slightly according to the cook or the season.

Basic Vinaigrette

Basic but certainly not boring, this vinaigrette will dress any salad with style.

½ cup vinegar
1 shallot, peeled and minced
Salt and pepper
1½ to 2 cups oil

Combine vinegar, shallot, and salt and pepper to taste in a stainless steel bowl. Whisk in oil in a steady stream.

Yields 2 cups

Roasted Shallot Vinaigrette

6 shallots, peeled
4 cloves garlic, peeled
¾ cup plus 1 tablespoon olive oil (not extra virgin)
¼ cup shallot red wine vinegar
1½ tablespoons chopped mixed fresh herbs (equal parts rosemary, thyme, parsley, oregano and/or lavender)
½ teaspoon salt
1 tablespoon fine ground mustard (We like Gulpener's Old Dutch.)

Preheat oven to 350°. Toss shallots and garlic with 1 tablespoon oil. Place in a baking dish and cover with aluminum foil. Roast for 45 minutes or until shallots are soft.

Place cooked shallots and garlic in a blender or food processor. Add vinegar, herbs, salt, and mustard and puree. With motor running, add remaining oil in a slow, steady stream.

Yields 1½ cups

Vegetable Marinade

Looking for the perfect accompaniment for main dish meats, chicken, or fish? Skewer assorted vegetables, marinate overnight, and then roast or grill. Perfection achieved!

1 tablespoon balsamic vinegar
1 tablespoon soy sauce
2 tablespoons olive oil
½ teaspoon sesame seed oil
1½ teaspoons lemon zest
Black pepper

Whisk together all ingredients, including black pepper to taste. Pour over your favorite vegetables and marinate in refrigerator for 30 minutes to 2 hours.

Meat Marinade

Marinate meat in a glass, stainless steel, or ceramic container in the refrigerator for at least 3 hours or, ideally, up to 48 hours.

2 teaspoons chopped garlic
1 teaspoon grated ginger
4½ teaspoons soy sauce
1 tablespoon dry sherry
1 tablespoon sesame seed oil
4½ teaspoons brown sugar
2 tablespoons sesame seeds

Combine garlic and ginger in a food processor and puree. Transfer mixture to a mixing bowl. Whisk in remaining ingredients. Pour over your favorite meat and marinate in refrigerator for 3 to 5 hours or overnight.

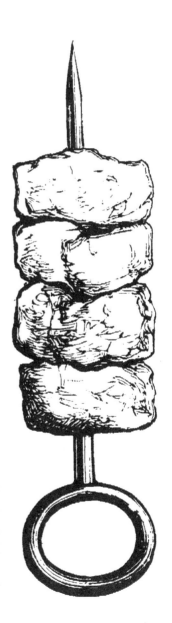

Ganache

For Milk Chocolate Ganache, substitute milk chocolate for semi-sweet.

8 ounces cream
8 ounces semi-sweet chocolate

Heat cream over medium heat until very hot but not boiling. Place chocolate in a bowl. Pour hot cream over chocolate. Mix with a spatula until smooth. Use warm as a glaze or cool. Store in an airtight container in refrigerator for up to 1 week.

Chocolate Sauce

6 ounces semi-sweet chocolate
¾ cup butter, cut into cubes
¼ cup milk or light cream

Melt chocolate and butter in a saucepan over medium heat. Meanwhile, bring milk or light cream to a boil. Whisk milk into chocolate. Stir to combine. Serve warm.

Caramel

¾ cup sugar
¼ cup water

Combine sugar and water in a heavy saucepan and bring to a boil, cooking until sugar turns a honey color. Remove from heat. (The caramel will continue to cook and brown as it cools.)

Pâté Brisée

Pâté brisée is the French equivalent of a classic short pastry crust. It is used for fruit tarts, baked dumplings, and other desserts (such as Rhubarb-Raspberry Galette on page 213).

1⅔ cups all-purpose flour
½ teaspoon salt
½ cup unsalted butter
1 egg, lightly beaten
2 teaspoons water (approximate)

Sift flour and salt into a bowl. Cut in butter until mixture resembles breadcrumbs. Add egg to mixture and enough water to form a firm dough. Shape dough into a ball and chill for 30 minutes. Bake as directed in recipe.

Baked Tart Shell

1½ cups all-purpose flour
¼ cup sugar
Pinch of salt
¾ cup unsalted butter, cut into ½-inch pieces
1 large egg

Preheat oven to 375°. Butter a 10-inch tart pan with removable bottom. Combine flour, sugar, and salt in a food processor and pulse. Add butter and pulse until mixture resembles coarse meal. Add egg and pulse until incorporated.

Pat dough into a ball on a lightly floured surface and place between 2 sheets of parchment or wax paper. Roll dough to a 12-inch disk. Transfer disk and paper to a baking sheet and refrigerate until firm, about 15 minutes. Peel off top paper, invert dough onto pan, and peel off bottom paper. Fit dough into pan and chill for 10 minutes. Prick dough all over with a fork and bake on middle rack of oven for 20 minutes until golden brown. Cool on a wire rack.

Short pastries contain a lot of fat which results in a crumbly texture and a melt-in-your-mouth richness. A small amount of water is added as a binding agent. The liquid and a high baking temperature give the pastry a satisfying crispness. Work in a cool environment and be sure to not overhandle the dough or you'll end up with a heavy, tough pastry.

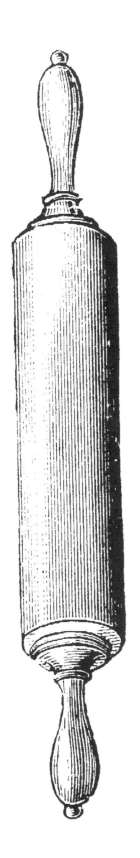

Pâte Sucrée (Sweet Pastry)

A lightly sweetened pastry dough enriched with egg yolks, pâte sucrée is excellent for tarts (such as Alsatian Apple Tart on page 208) and sweet pastries.

1⅔ cups all-purpose flour
½ cup unsalted butter
¼ cup superfine sugar
2 egg yolks
¼ teaspoon vanilla extract

Sift flour into a bowl. Cut in butter until mixture resembles breadcrumbs. Stir in sugar. In a separate bowl, lightly whisk egg yolks and vanilla. Add yolks to flour mixture and combine to form a dough. Press dough into a ball and chill for 30 minutes. Bake as directed in recipe.

Basic Tart Shell

1 egg, lightly beaten
¼ cup confectioners' sugar
½ cup butter, cut into cubes and softened
Pinch of salt
1½ cups flour

Place egg, sugar, butter, and salt in a food processor and pulse for a few seconds. Add flour, ½ cup at a time, and continue pulsing until all flour is combined and dough just holds together. Remove dough from processor and knead into a disk. Refrigerate until well chilled.

Roll out chilled dough on a lightly floured work surface until dough is slightly larger than an inverted 9- or 10-inch tart pan. Carefully fold pastry in half, transfer to pan, and unfold. Press firmly into bottom and up sides of pan. Prick bottom with a fork. Bake as directed in recipe.

Pastry Cream

Pastry cream is extremely versatile. It can be used as a filling for cakes, cream puffs, and eclairs; as a topping for pastry; or thinned and served as a sauce. It acts as a delicious "glue" in Croquembouche (see page 234) and Paris-Brest (see page 231).

10 egg yolks
1¼ cups sugar
½ cup flour
½ cup cornstarch
1 quart milk
1 teaspoon vanilla extract
⅓ cup butter

Whisk together yolks, sugar, flour, and cornstarch in a mixing bowl. Place milk and vanilla in a saucepan and bring to a boil. Slowly add one-third hot milk to egg mixture, whisking quickly. Pour mixture back into saucepan. Cook over medium heat until mixture comes to a boil and thickens. Swirl in butter. Strain into a bowl, cover, and cool completely. Refrigerate for up to 3 days.

Mango Compote

1 mango, peeled and diced
3 scallions, sliced
½ red pepper, diced
¼ cup rice vinegar
2 tablespoons olive oil
Salt and pepper

Combine all ingredients in a bowl and mix thoroughly. Refrigerate for at least 30 minutes so flavors will marry.

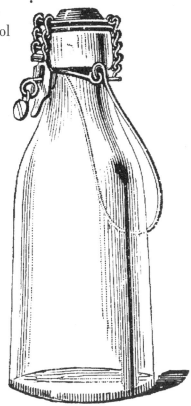

Choux Paste

Often called pastry, choux paste or "pâte à choux" is actually a soft paste that forms a crisp risen "pastry" when baked. It can be piped or spooned into shapes to hold chocolate, whipped cream, pastry cream, custard, fruit fillings, or ice cream.

1 cup water

½ cup butter

1 cup flour

1 tablespoon sugar

1 teaspoon salt

4 eggs

Combine water and butter in a saucepan and bring to a boil. Reduce heat to low. Add flour, sugar, and salt. Mix with a wooden spoon until mixture is dry and pulls away from the sides of pan. Remove pan from heat. Stir in eggs, one at a time, mixing well to thoroughly incorporate between each addition. Use as directed in recipe.

Yields about 2½ cups dough

To make cream puffs with choux paste

Preheat oven to 400°. Line a baking sheet with parchment paper. Place choux paste in a pastry bag fitted with a ½-inch plain tube. Pipe 1-inch mounds onto the baking sheet, 1 inch apart. Brush with egg wash. Bake for 20 to 25 minutes or until puffs are firm and brown. Pierce bottoms of each puff with the tip of a small knife. Fill with Pastry Cream (Recipe appears on page 298.) or Sweet Whipped Cream (Recipe appears on page 227.).

See the recipes for Paris-Brest (page 231) and Croquembouche (page 234) for other ideas on how to use and bake choux paste.

Lavender Orange Sauce

Juice of 3 oranges

1 tablespoon Grand Marnier

1 tablespoon lavender

¼ cup butter

Bring orange juice, Grand Marnier, and lavender to a boil in a heavy saucepan. When mixture reduces and is syrupy, stir in butter.

from the cooking school at la campagne ~ from the cooking school at la campagne ~ from the cooking school at la campagne ~ from the cooking school at la campagne ~ from the cooking school at la campagne ~ from the cooking school at la campagne ~ from the cooking school at la campagne ~ from the cooking school at la campagne ~ from the cooking school at la campagne ~ from the cooking school at la campagne ~ from the cooking school at la campagne ~ from the cooking school at la campagne ~ from the

index

Additional copies of
From The Cooking School at La Campagne
may be ordered by phone, fax, or mail.

Order Form

Please send me _____ copies of **From The Cooking School at La Campagne** at $16.95 per copy.

_____ Book amount total

_____ Sales tax: New Jersey addresses, please add $1.01

_____ Shipping: $3 for first book; $1 for each additional book

_____ Total amount enclosed

Name _____

Address _____

City/State/ZIP _____

Phone _____

Credit Card # _____ Exp. _____

Name on Card _____

Checks, money orders, and credit cards (American Express, Visa, MasterCard, and Diner's Club) accepted for payment.

By Phone: Call 856-429-7647
By Fax: Fax this order form to 856-429-0037
By Mail: Mail this order form to: La Campagne
　　　　　　　　　　　　　　　　Book Processing
　　　　　　　　　　　　　　　　312 Kresson Road
　　　　　　　　　　　　　　　　Cherry Hill, NJ 08034

Gift copies and packages are available! Call for details.

About the author

John Byrne is the proprietor of La Campagne. He has worked his entire professional life in the food industry and was the former Vice President of Ridgewell's Catering. He is a member of the Executive Board of the New Jersey Restaurant Association. An avid but lousy golfer and fisherman, John lives in Haddonfield, New Jersey, with his wife Dorothy.